D0629998

Computer Science Project Work

Springer
London
Berlin
Heidelberg
New York
Barcelona
Hong Kong
Milan
Paris
Singapore
Tokyo

Sally Fincher, Marian Petre and Martyn Clark (Eds)

Computer Science Project Work

Principles and Pragmatics

 Springer

Sally Fincher, BA, MA, LHG
Computing Laboratory, University of Kent at Canterbury, Canterbury,
Kent, CT2 7NF

Marian Petre, BA, Dip. Advanced Studies Computing, PhD
The Open University, Walton Hall, Milton Keynes, MK7 6AA

Martyn Clark, BA, MA, MSc
School of Computer Studies, University of Leeds, Leeds, LS2 9JT

ISBN 1-85233-357-X Springer-Verlag London Berlin Heidelberg

British Library Cataloguing in Publication Data
Computer science project work : principles and pragmatics
    1. Computer science – Study and teaching (Higher) – Activity
    programs – Great Britain 2. Project method in teaching
    I. Fincher, Sally II. Petre, Marian III. Clark, Martyn
    004'.0711'41
    ISBN 185233357X

Library of Congress Cataloging-in-Publication Data
Computer science project work : principles and pragmatics/Sally Fincher,
Marian Petre, and Martyn Clark (eds.)
    p. cm
    ISBN 1-85233-357-X (alk. paper)
    1. Computer science. 2. Industrial project management. I.Fincher, Sally, 1959-
    II.Petre, Marian, 1959- III. Clark, Martyn, 1961-
    QA76.C57325 2001
    004'.068'8—dc21   00-063511

Printed in Great Britain

Typeset by Florence Production Ltd, Stoodleigh, Devon
Printed and bound at The Cromwell Press, Trowbridge, UK
34/3830-543210 Printed on acid-free paper SPIN 10776394

Contents

Preface

Why Computing (as an Academic Discipline) Does Projects

Computing is concerned with the understanding, design and exploitation of computation and computer technology. It is a discipline that blends elegant theories (derived from a range of other disciplines that includes mathematics, engineering, psychology, graphical design and well-founded experimental insight) with the solution of immediate practical problems; it combines the ethos of the scholar with that of the professional; it underpins the development of both small-scale and large-scale systems that support organizational goals; it helps individuals in their everyday lives; it is ubiquitous and diversely applied to a range of applications, and yet important components are invisible to the naked eye (2000a).

The computer is without doubt the most significant technological development of the twentieth century. The consequences of its development and its use in conjunction with the technology of telecommunications have pervaded every aspect of life in the late twentieth century, and will continue to do so for the foreseeable future. These consequences have been felt particularly in education, where large numbers of programs are available to the large numbers of students who seek places on them; even so, the supply cannot keep pace with employers' demands for students with computing knowledge.

The perception of computing as a practical discipline carries with it the notion that there are other disciplines that are of a less practical (or more theoretical) nature. The casual observer perceives that "practical work" or "projects" are more naturally associated with practical disciplines than with more theoretical ones, but this represents too superficial an observation. From a teaching perspective, it is possible to characterize different disciplines as having a more practical or more theoretical perspective, but effective learning is based in activity, not in disciplinary orientation.

Historically, regardless of the subject to be learnt (that is including what we would today class as subjects having a less practical bias) learning has been closely related to the real work of professionals, tradesmen, artisans, independent scholars and clerics, situated in the context of a community of practice (Lave and Wenger, 1991; Wenger, 1998). When a young person was found able to make an independent contribution to this field of knowledge, they would prepare a master "piece" and, with the consent of the masters, graduate to become a member of a trade, order, profession or guild; thus their professional community legitimized their learning. In the modern university, there is work which can be seen in this apprenticeship tradition; not only, obviously, in subjects which relate to professional practice (the use of the atelier system in architecture and the laboratory-based practices of the biological and physical sciences, for example) but also in teaching and learning activities within the social sciences and the humanities (debates and moots in law and the craft of constructing a syllogism or other form of argument in philosophy, for example).

For the discipline of computing, the particular "pull" of industrial practice is very real, widely recognized and commonly addressed within the curriculum.

Because computing is an integrated discipline, it is essential for undergraduate programs to emphasize the practical aspects of the discipline along with the theoretical ones. Today, much of the practical knowledge associated with computing exists in the form of professional practices that exist in industry. To work successfully in those environments, students must be exposed to those practices as part of their education. These practices, moreover, extend beyond computing-specific skills to encompass a wide range of activities including management, ethics and values, written and oral communication, and the ability to work as part of a team. (2000b)

Project work in computing therefore arises in two ways: in common with almost all disciplines, it is used as a vehicle for effective learning, and in common with all disciplines with a practical application, it is used to demonstrate the mastery of skills appropriate to professional practice.

There is a broad range of styles of project work within computing curricula, but three main types are worthy of special mention:

- for the reinforcement of learning, the small piece of project work closely associated with a specific aspect of the curriculum (for example, the writing of a program, the design of a database, the construction of a piece of hardware) is often undertaken, typically over a relatively small timescale; a single-subject degree program in computing may contain many such projects
- to demonstrate mastery of skills, a larger project is often undertaken; this type of project is often used to demonstrate that the student can integrate knowledge acquired from different parts of their program towards some defined end, rather in the nature of the "master piece" produced by the apprentice
- finally, there are projects which are undertaken by teams of students working together, more closely modeling modern professional practice.

Incorporating these different types of project into the computing curriculum brings with it a variety of problems, the exploration of which form the subject matter for this book.

The role of project work in demonstrating mastery of skills appropriate to professional practice is given added force within the computing curriculum through the influence of professional bodies – within the UK, the British Computer Society (BCS) and the Institution of Electrical Engineers (IEE); in the USA, the Accreditation Board for Engineering and Technology (ABET) performs a similar accrediting (although not chartering) role. The role of professional bodies typically includes a responsibility, enshrined in the UK through Royal Charter, to establish and maintain appropriate standards of education and experience for those engaged in a profession, and to encourage education and training in matters associated with the advancement of subjects relevant to the profession. In furtherance of this responsibility, educational establishments and professional bodies can collaborate in the accreditation of degree programs under guidelines laid out in the Standards And Routes To Registration (SARTOR) of the Engineering Council (1997), which requires all courses leading to Chartered Engineer status to "embody and integrate theoretical, practical and project work".

Such accreditation typically includes the requirement that degree programs contain a practical, problem-solving project designed to demonstrate professional competence in the development of a suitable application. An engineering approach, which focuses on the specification, design, implementation, testing, and evaluation of an artifact is often required. This emphasis on problem solving is (in computing years) very ancient. The 1968 Association for Computing Machinery (ACM) monograph on *University Education in Computing Science* (Finerman, 1968) describes its importance:

The second capability to be considered is that of problem solving. Specifically, this means the ability to grapple with empirical situations involving large and complex systems. For the terminal student, it is felt to be of prime importance that a computer science program instills this capability. The most critical aspect (somehow) to put the student into the kind of situation that he (sic) may expect to encounter in an industrial or research context. There are several ways (some already mentioned) that this might be done. A year's course dealing empirically with systems problems is one possibility; a Master's project or thesis is another. In some sense, these alternatives could be said to be equivalent . . . The feature of the problem-solving capability – being able to describe adequately the problem and its alternative solution methods – is very important; it is strongly suggested that it be taken into account in designing a Master's program.

More recently, several countries have engaged in activities that attempt to define the nature of computing (and other subjects) as academic disciplines. Within the UK this has, in part, taken the form of benchmarking standards which describe the nature and characteristics of degree programs in specific subjects, represent the general expectations about the standards required for the award of qualifications at given levels, and articulate the attributes and capabilities that those possessing such qualifications should be able to demonstrate. Within computing, the benchmarking standards (2000a) expect that students of computing will engage in "a major activity allowing students to demonstrate ability in applying practical and analytical skills (as they are present in the course as a whole)" and that students will acquire a range of practical abilities. In the USA the ACM and the Institute of Electrical and Electronics Engineers Computer Society (IEEE-CS) have had a large input to (and impact on) the computing curricula. Their joint task force reported in *Computing Curricula 1991*, ". . . laboratory projects emphasize the synthesis of practical solutions to problems and thus require students to evaluate alternatives, costs, and performance in the context of real-world constraints. Students develop the ability to make these evaluations by seeing and discussing example designs as well as receiving feedback on their own designs". At the time of writing, a new joint task force on the *Year 2001 Model Curricula for Computing (CC-2001)* has been formed to review the 1991 curricula and develop a revised and enhanced version for the Year 2001 that "addresses developments in computing technologies in the past decade and will sustain through the next decade" (2000b).

It is therefore unsurprising that project work is a central component of computing courses.

Why Computing Departments Do Projects

Many stakeholders in the discipline believe that an "apprenticeship approach" is a key component of inculcating learners into the discipline. Project work is not an apprenticeship in the traditional sense, partly because the power relationship between master and apprentice is missing or obfuscated and partly because it is inappropriate for the 21st century educational climate; we do not expect the passive learning behaviors of apprentices in our students, nor that their successes will be dependent on patronage:

An architect or draftsman working for an architectural firm would most likely have been trained by working directly for an architect. His first assignments might be to trace designs done by more experienced people in the office ... In this way the architectural apprentice began to work with the actual material of drawings and building designs without being in a position to make decisions. Through repetitive copying, however, he did begin to learn a language, of plan, elevation and detail. Within the office, those who were more successful were gradually given positions of more responsibility, eventually perhaps taken under the wing of the principal designer, and asked to do buildings on their own. (Davis, 1999)

However, the craft-skills *model* is still valuable within higher education, because learning computing cannot be done solely by bookwork:

Every discipline has its distinctive ways of knowing, which it identifies with the activities it regards as its own: anthropologists do fieldwork, architects design buildings, monks meditate, and carpenters make things out of wood. Each discipline wears its defining activity as a badge of pride in a craftworker's embodied competence ... [our] distinctive activity is building things, specifically computers and computer programs. Building things, like fieldwork and meditation and design cannot be reduced to the reading and writing of books. To the contrary, it is an enterprise grounded in a routine daily practice. Sitting in the lab and working on gadgets or circuits or programs, it is an inescapable fact that some things can be built and others cannot ... (Agre, 1997)

A key aspect of "building things" is the mastery of complexity. Starting from easy pieces, a student acquires a range of individual skills. In computing terms, these skills might be the ability to write a proof, draw a plan, code simple programs, or wire up a circuit. As the individual skills are mastered, the student can begin to understand which skills would be appropriate in which context and thereby develop design and problem-solving skills. Finally, the individual skills and the design skills can be deployed in the construction of larger pieces more representative of the sort of systems students observe on their desktop computers. Many computing courses, particularly those gaining accreditation from professional bodies, demand that students demonstrate their mastery of the subject by the construction of demonstrably working artifacts. Valuable experience can also be obtained if students acquire individual skills short of complete mastery (in the traditional apprenticeship sense); such experience may be particularly valuable for those studying computing in combination with other subjects.

Projects are therefore an important tool in educating students in the mastery of the complexities inherent in modern-day computing systems. They can give insight into the sort of systems that students observe on their desktop computers, and can help bridge the gap between systems they use and systems they construct. Students are also able to bring together a range of disparate elements of the curriculum (not just skill-related elements) from across subject areas and years into a single project.

Additionally, for the computing student, project work can occupy a relatively long time within the degree program (albeit of much shorter duration than the traditional apprenticeship). Thus students, while constrained to follow a syllabus within the curriculum, can have more freedom to pursue their own interests within the context of project work. Staff, too, can also develop their own interests, allowing students to contribute significantly to research, scholarship, departmental and university infrastructure.

Finally, for the employer, project work is used as evidence of ability and experience, as a discriminator and an interview topic. Thus for the student who chooses to make their career in the computing profession, project work can launch a career in a way analogous to the "master piece" of the apprentice.

Ways To Use This Book

Talking about teaching and learning practice, especially with regard to changing practice is difficult, and is difficult for a number of reasons:

- knowing "what's out there", what other people do
- knowing what is possible, what you can change
- getting the information in the right form to allow you to make a change.

In writing this book (and in the work that informed it) we squarely address these issues by concentrating on the identification of principles which can orientate and guide the practitioner and distilling practice so that change can be achieved in a pragmatic fashion.

Knowing What's Out There

Pedagogic information is notoriously difficult to locate. There are several potential explanations for why this should be so. Firstly, teaching remains a fundamentally private activity, concealed behind the classroom door. Secondly, it may be difficult to press friends and colleagues for sufficiently detailed descriptions of practice without appearing to be stealing or poaching their ideas. This becomes especially problematic if there is a local climate where teaching is neither a rewarded nor a highly regarded activity. Further, there may be institutional-level prohibitions about what may or may not be published to "outsiders". By engaging in a large-scale data collection of project work practices from all UK and some overseas computing departments we present (in Part One) a new body of material. We do not provide data in the sense of inventing or discovering new practices, but, by gathering them in a standardized and comparable way, we create new information which was previously unavailable to the practitioner.

Knowing What Is Possible, What You Can change

Changing project practice is very difficult – staff have highly personal ideas about what is a project and why projects are done – and the combined forces of momentum and sentiment prevent revolutionary change. The way in which we present the data in Part One shows not only the content of project work practice but also how this content may be combined, and the principles of its use. This particularly helps for two reasons.

First, we are able to present more material. Most practitioners would be hard pressed to locate a similar quantity of practice and experience from their own experience or from within their own network of professional colleagues. Secondly, we are able to present a greater variety of material. It is obvious that our friends and colleagues tend to be drawn from similar areas. By using them as sources of information it is difficult to find material which is truly different from our own. Although local practice may not be satisfactory, it is often difficult to "get out of the box" of existing thinking. Part One provides a very wide range of materials and practice, from every kind of institutional perspective. Lastly, the organization of Part One uniquely gives the opportunity of identifying patterns of practice of many combinations and principles.

Knowing How To Change

In seeing a large body of assembled material, and assessing the parts, the combinations and the articulating principles of project work, we afford and assist reflection on our own practice. Such reflection may allow us to identify weak spots in current practice. However, once a need is identified, what the academic practitioner wants is a solution to plug that gap. In the course of gathering project work data, by holding workshops and conferences, and through talking to people about what they did, we came to find out about a lot of interesting things that were going on. Having located these, we then strove to find a way to pass them on with the maximum chance of success. Best practice in terms of transfer was characterized to us as, "having someone give you nifty ideas with the bugs ironed out". We worked on a method and a form for doing this, and the resulting ideas are presented as "bundles" in Part Two.

We have worked to identify, and then address, fundamental issues in the identification of, and transfer of, project work practice. Here we present a comprehensive and coherent collection of proven materials. We hope that you find it useful.

If You're Not in the Computing Discipline

We only looked at project work within computing science. We only gathered data from computing departments and (in the main) talked only to computing academics or computing employers. This meant that when we first started to characterize and categorize pieces of practice the obvious way to do it was in regard to what the students had to produce:

- did they have to build a piece of software, and, if so, how big, how complicated?
- did they work so that they experienced the whole of the software life-cycle, or could they do a project just, say, in the design phase?
- did they have to work in teams, and, if so, did they mimic the roles required in professional practice?
- were they expected to learn and use existing commercial tools and applications, or write their own?

Of course, occasionally, we would find ourselves in the position of telling people from other disciplines what we were doing. Then it would make no sense to talk about the parts that made computing projects unique, or at least specific to computing. So we'd talk about more general things – the aims and objectives, the methods of supervision and assessment. When we talked at this level, we found a remarkable degree of commonality.

Paradoxically, for those outside computing, it seems to be better if you read the deliverables mechanisms first. In this way, your understanding of what computing requires from project work will inform the project work processes we describe and allow you to make a mapping to the specific deliverables of your discipline. There are other books, focused on other disciplines, which might then help to "bridge the gap" of disciplinary-specific endeavor (Luck, 1999; Allison et al., 1996; Bell, 1993).

The Parts of This Book

This book is organized in two halves, with different sorts of information in each half. In each half the information, expected audience and style are very different, but the subject matter is the same. So, you will find sections on, say, "assessment" in Part One *and* in Part Two. These sections do not duplicate, but complement, each other.

The first half is figured as a reference manual, compiled from data collected in a nationwide survey. It contains two types of information: case studies and mechanisms.

Composite case studies do not exist anywhere "in the real world" in their entirety; they are compounds of what we found to be "standard practice".

When we conducted the survey we were interested to note the (standard) paradoxical response. Part one of this response was "I have no idea what happens in other institutions". Then, when we told them what did happen elsewhere, and, often, that their own practice was in the same pattern *no one was surprised*.

In the same way, we do not anticipate that much in the first half of the book will be surprising: it is a compilation, abstraction and distillation of standard practice. The composite case studies represent typical project courses and their typical place within the curriculum. Thus, software-engineering-focused group projects most commonly occur in the middle of a program. So, we have a composite case study which is called "The second year group project". Composite case studies are, largely, organized on their place within the curriculum.

Mechanisms, however, slice the data another way. Here aspects of project work are examined across all possible situations in which they may occur. To take an example, allocation occurs in all forms of project work – and there are standard ways of accomplishing it. The mechanism section that relates to allocation aims to provide the entire continuum of standard ways to allocate students to supervisors or students to projects or supervisors to students/projects.

Together composite case studies and mechanisms aim to be a comprehensive representation of how these things are commonly done in UK higher education.

The other sort of information which is in the first half of the book is encompassed in **specific case studies**. These are single examples, from single instances, treated in a more in-depth and contextualized fashion. They illustrate a particular emphasis on one method or approach and are always exemplary or illustrative of especially interesting aspects of project work.

Thus, the aims of the first half of the book are to be comprehensive, to catalog the range of practice, to show standard practice (which we expect to be unsurprising), and to show interesting instances in more detail. Unfortunately, this means that it is unlikely that anyone would want to read this from start to finish. It is a work to "dip into" when need or interest dictate. It may be most useful for those organizing (designing, sustaining or redesigning) projects for an entire department (the project coordinator). It provides the breadth of experience and summation of advantages/disadvantages of each approach that gives a firm foundation for considered decision making.

The second half is different, although it deals with the same subject matter. It is conceived as a "user manual", something that matches the inexperienced, sometimes rather daunted, recipient of a new process. The user manual is not a unique genre. Many practical subjects have devised ways to pass knowledge from person to person without their ever meeting or interacting in an immediate way. Car maintenance manuals and cookbooks, are very popular expressions of this genre. However, the approach has limitations:

> One of the differences about the universe of cooking as portrayed in beginner's cookbooks and as we acquire it in real life is that in the former knowledge progresses in an orderly fashion, while in real life it arrives in unique chunks of experience . . . and those in no particular order. In this regard, it is more like doing a jigsaw puzzle: putting your hand on just the right piece can link several other unconnected-seeming pieces together in a coherent pattern. (Thorne and Thorne, 1998)

Indeed, Part One is very much a compendium of knowledge which "progresses in an orderly fashion". Part Two is both more informal and directed at engaging the problems of the practice, concerned with addressing the practitioner "on the ground". There is no attempt in the second half for the coverage to be complete. It is precisely and deliberately non-comprehensive, a combination of intention and practice.

References

(1997) Engineering Council.

(2000a) Quality Assurance Agency for Higher Education, UK.

(2000b) ACM and IEEE Computer Society, Chapter5 "Principles".

Agre, P. E. (1997) *Computation and Human Experience*, Cambridge University Press, Cambridge.

Allison, B., O'Sullivan, T., Owen, A., Rice, J., Rothwell, A. and Saunders, C. (1996) *Research Skills for Students*, Kogan Page, London.

Bell, J. (1993) *Doing your Research Project: A Guide for First-Time Researchers in Education and Social Sciences*, Open University Press, Buckingham.

Davis, H. (1999) *The Culture of Building*, Oxford University Press, New York.

Finerman, A. (Ed.) (1968) *University Education in Computing Science*, Academic Press, New York.

Lave, J. and Wenger, E. (1991) *Situated Learning: Legitimate Peripheral Participation*, Cambridge University Press, Cambridge.

Luck, M. (1999) *Your Student Research Project*, Gower, Hampshire.

Thorne, J. and Thorne, M. L. (1998) *Outlaw Cook*, Prospect Books, Devon.

Wenger, E. (1998) *Communities of Practice: Learning, Meaning, and Identity*, Cambridge University Press, Cambridge.

Acknowledgements

This book is one result of work of the Effective Projectwork in Computer Science (EPCoS) consortium. EPCoS was funded in the first phase of the UK Higher Education Funding Council for England (HEFCE) Fund for Development of Teaching and Learning (FDTL) initiative from 1996–1999, reference 12/96.

The consortium was led by David Bateman and Sally Fincher from the Computer Science Discipline Network, based at the University of Kent. Members of the consortium were: Brian Lings and Wendy Milne from the University of Exeter, Ian Utting from the University of Kent, Roger Boyle and Martyn Clark from the University of Leeds, Peter Capon from the University of Manchester, Marian Petre from the Open University, Gwil Edmunds and Rachel Harrison from the University of Southampton, Malcolm Birtle from the University of Teesside, and Keith Mander from the University of York.

Over the life of the project we were assisted by many others. Due especial mention are Fiona Hovenden, who was our Development Officer in the first year, and Mike McMillan-Andrews who supported us in many invaluable, practical ways from helping with mailshots to managing the website. We were supported at a different level by the input from our Steering Committee: Professor Derek Fraser, Vice Chancellor of the University of Teesside, Professor Diana Laurillard, Pro-Vice Chancellor of the Open University, and Professor John Slater, Pro-Vice Chancellor of the University of Kent. Their advice and support truly steered us through an (occasionally) sticky course. Over the life of the project (and beyond) the quality of advice and support we received from the FDTL National Coordination Team, especially Carole Baume, was exemplary.

Finally, there is no doubt that the consortium would have folded well before we reached this point if it had not been for the vision, kindness and emotional support of David Bateman – who was also adept at knowing when to apply more tangible forms of support ranging from a pat on the back to buying his round. Thank you, David.

This book was put together by a subgroup of the consortium: Roger Boyle, Martyn Clark, Sally Fincher, Marian Petre, Keith Mander, and Ian Utting. We drew on the work of EPCoS; not only the contributions of consortium partners, but also on data from our survey and material gathered from EPCoS conferences and workshops. We gratefully acknowledge all these inputs (witting or unwitting). Any credit must be given to the originators of those ideas; all mistakes and errors are properly ours.

Part

Introduction

It is axiomatic that teaching practice varies enormously from one institution to another. Part One describes a wide range of materials and practice, from a variety of perspectives, derived from an analysis of actual practice at over 50 institutions. The aim is to indicate the breadth of the territory of project work, to show what kinds of features appear, and to enumerate the different features that distinguish one sort of project from another.

The mapping undertaken in Part One recognizes that project work is composed of: a number of *elements*, expressing an *educational form*, which must be made to work in *context*. Elements, form, and context are interdependent, and the characterization of any one example must include all three – although that is not necessarily how people naturally think about their practice (which is why this book also includes Part Two). Part One gives attention to each of the three, in order to expose and characterize them.

Part One:

- characterizes common project *forms* (composite case studies)
- maps out *elements* of practice abstracted from context (mechanisms)
- gives examples of practice in *context* (particular case studies).

In assembling a body of authentic examples, we aim to provide a resource in a simple, standard format to make exploration and comparison feasible.

What Is a Composite Case Study?

It is the selection of certain combinations of elements which characterizes a particular project form. The composite case studies are composed from many individual examples of commonly encountered, straightforward ways of undertaking project work. They are constructed to reveal the common form and reflect standard practice from all (and none) of the contributing examples. The case studies have been composed *because* their form is typical and hence they should be familiar to many practitioners: what is standard is no surprise.

The format for the case studies is derived from how practitioners describe their work to each other, and the information they use to characterize their projects. These case studies consist of two parts: a header and constituent sections. The standard format makes it easier to pick out and compare particular elements across the various forms.

The Header

The header provides an "at a glance" overview of the practice which the case study encompasses:

Individual or group?	Describes whether the instance is usually for individuals or groups and, if groups, the number of students typically involved.
Year	Denotes the place within the curriculum in which the instance is commonly located.
Assessment	Gives the typical assessment objectives.
Pedagogic focus	Describes the common reasons for undertaking a project of this type.
Special characteristics	Aspects which are particularly (sometimes uniquely) relevant to work of this nature.
Key problem	A characteristic difficulty associated with this approach.

The Constituent Sections

The text of the composites is divided under common subheadings to facilitate easy comparability across examples. Of course, there are some subheadings that are only useful to particular composites, but, in general, each has the same elements. The subheadings are:

Size and duration	Typical contact hours per week, duration, and scale of project
Context	A sketch of the origins and "flavor" of the project. Context may be cultural, environmental, historical or a combination of these elements.
Objectives/aims/ pedagogic focus	What it is intended that students will learn from a project of this type
Topics (allocation)	The ways in which topics are assigned between supervisors and students
Supervision	The nature of the interaction between students and supervisors
Assignment to groups	(Obviously not applicable to instances of individual project work)
Student process	How students are expected to work and to manage the project
Deliverables	What students are required to produce
Assessment	Basis for assessment, typical assessment criteria and strategies
Cited keys to success	Quotes from practitioners or other anecdotal evidence

Broadly, the composite case studies are ordered on the place in which they commonly occur in the curriculum (first year, second year, etc.).

What Are Mechanisms?

The "mechanisms" section was constructed by abstracting specific, small elements of project work practice from many real examples. Any element may be satisfied by a number of different teaching and learning mechanisms (for example, the element "allocation of students to teams" may be satisfied in a number of ways). In this section, we aim:

- to map the *range* of the usual ways to implement a specific element
- to *highlight the trade-offs* that might be considered in choosing one way of doing things over another.

Consequently, this section can be particularly useful when you know what it is that you want to change and can help you to decide what to change *to*.

These two complementary aims are reflected in the presentation of the mechanisms, which comprise a general description, followed by a discussion of advantages and disadvantages associated with their use. The advantages and disadvantages are important because it is by looking at these that a practitioner can tell whether the practice described may be of value. It is the consideration of advantages and disadvantages that exposes how the mechanism might relate to a particular context.

What Are Specific Case Studies?

All the specific case studies are detailed descriptions of projects, taken from a variety of institutional contexts and settings. Each has been chosen because it displays an unusual or particularly interesting approach. The specific case studies utilize the same format as the composites.

Whilst composite case studies and mechanisms (especially when read in conjunction) provide a charting of the territory of project work, the specific case studies fill in some of the richness that was stripped away in the abstractions and compositions. More importantly, they illustrate the ways in which context impinges on mechanism choices, the way mechanism choices are interdependent, and the ways in which form and mechanism influence each other. The choices are not random or independent; the specific case studies show how elements, form and context interrelate to give projects their particular character.

Project Models

A project is shaped by its educational aims. What the project is meant to accomplish (or what the students are meant to learn through doing the project) governs the choice of mechanisms for any particular instance of project work. In a sense, "form follows function": what the project is "for" constrains which sorts of formats, deliverables, assessment and so on are appropriate. The "project models" described in this section are simply thumbnail sketches of the educational aims and focus of different types of project. These models can be interpreted and realized in a variety of ways, using a variety of mechanisms. The models provide a view on projects through their role in the curriculum (rather than the stage in the program at which they are presented). They do not fulfill the same function as the later case studies, but are presented here as a more abstract consideration of the roles of projects in a curriculum.

Research

Overall aim: Theoretically grounded project work, which contributes to a research discourse using appropriate methods and reporting.

Research projects mirror the traditional research model of the natural sciences, introducing students to research methods, research standards, and research discourse. Computing science research projects have theory as a necessary component. Although an exceptional student project might extend or challenge existing theory in some fashion, the theory component is more usually realised as a demonstration of theory through focused application, or the "re-contextualization" of theory through a novel application – and hence demonstration of the student's grasp of the advanced concepts involved. In this sense, computing science research projects are usually largely "practical", while theoretically grounded. The project work must be situated in the existing research discourse, and so these projects normally include a literature survey as a major component. As in the natural sciences, student research projects may be designed to contribute to a research agenda in the department, adding incrementally to a program of research planned by a member of faculty. The main deliverable is the project report or dissertation.

Product Development – Design and Build

Overall aim: To design, implement, and test a software product.

"Design and build" projects focus on product development, and assessment is usually product oriented. The aim is to complete a whole development cycle, from the identification and specification of the product, through design, to prototyping and testing. Design and build projects often draw topics from the "real world", either by basing proposals on observation of how things work, or by bringing in acting or actual clients.

Software Engineering

Overall aim: To follow a software engineering development methodology (following the software engineering life-cycle through specification, implementation, documentation, and testing) on a mid- to large-scale software engineering problem.

Software engineering projects are typically team projects undertaking a medium to large software engineering problem. The work focuses on following some software engineering development model or methodology; students are typically required to document their passage through the software engineering life-cycle. The projects are largely technical, but they also require the technical work to be "packaged" appropriately, realizing standards of practice for project management and software development, demonstrating approved methodology, and addressing professional issues.

Application-based

Overall aim: To create a software product within the context of existing software products: understanding, using, and integrating the various software effectively.

Application-based projects involve creating software in the context of an existing system or set of tools, such as information systems, databases, etc. This requires mastery of existing systems with sufficient insight to integrate new functions appropriately, to use existing pieces of software in concert, to create new functionality without "reinventing the wheel" – or introducing problems. Such projects usually arise from "real" problems, and testing and evaluation are important components of the project work. A great deal of consultancy work in the "real world" is application based, and so these projects emulate an aspect of professional practice.

Team Projects, Process-based

Overall aim: To experience group processes and teamwork (including decision making, communication and cooperation, role taking) in the execution of a development project.

Process-based team projects focus on cooperative development and group process. Assessment is typically process-oriented, examining role taking within the team, project management, decision making, record keeping and documentation, and the development of individual strengths and interpersonal skills. Projects are typically software engineering projects, and management structures and processes may be specified. Process-based projects may be built around product development, but the success of the product is secondary to the experience of the process, and some process-based projects are designed so that students can experience setbacks and failure.

Capstone, Integrative

Overall aim: To integrate and consolidate acquired concepts and skills through use on project work.

Integrative projects are called "capstone" projects in the US, referring to the coping stone that completes a wall and ties together the final layer of the structure. Ideally, these projects are learning experiences. The aim is to concretize concepts by putting them to use, to connect concepts to the skills that use and embody them, and to integrate concepts by using them in concert to accomplish the project and hence make sense of them "as a whole". Integrative projects may focus on problem solving rather than product building. Capstone projects are typically final-year projects, but they may be used to integrate preceding work at any time in the curriculum.

Culminating, Demonstrative

Overall aim: To demonstrate acquired skills.

Culminating projects are designed to allow students to demonstrate the technical skills they have acquired. They are typically technically demanding projects that require students to "show their stuff" in a number of key areas through the development of a system or prototype.

Industrial Projects

Overall aim: To glimpse the "real world" of industrial practice (including constraints, decision making, standards, and management) through interaction with industry on a project.

The aim of industrial projects is to influence student attitudes and behavior by including industrial experience, either by sending students into industry, or by bringing industrialists into the university to lead students. Students often give more credence to messages delivered by those "at the coal face" than by academics, whom they view as being removed from the real world. The involvement of industry in student projects can refocus students' attention, helping them take seriously non-technical issues, constraints on development, and professional standards. The role of industry may vary, from providing problems, to providing instruction or supervision, or to taking realistic roles as project managers or clients. Further, students may be placed temporarily in the workplace, giving them a chance of direct experience.

Project Choice

It can be bewildering trying to make appropriate choices of project aim, form, and component. It might be thought that "anything goes" and that mixing and matching mechanisms to models will provide equally acceptable results. In some aspects, this is perfectly true; for other aspects, there are specific mechanisms that are strongly associated with a particular form or model of project, to the extent that it would be perverse to substitute something else. The following chart presents some of these associations which we captured in our data. The chart is it is not meant to be comprehensive – these are not the only choices, just the "most typical" within our data set.

KEY TO TABLE

The boxes contain named mechanisms (from the possible range) which are typically found associated with a given project type. Additionally:

CHOOSE ONE: indicates that there isn't a defining aspect

italics: an entry in italics indicates that choice here depends on other choices (form or model of project)

bullet points: mechanisms are listed in "most typical" order

parentheses: indicates a "less typical" option, i.e. use of this mechanism has been observed in this situation, but not as commonly as others.

	topic allocation	supervisor allocation	allocation of students to groups	supervisor roles	supervision meetings composition
final-year individual	CHOOSE ONE • assigned individual • students propose • negotiated choice of set topics	CHOOSE ONE existing relationships students choose supervisors choose student profile	N/A	• observer / commentator project manager mentor	individual collective
second-year group	one topic for all aspects of one topic choice of set topics	• arbitrary team supervision pool supervision	CHOOSE ONE self-selection allocation by ability	CHOOSE ONE *related to project model*	collective whole group project leaders
taught M.Sc.	• students propose assigned individual	• supervisors choose existing relationships supervisors invite	N/A	observer / commentator	individual
project with handover	aspects of one topic	arbitrary team supervision existing relationships	self-selection allocation across abilities	• observer / commentator	CHOOSE ONE collective whole group project leaders
research-type	CHOOSE ONE negotiated within constraints students propose choice of set topics	supervisors choose supervisors invite	N/A	observer / commentator mentor project leader master	individual collective
design and build	assigned choice of set topics negotiated	arbitrary	CHOOSE ONE *(or more)*	CHOOSE ONE *roles depend on location of project in the curriculum*	individual *or* group *(as appropriate)* collective
project with industrial involvemen	negotiated with client & supervisor one topic for all aspects of one topic	arbitrary	CHOOSE ONE allocation across abilities	observer / commentator mentor technical guru	whole group project leaders
project with client	negotiated with client & supervisor thereafter . . . CHOOSE ONE	*supervisor allocation usually follows client assignment, which may follow topic assignment*	CHOOSE ONE self-selection	observer / commentator project manager	whole group collective project leaders
professional bodies' model	CHOOSE ONE	CHOOSE ONE	N/A	observer / commentator mentor	individual
process-based	CHOOSE ONE one topic for all choice of set topics negotiated	arbitrary existing relationships team supervision	self-selection allocation across abilities demographic dist. dis-affinity	observer / commentator project manager client teacher	whole group collective (project leaders)
integrative/ capstone	one topic for all choice of set topics (students propose) (negotiated)	supervisors choose students choose student profile	N/A	observer / commentator mentor	individual

time for meetings	student roles in groups	assessment: who marks	assessment: basis	staff deployment
prescribed catch-as-catch-can appointments only	N/A	supervisor + one	summary formative	everyone pulling in
prescribed office hours	CHOOSE ONE	CHOOSE ONE supervisor self assessment peer assessment	CHOOSE ONE	small group graduate students
prescribed appointments only	N/A	supervisor + one moderator	summary formative	everyone beyond the dept. industrial involvement
prescribed appointments only	self-organizing rotating	supervisor peer assessment	summary	small group
prescribed catch-as-catch-can	N/A	supervisor + one	summary formative	small group graduate students
prescribed office hours *(group projects)* catch-as-catch-can *(individual projects)*	self-organizing	supervisor supervisor + one peer assessment	CHOOSE ONE *depends on the role in the curriculum*	CHOOSE ONE *depends on the role in the curriculum*
prescribed appointments only office hours	self-organizing supervisor-appointed	supervisor external party	summary	small group industrial involvement
prescribed catch-as-catch-can	self-organizing negotiated	supervisor external party	summary continuous formative	small group
prescribed	N/A	supervisor supervisor + one	summary	everyone pulling in
prescribed appointments only	CHOOSE ONE rotating	supervisor supervisor + one self assessment peer assessment	CHOOSE ONE summary continuous formative	small group
prescribed catch-as-catch-can	N/A	supervisor + one	summary	everyone pulling in

1 Composite Case Studies

Composite Case Studies

1.1 Final-year Individual Project

○   ○   ○   ○

Individual or group?	individual
Year	final (3 or 4)
Assessment	usually focused on deliverables
Pedagogic focus	substantial, independent software development
Special characteristics	student-supervisor relationship
Key problem	supervising and assessing many different topics

Size and Duration

Typically arranged as a part-time effort extended over 2–3 terms (i.e. 6 months to a year), but can be cast as an intensive project run full-time during one term. Expected student hours per week range from 6–35. Cohorts range from 12–300, with most in the 60–100 range.

Context

Many computing science faculty members come from the natural sciences, where the final-year project has always been a feature of undergraduate education. In the natural science curriculum, it has a clear purpose: preparation for research within that discipline. Students there typically work in the supervisor's area of expertise, contributing a small piece to a larger research effort, and hence contributing to departmental research. So the focus is on the practice of the discipline (e.g. actualizing physics). Because the practice of computing science is different from the practice of the natural sciences, the project model has been adapted.

Computing science final-year projects are typically student-chosen, student-focused projects, making no contribution to ongoing research in the department. They follow different models:

- the research basis, or
- the culminating, integrative basis, or
- the apprenticeship, design and build basis.

Whatever the model, they are designed as a demonstration of practice, attracting importance as professional, industrial preparation. They are important evidence for potential employers ". . . more important than [degree] classification". Hence the position and importance of the final-year project has been consolidated through pressure from employers, professional bodies and their accreditation programs. The project is substantial; it can represent 20–66% of coursework for the year, and 10–33% of the degree. In most departments, failing the final-year project entails failing the degree.

There are many pressures on project constitution, for example:

- increasing student numbers (i.e. staff supervising multiple projects)
- professional bodies' requirements about the nature of the project (e.g. students required to experience the whole software project life-cycle)
- fast-changing technology means supervisors have to "up-skill" or students are constrained to "out-of-date" topics.

Yet the "shape" of the final-year project still derives from a time of elite education, when staff:student ratios were favorable and resources were relatively ample. As such, they are resource hungry, and recent innovations focus on bringing costs in line with current resourcing.

Clearly, the staff load attendant on individual projects is enormous. Scale is probably the major issue; there is a limit to how many projects one faculty member can supervise adequately. The more staff who are involved, the greater the monitoring and consistency load. With fewer students it would be easier to monitor the suitability of a project idea and to gain greater consistency in marking. More students make both of these harder.

Technical resources must be available to accommodate demand. Constraints on software, platforms, and other materials are usually built into the environment; students may only use what is available and supported. Many students – typically 50% – work using their own computers, in addition to those in the laboratory.

Many departments have explicit course prerequisites, such as software engineering, although prerequisites are more typically implicit, given degree requirements and the placement of the project in the final year. Some departments run individual projects within a course structure, so that in addition to supervisory sessions students attend lectures associated with project work (e.g. research methods, project management, presentation skills) or meetings addressing general project issues.

Objectives/Aims/Pedagogic Focus

The final-year project is fundamentally a demonstration of technical competence, encompassing problem solving and software development. For example, students may be asked to identify a number of topic choices, of which one is assigned based on supervisor availability.

Supervision

Final-year projects are almost all characterized by a single student–single supervisor relationship, and a roughly equal emphasis on individual achievement and the supervisory relationship, i.e. the project is about the growth of the student as a practitioner, and the supervisor nurtures it. Supervision is typically intended to be "light-handed": "supervisors are expected to help students to 'help themselves' . . ." and "supervisors should be advisors rather than directors of the student's work . . .". Supervisors typically provide high-level guidance on project planning and management. They may give technical or managerial input as required. They may suggest sources of information, methods and techniques, writing tips. They may provide critiques of deliverables or intermediate products.

Some institutions operate hierarchical monitoring arrangements, with supervisors being overseen by leaders, and a few operate limited joint supervision arrangements. Collective or joint supervision is usually designed to reduce demand on supervisory staff or to give access to specialist expertise. Most students also have access to technical support, some to specialist technical support or laboratory assistants.

Contact time ranges from 10 minutes per week to 1 hour per week, with 30- or 60-minute sessions most common.

Student Process

The student process varies, within the common framework of the student-supervisor relationship. The amount of negotiation varies, usually constrained to the topic, but potentially covering every aspect of the project, including learning objectives, milestones, deliverables, and assessment.

Occasionally, a project structure is prescribed. For example, the student may be required to demonstrate adherence to the waterfall model of software development, or to work within a development discipline such as the Personal Software Process (PSP) (Humphreys, 1997). More often, it is simply specified that the student conforms to some recognized methodology. Milestones and intermediate products are sometimes specified.

Deliverables

Virtually all final-year projects require:

- a final report (typically 8,000–12,000 words) and
- a software product (number of lines of code varies greatly, from 1,000s to 10,000s).

The next most common deliverable is:

- an oral presentation, or
- a software demonstration.

Other deliverables are less common, but can include some or all of:

- a specification
- an abstract or project synopsis
- a work plan and schedule
- user documentation
- a project log or journal, a portfolio of working documents
- a progress report
- a survey of theoretical background and literature, or a reading list.

Assessment

The most common assessment model involves the supervisor, a second marker (either a second supervisor or a moderator), and the potential for a third marker if the first two differ significantly.

The mark is usually apportioned to stated categories, either to deliverables (e.g. final report, software, and presentation) or to elements of the work (e.g. output, initiative, planning, presentation). Most departments have marking criteria or exemplars.

The biggest difficulty in assessment is maintaining equity, given the variety of problems and the number of students and supervisors. The three main factors are:

- controlling the level of difficulty and complexity of the problem – or taking it into account in assessment
- assessing supervisor input into the work
- monitoring consistency among all staff involved.

Cited Keys to Success

Success relies crucially on "student motivation and staff dedication". The linchpin of the final-year project is good supervision. Other factors cited include:

- "The heavy involvement of research assistants' expertise"
- "Persistence, management of project"
- "Good quality project ideas"
- "Students devoting the required time to the project"
- "Insisting that [students] keep the project moving at a steady pace"
- "Emphasis placed on importance of project"
- "With large numbers of students it is important to write down what you expect of students and how they can accomplish that. Word of mouth is no longer reliable enough as a means of communicating what a final-year project is about to a large group of students."

References

Humphreys, W. S. (1997) *Introduction to the personal software process*, Addison-Wesley, Reading, Mass.

1.2 Second-year Group Project

○ ○ ○ ○

Individual or group?	group (4–5 to 7–8)
Year	2
Assessment	usually individual, based on deliverables
Pedagogic focus	introduction to group working and a "complete" system
Special characteristics	group work
Key problem	assessing individual performance within groups

Size and Duration

Typical teams fall in the range of 4–5 to 7–8 members. The student time commitment varies from 1–3 hours per week for 12–15 weeks, to 12 hours per week for two terms (i.e. 24 weeks).

Context

Second-year projects are typically well established within their institutions, having been used for 5–20 years. Nearly all instances are considered successful; they provide an early and salutary introduction to teamwork at a time when the faculty wants students to look beyond the scope of their own code. The larger projects are usually seen by students and staff as having real importance in the degree. The value of group projects is enhanced by industry interest and the increasing value prospective employers put on teamwork and communication skills.

Group projects are typically offered in the second year because, "The first year would be too early, since they are assumed not to have enough experience of programming or the principles of software engineering. The third year would be too late, mainly because we want them to undertake individual projects which are technically more challenging at that stage."

Second-year projects are constructed in different ways, to build on different aspects of or perspectives on group work. The most common form is the simplest: students working in groups over a number of weeks. Variations are usually intended to increase the "realism" of the experience by mimicking some part of industrial practice, for example:

- intensive group project (sole activity, concentrated into one or two weeks)
- buyer/seller (introducing concepts and issues of software integration): "Halfway through the project, each group has to 'sell' its software to another group, and to 'purchase' the software of another group in order to create the complete software system required. The groups have to address issues of effective advertising of their own 'product' and how to assess the offerings of other groups."
- explicit client (emphasizing the business context): "Real clients. Real bank accounts. Real company."

Projects are often set in the context of scheduled laboratories and project classes. Some programming knowledge, but usually little other technical or project management knowledge is assumed. The project usually follows or is concurrent with a software engineering course.

Some tools or techniques are usually prescribed (e.g. programming language, platform, management scheme) – or just constrained by availability.

The main quality issues are those usually associated with group work: equity, coping with sub-optimal group dynamics, individual variation. "Individual high achievers can find team working difficult, and weakly motivated students find the approach difficult."

Objectives/Aims/Pedagogic Focus

The second-year group project is typically considered important because, "It is the only place where students get involved in large-scale group work." Hence, it is seen as providing:

- an introduction to group working, exposure to issues of team organization, approximation of industry practice
- experience of developing a small "complete" system, introduction to code integration, experience of a software development environment
- experience of programming something more substantial than previous assignments
- planning, scheduling, time management, progress monitoring
- experience of producing documentation
- an opportunity to make concrete and consolidate software engineering issues raised in other courses
- experience of client negotiations
- an opportunity to evaluate tools, methods, and software
- a chance to learn from mistakes.

Technical objectives include:

- project planning

- product definition
- design
- prototyping
- implementation
- integration
- testing
- software delivery.

Non-technical objectives include:

- communication
- ability to manage group activity
- ability to manage personal activity in a group context
- advertizing a product
- ability to manage meetings
- report writing
- oral presentation.

Topics (Allocation)

Project topics are typically prescribed, or made by selection from a prescribed list, but a variety of topic allocation mechanisms may be used. The type of prescription depends on the course design, e.g.

- buyer/seller arrangements require at least two topics, so that teams have something to market
- integrated mega-project arrangements require appropriate coverage, hence each team is allocated a particular part of a large problem .

Occasionally the project is specified by an external client.

"Project topics are prescribed mainly to insure comparable and sufficient difficulty and complexity ... The topics ... always involve the use of a distributed database, graphic user interface and communications facilities. The topics are always beyond the capability of an individual, or teams, given the resource constraints. This is to encourage teams to negotiate the scope of deliverables and to prevent one team member doing all the work."

Supervision

Supervision is usually assigned. Supervision is usually on a weekly meeting basis, sometimes on a class basis. Contact time normally ranges from 1–3 hours per week per group.

The supervisor's role depends on how the project is cast. For a generic software engineering task, supervision is usually in the form of high-level guidance, monitoring and troubleshooting, rather than instruction per se. A design and build project embedded in a notional business environment is more likely to include client and line manager roles, and, occasionally, the supervisor acts as "customer".

What is seen in supervision practice in second-year group projects shows wide variation, but there is a typical relationship between the nature of the project scenario and the role (or roles) the supervisor plays.

There is usually a project coordinator who monitors the projects and supervision overall to ensure progress, consistency, and quality.

Assignment to Groups

Groups may be self-assembled or assigned. Various assignment schemes are employed, e.g.

- arbitrary
- tutorial groups
- demographic dispersal
- by or across ability and/or skills
- affinity (or dis-affinity).

Student Process

Management structure varies. Groups usually manage themselves, although sometimes the supervisor takes a more active role. Sometimes groups are required to negotiate their approach and their group structure and hence to have it approved. Often, key roles are stipulated (e.g. team leader, financial controller, recorder, librarian, quality controller, liaison) – depending on the nature of the project and context. Often there is a rotating role, e.g. chair, organizer, recorder.

Organization is typically described as "democratic". The structure of the organization and the assignment of roles are typically chosen by the group. For example:

- "Each group evolves its own structure and method of working. Part of the learning process is to discover the advantages and/or disadvantages of the structure they choose."
- "The life-cycle to be employed is negotiable so long as processes of specification, design and validation can be seen . . . No methods are prescribed, but recognizable methods are expected to be adopted (negotiated) by the teams."

Collaboration is usually face-to-face, supported by email.

Deliverables

The requirement and assessment of deliverables varies from case to case, but the overall pattern is fairly consistent, relying on some subset of:

Individual Deliverables:

- individual report
- logbook or diary

Group Deliverables:

- documentation of group organization and management (e.g. agenda, minutes of meetings)
- documentation of process (specification, project plan, design documentation, library and inspection records)
- software (prototype, operational system)
- test documentation
- user documentation
- face-to-face presentation
- sales and purchase strategies.

Assessment

Assessment is typically individual (on the basis of individual and group deliverables), with some component of the mark based on the group output, e.g. 50% joint (software product and documentation) and 50% individual (final report). "Group marks only modified if student disowned by group. Students are told 'it is not fair' and marks are sufficiently unimportant for them to accept this."

Assessment usually takes into account a variety of factors, e.g. software quality, presentation, group organization and management, report writing, project planning, design, individual contribution to the group, communication.

Some institutions assess each deliverable in phases. Some assess only summatively. Assessment is typically criterion based, using a marking scheme which specifies how many marks should be given to a particular aspect of the work.

Students are often asked to keep a logbook or diary, as part of their report. There is typically (not always) some element of self-assessment, e.g.

- group agrees "self-assessment percentages" for portion of total effort contributed by each member of the group, and this percentage is used to compute the individual's mark
- deliverable components are given a marks tariff; hence, weaker students can avoid more complex deliverables
- team may be able to penalize or sanction under-performers (e.g. yellow card/red card system).

Peer assessment is usually limited:

- negotiation process (for buy-in systems) may be peer assessed
- formative peer assessment as part of quality control using inspections.

Assessment is typically by the supervisor and one other member of staff.

Cited Keys to Success:

- good group self-management
- a suitable technical level
- "Real clients. Real bank accounts. Real company."
- "The willingness of tutors to accept a gradual transfer of control and responsibility for learning from tutors to students."

1.3 Taught M.Sc. Project

○ ○ ○ ○

Individual or group?	individual
Year	postgraduate
Assessment	based on the dissertation
Pedagogic focus	demonstration of subject mastery, academic skills, and the potential for individual contribution
Special characteristics	original work is expected
Key problem	getting the students to come to terms with what's required

Size and Duration

M.Sc. projects typically take up a substantial portion of a student's time, usually half of their time over two terms (i.e. 50% of 24 weeks), or all of their time over one term (such as the three months over their final summer).

Context

The M.Sc. project is the culminating project for the taught master's degree, either a "conversion" to a new subject for a student with a degree in another, perhaps unrelated subject, or an advanced degree focusing on a specialism within the domain, perhaps on an emergent area. A master's degree conveys that the holder has the knowledge with which to practice a craft independently, without submitting to the supervision of others more experienced. Hence the project is the demonstration of mastery of the subject and its skills, of the student's understanding of academic work (including an ordered, critical and reasoned exposition of knowledge), their independent ability to analyze an issue, and to design and execute a program of work, whether research or development. As a "rough guide", an M.Sc. project must demonstrate appropriate technical skill, but it also usually requires a significant theoretical component and so often has some aspirations as research preparation.

Projects can take different forms:

- *design and build:* the design, implementation and evaluation of a system or subsystem, perhaps applying a novel principle, or perhaps applying a known technique in a new context
- *evaluation:* an evaluation of a particular system or comparison of alternative systems, perhaps in a particular context of use with implications for an overriding issue, perhaps in the context of critiquing one or comparing a variety of evaluation methodologies, or perhaps in the context of illuminating aspects of theory
- *theoretical analysis:* an analysis of particular policies, strategies, techniques, or theories, usually with some further proposals
- *empirical:* investigation into particular systems or practice using empirical techniques.

Projects may also involve industry through students' own employers or as external "clients". Some will receive additional support in this context, others will be constrained in which avenues they may investigate.

M.Sc. projects are usually well established in their institutions and are usually similar in structure. Commonly, the project has a supervisor, who oversees the work but does not usually manage it, and an internal examiner, who assesses and provides feedback on specific deliverables but has no other contact with the student.

The assessment of dissertations can be a subjective and personal business, relying on the supervisor's experience and perspective. Different parties may interpret the M.Sc. standards and requirements differently. Maintaining consistency among markers may be difficult if perspectives vary too widely, and disagreements necessitate even greater resource demands, since a third party must give close attention to a substantial document.

The project process may be a "closed" one, not easily accessible to monitoring, focused as it is on the student's independent work and on the student-supervisor interaction. Hence, it may be difficult to detect problems early enough in the process to remedy. The nature and standard of supervision may vary significantly among staff, and similarly the nature and standard of feedback from the internal examiner may vary significantly, potentially having substantial impact on the student's progress. The supervisor and internal examiner must find a compatible perspective, so that students are not "caught in the middle" with conflicting advice.

M.Sc. projects are labor intensive for supervisors and internal examiners, hence having significant resource implications for departments. The proposal process alone can be extremely demanding, even before the student is accepted for project work and a supervisor is assigned. Making matches between students (and their topics) and supervisors can be problematic; if suitable "marriages" cannot be made, then students may be required to change topic or approach in order to be accommodated within available expertise. The load on staff may be uneven, depending on student interests in a given term (influencing how many projects a supervisor takes on), student ability and maturity (influencing the individual demand on the supervisor), and complexity of the project.

Objectives/Aims/Pedagogic Focus

The aim of the M.Sc. project is to demonstrate that students can carry out work independently:

- to analyze an issue and identify a topic
- to design and execute a substantial program of work
- to find and assimilate topical information, both theoretical and technical
- to make use of what they've learned on the M.Sc. course
- to select and apply appropriate methods or methodology (in investigation, generation, and evaluation)
- to keep records and produce suitable documentation
- to present work both orally and in writing in appropriate, ordered, scholarly form
- to reason critically, both about preceding work and about their own.

Topics (Allocation)

Project topics are typically proposed by the student through a written proposal and subsequent negotiation process. Projects are usually concerned with academic or practical areas, often drawn from the student's past experience or work environment. Alternatively, project topics may be assigned or selected from a list, when pressure of numbers or other resources make student proposals infeasible. Projects are usually required to have a theoretical component as well as a practical one, and students are usually required to set the project in the context of related work.

Supervision

Supervision is often assigned on the basis of the student's proposal. Often there is a brokering period, when supervisors with appropriate expertise are sought for the topics that have been proposed, and when topics are renegotiated in terms of available supervision. In other cases (for example, where numbers are high), this sort of proposal-and-brokering may be impracticable, and other mechanisms are used to assign supervisors.

Supervision is usually individual, involving regular face-to-face meetings, email, and other contact. The supervisor acts as observer/commentator and often mentor, providing strategic guidance, monitoring and troubleshooting, but the initiative usually remains with the student. The supervisor may critique student plans and usually provides detailed feedback on interim reports and dissertation drafts. In particular, supervisors usually track the project management, guiding students to maintain an appropriate pace to achieve the project objectives. Students often come to conversion degrees from outside academia, and so supervision often includes instruction in applying the academic, scientific, and engineering standards expected.

Supervision is often on an "as needed" basis, with only infrequent scheduled meetings, but closer supervision can be arranged, with contact of the order of $1/2$–1 hour per week. M.Sc. projects are often conducted during the summer months, when staff availability may be sporadic.

In "supervisor plus another" arrangements, the internal examiner usually comments on interim reports and assesses the dissertation, with no other contact with the student and often no other contact with the supervisor. Feedback on interim reports is intended to guide the student about achieving an appropriate standard (and success overall). The internal examiner's feedback may be filtered through the supervisor, so that the student receives a consistent "story".

Student Process

The M.Sc. project is meant to be independent work, and so the students usually manage themselves, although reporting to the supervisor. The level of supervisor intervention depends on the "maturity" of the student. Work is usually "staged" in some way, often by the specification of one or more interim reports that both foreshadow the dissertation and reflect on the process and progress of the project. Often students are responsible for identifying and acquiring resources, from software to technical advice.

The student may be asked to follow methodologies presented elsewhere in the course. For example, a software development methodology might have to be implemented in design and build projects, or library research techniques might have to be used in the literature survey, or evaluation techniques might provide a basis from which a suitable evaluation plan is to be assembled.

Deliverables

The pattern of deliverables is fairly consistent:

- one or more interim reports, which may include work plans, research strategies and methodologies, sample software or essays, documentation of process (specification, project plan, design documentation, library and inspection records), self-critique; the interim reports are usually meant to be formative, providing a vehicle for teaching and guidance
- the dissertation, 10,000–15,000 words, which must usually include a literature survey as well as a comprehensive presentation of the project work in its own terms. Hence, a design and build project might include specification and design rationale, software, test and user documentation, and an evaluation report. A research project might include elaboration of theories or techniques; case studies, survey data or other situated empirical evidence; demonstrations of concepts, for example application of a concept in a new context; prototype implementations and test data, including statistical or other analysis.

Assessment

Assessment is usually done by the supervisor and internal examiner. Often there is a third party who monitors quality, for example by reviewing assessment over a number of projects. In the case of disagreements between supervisor and internal examiner, there may be a third marker, either another examiner or the monitor.

Students may be asked to sit oral examinations, particularly where there is some question about the dissertation or work, but oral examinations at M.Sc. level are not usual.

The assessment is normally based on published criteria, often with a marking scheme (guideline or required). These often suggest weightings among criteria such as: originality, adequacy and pertinence of literature survey, appropriateness and application of methods, use of evidence, technical/scientific analysis and argument, structure and organization, standard of writing and presentation.

Dissertations are usually rated as falling within categories such as:

- acceptable
- acceptable subject to minor corrections (within a time limit)
- unacceptable, but permitting resubmission (within a time limit) subject to major corrections
- unacceptable.

Some grading systems have categories:

- pass
- merit
- distinction.

Cited Keys to Success

The keys to the M.Sc. project are good screening of proposals and effective supervision.

The proposal sets out the scope of the project, the initial strategies, and the plan of work. Many deficiencies are detectable at this stage, and it is in the students' interests as well as the department's not to accept substandard proposals.

The supervisor can be considered the guardian of progress. Many deficiencies can be addressed during the course of a project, if they are detected early and addressed vigorously, and this requires the vigilance of the supervisor within a good student-supervisor relationship (i.e. one in which the student keeps the supervisor informed). The internal examiner can provide valuable input, clarifying which deficiencies must be addressed (and how) in order for work to achieve the required standard, as well as suggesting other perspectives or improvements. Students have trouble with pacing and organizing work of this scale; good supervision can keep them on the right track.

Students cite the availability of instructive examples (both good and bad) as contributing to their understanding of what is expected, both in form and in standard. Clear documentation of the expectations and criteria also help.

1.4 Project with Handover (a.k.a. "Software Hut")

○ ○ ○ ○

Individual or group?	usually groups of 3–6
Year	2 or 4
Assessment	individual and peer
Pedagogic focus	learning about working with other people's code.
Special characteristics	reliance of students on others' work and, in competitive version, the economic environment
Key problem	finding and dividing a suitable topic

Size and Duration

The handover model has been used with both individuals and groups, but it is usually applied to group working. The handover project is usually designed in phases and usually covers the better part of a term (i.e. 8–12 weeks).

Context

The notion of the handover project arose from the desire to make academic project work relevant to an industrial environment, where software engineers must understand, rely on, and integrate their own code with code they did not write, and where specifications are often imprecise, incomplete, and ambiguous, requiring demystification.

There are two main interpretations of this form of project: competitive (i.e. the "Software Hut" (Horning and Wortman, 1977)) and non-competitive. Both have the essential requirement to produce software components with specified interfaces, so that a working system can be formed by the combination of components that are the efforts of more than one group. Both are usually designed in phases, so that different aspects of development (component implementation, integration of a system, modification of an integrated system) are experienced, and hence different consequences of combining code written by different people are encountered.

The competitive version adds to the handover element an equally important element of an "economic environment", with "tendering" for handover, so that students compete for the opportunity to include their component in a system – and students compete to assemble the best system within the economic constraints. Hence the task is not just technical, but also social and economic, requiring students to juggle constraints in order to produce and "buy" and "sell" components which are competitive in several dimensions (e.g. efficiency, cost, reliability, "sex appeal"), in order to construct an effective, maintainable product. In a competitive scheme, the cohort must be large enough for the competition to be viable. The success of the whole relies on the effective identification of a topic and its fair division into comparable components.

Teachers regularly report that relevance is a motivator. Competitive schemes – especially those that are "game-like" – often also boast benefits in motivation and enthusiasm. In competitive trading schemes such as the Software Hut, priorities and standards (e.g. for testing and documentation) often sort themselves out in terms of market demands. The business of handover insures that students are exposed to at least some code written by others, so that they may compare approaches and design choices and begin to assess consequences.

Objectives/Aims/Pedagogic Focus

The aims of the handover relate to providing "realistic experience":

- giving students various experiences of working with (integrating, maintaining, modifying) code written by other people and hence observing the consequences of different design and implementation decisions and approaches
- giving students experience of working on a project too large for one person and, hence, relying on and integrating with code produced by others
- increasing the "realism" of projects, at least in terms of imposing environmental constraints.

Within those aims fall objectives to do with attending to the requirements of maintainable code, e.g.

- comprehending code written by others
- analyzing consequences of decisions at different stages and levels (for existing code)
- anticipating consequences of decisions at different stages and levels (for new code) and making choices that serve integration
- defining and observing interface specifications
- assessing reliability and efficiency
- balancing costs (e.g. generality, maintainability, efficiency, speed of production)
- providing effective documentation.

Additional objectives relate to group working and the professional software development process.

Topics (Allocation)

Topics are typically assigned to aspects of a given problem, because the handover requires overall orchestration. Problems must be planned carefully, so that the components or modules are designed to be of about the same magnitude and to have a well-defined interface. For example, projects may be "front-end/back-end", with one team taking the user interface, and another designing the underlying processing.

Supervision

Much of the "supervision" occurs in the preparation: establishing an appropriate topic with appropriate parameters and within an appropriate structure. Thereafter, supervision may well be mainly monitoring: ensuring that work progresses, allowing students to learn from their own experience. This usually involves weekly contact (e.g. through meetings or classes) of $1/2$–1 hour, but little direct input into student work. If there is more than one supervisor per cohort, supervision must be well coordinated and well attuned to the handover structure. Supervision is usually assigned.

Assignment to Groups

Groups are usually self selected, but they may be assigned or adjusted in order to balance the teams in the interests of a lively "economy". In non-competitive schemes, the "partner teams" may be assigned in advance, so that each team knows who will receive its software.

Student Process

Handover projects are usually arranged in phases, covering different aspects of the handover experience. The original Software Hut model (Horning and Wortman, 1977), for example, had three phases:

Phase A (days 1–29): Each hut is to design, implement, validate, document, and otherwise prepare for sale either Module X or Module Y of the attached specification;

Phase B (days 29–50): Each hut is to write a driver program and integrate Modules X and Y purchased from two other huts, and prepare the resulting system for sale;

Phase C (days 50–64): Each hut is to purchase a system (not containing its own module) from another hut, modify it according to revised specifications (to be provided on Day 53), and prepare the revised system for sale.

In this way, each hut (i.e. team) could start afresh at the beginning of each phase, potentially using code much better than their own. The trading was set within an economic system which gave each hut a budget, which rewarded successful completion of each phase with additional funds, and which imposed financial penalties for delays and errors.

Within the handover structure, team structures and processes are usually left to the students to determine.

Deliverables

Handover products:

- software component
- software demonstration
- software documentation, including installation and user manuals, evidence of testing
- integrated software system.

Additional academic deliverables:

- profit and loss statements
- team process documentation
- individual reports, perhaps including reflections on process, evidence of individual contribution, project log.

Assessment

Assessment is usually a mix of supervisor assessment based on deliverables (some of which may document the development and handover processes) and peer assessment.

The handover provides an opportunity for peer assessment, since each team must gain familiarity with other teams' software and become well acquainted with the software they integrate or modify. Competitive systems provide an in-built mechanism for peer assessment: trading profit is in effect a reflection of peer group assessment. With more than one team addressing any given component, each team can assess another's solution to the same topic.

External input may be brought into assessment, with an industry collaborator (perhaps the originator of the overall project topic) reviewing the products. This also gives an opportunity for another form of competition, since an external assessor may identify a "best" product.

Cited Keys to Success:

- designing the project fairly, with balanced components
- retaining the "game". Horning and Wortman observed, "It has been our

experience that as we increase the realism of the project we also tend to increase the amount of strife and student discontent". (p. 328)

References

Horning, J. J. and Wortman, D. B. (1977) *IEEE Transactions on Software Engineering*, **SE-3**, 325–330.

1.5 Research-type Project

○   ○   ○   ○

Individual or group?	usually individual
Year	2, 3, or 4
Assessment	based on deliverables
Pedagogic focus	developing critical thinking and research skills
Special characteristics	possible involvement in research program
Key problem	topic scope: identifying interesting topics that are small, well defined, and "off the critical path"

Size and Duration

The research-type project is used at different stages in the curriculum, usually (although not always) as an individual project. The later it occurs in the curriculum, the more time is usually given to it, and the higher the expectations of its outcomes. Research-type projects tend to last from half a term (6 weeks) to 2 terms (24 weeks).

Context

Research projects mirror the traditional research model of the natural sciences, introducing students to research methods, research standards, and research discourse. It is the most "academic" style of project, having theory and the critique of ideas as essential elements. The research-type project in computing science tries to marry theory with practice, often requiring students to build on theory in examining extensions, reapplications, or innovations in practice.

In some departments, it is possible to embed research-type projects in greater, ongoing research programs, so that students may be exposed to the environment of research and may benefit from the existing community of knowledge and discussion. The benefit may be mutual, with students making genuine contributions to the research program, while learning and gaining motivation from the other researchers. Student projects can, for example, be used to demonstrate the feasibility of research ideas that can then be carried forward by others. Bids for external funding are often more successful if feasibility has been demonstrated. Research projects can give impetus to others' research, e.g. where a student provides facilities that further a doctoral student's work, or where induction of the student into the research program sharpens the doctoral student's thinking. Student projects can produce tools which assist and enhance other research (e.g. demonstrators, simulators, test harnesses, improved user interfaces) without being critical for it. However, care must be taken that students are not exploited. The best student work of this type leads to publications.

Situating research projects within research programs can enable the faculty to draw on non-teaching resources to spread the supervisory load, for example where technical support is provided by research assistants and research fellows working in the program.

Objectives/Aims/Pedagogic Focus

The focus of research projects is to develop the skills of independent investigation and research by means of supervised project work. The aim is to encourage students to take an interest in critical inquiry, to develop research techniques and problem solving skills, and to take responsibility for their own learning. Objectives may include:

- contributing to understanding and demonstrating this contribution through some implementation or some improvement of techniques
- reading and critiquing the research literature – developing critical skills for selection, integration and interpretation
- learning how to evaluate others' claims and hence how to present their own appropriately
- learning research techniques
- choosing and applying appropriate methods or methodology
- assimilating concepts and conceptual structures
- proposing a development of the concepts: e.g. an extension, refinement, new application
- developing problem-solving skills
- developing writing and presentation skills
- making a plan and following it through.

Topics (Allocation)

Projects associated with larger research programs must usually be small and well defined. Student projects must be "off the critical path"; the outcome of the research program must not depend on the outcome of the student work. There are many types of useful but non-critical topics, including:

- feasibility studies and early prototypes (demonstrations of principle), exploration and testing of untried ideas, establishing context and precedent for new or untried ideas

- peripheral or spin-off topics
- enhancements and auxiliary tools (e.g. simulators, test harnesses, improved user interfaces)
- demonstrations and applications based on research outcomes: providing evidence of the utility of the research ideas.

Depending on the number of students and supervisors involved, topic allocation may be problematic, and a variety of mechanisms are used, e.g.

- invitations by supervisors to students
- students seek supervisors/topics (Supervisor allocation and topic allocation are interrelated in this case. In effect, the student chooses a topic area through the choice of supervisor. Then, typically, the supervisor will influence the particular topic choice.)
- students bid for set topics from a list (Rationing of topics to even the distribution of topics and supervisor load can be handled various ways: bidding, first come-first served, a lottery, supervisor choice, etc.)
- negotiated across the cohort, so that the topic area is chosen based on student preferences, and particular topics are constrained to that area.

Supervision

The student-supervisor relationship is usually key in research projects, because the project work usually derives from the supervisor's interest and expertise. When students are contributing to a larger research effort, their research must relate to the whole and be informed by it, so that communication through supervision is essential. Supervision usually includes individual meetings with the supervisor on a regular (e.g. weekly) basis.

Student research projects are sometimes set within a group support structure, so that there are plenary meetings in which students doing research projects discuss their progress, can raise problems and issues, and can learn from other students' experiences.

Sometimes students benefit from the research program in which their research is situated, so that, for example, they may join meetings of the research team at which research and procedural issues are discussed. They may benefit from the community of researchers, drawing on doctoral students' and research assistants' knowledge of the area and on their technical knowledge, so that they have more sources (and more perspectives) than just their supervisor.

Supervision is typically on a weekly basis, with contact ranging from ½ –1 hour per week, although it may well be augmented by guidance from sources other than the supervisor.

Student Process

Research projects are largely the responsibility of the student, within the framework of regular supervision meetings. Usually students are asked to map out a work plan, but inexperience can make these ineffectual; adherence to the plan (or to a realistic alternative) often relies on good monitoring through supervision. Often students are given guidance (e.g. suggested milestones) based on typical progress, and examples of past projects (both good and bad) may be provided.

Deliverables

The main deliverable in most research projects is the final report, which encompasses the work of the project, for example summarizing the literature survey and giving the theoretical rationale for the project, demonstrating the ideas through the practical work, describing the particular implementation, and so on. Where appropriate, there may be a live demonstration of an implementation or prototype.

There may be a requirement for interim reports; usually these are more for the purposes of supervision than for assessment. Interim reports may include work plans and timetables, report of literature searches and annotated bibliography, critique of key issues, justification for prototype or demonstration, evaluation plan, etc.

Assessment

Assessment is usually based largely on the final report, although it may also take into account interim reports or other material. The supervisor is the primary marker; often there is a second marker and a scheme for resolving disagreements. The assessment scheme may take different aspects into account, for example:

- originality or contribution
- literature search and synthesis
- method
- use of technical knowledge
- technical or scientific analysis and argument
- presentation, including grammar, structure and organization.

Cited Keys to Success:

- engagement of staff
- student interest: there is potential for students to make a genuine contribution
- association with ongoing research programs.

1.6 "Design and Build" Project

○ ○ ○ ○

Individual or /group?	can be individual, more often groups of 3–5, or 4–7
Year	any
Assessment	product oriented
Pedagogic focus	analysis, design, and implementation of a software system
Special characteristics	"practising the craft"
Key problem	getting the right level of difficulty of the topic

Size and Duration

The "design and build" model applies at almost any level, and can be (is) interpreted at any scale, from a two-week class assignment, to a substantial, advanced group project covering two terms (i.e. 24 weeks).

Context

Design and build projects feature at all levels of the computing science curriculum, from very early, tiny, individual projects to mega-projects that integrate the software components developed by a number of groups, to substantial integrative projects that culminate a degree program. Whether "early" or "late", they are all characterized by the objective of designing and building software that runs, but they vary in other principal dimensions: scale, scope, number of participants, duration, supervisor input.

In its most common form, the design and build project is intended to simulate the approach of a traditional software development team in producing a substantial software system. Projects of this type vary depending on which "slice" of the development life-cycle is emphasized. Hence, some will start from requirements elicitation by the students and end with early prototyping (specify-design-implement), whereas others will start with a given specification and work through rigorous product testing (design-implement-test), still others will require an eval-uation against user requirements (specify-design-implement-evaluate). Yet at the core of each of the variants is the requirement to design and build a software system, usually within a recognized methodology and within a structure of deliverables.

The scope of the project at each stage may be restricted to fit within practical constraints.

Objectives/Aims/Pedagogic Focus

The focus of these projects is to "practice the craft" of computer science, to apply acquired skills and techniques – and to understand their significance and perti-nence. The majority of design and build projects aspire to produce a *substantial* software system. The objectives may include demonstration of any (or many) of the relevant skills and techniques, e.g.

- analyze, design and implement a substantial software system
- use a structured methodology in system development (e.g. design, imple-mentation and testing)
- plan and execute a professional test schedule
- estimate, plan, and manage time.

Further, design and build projects may aim to teach students to appreciate the need for a professional approach to all aspects of software development.

Topics (Allocation)

Project topics are usually assigned, or a list of topics is assigned from which students may choose. Less often, topics are by negotiation, but the problems of getting the scale, scope, and complexity of the topic right usually militate against pure student selection of topic.

Depending on the course design, individual topics may fit into a greater scheme, so that for example:

- a current topic may build on previous project work and must integrate with it, or
- each topic may be a component of a larger system, or
- some buyer/seller arrangement may operate [see, e.g., 1.4 *Project with Handover*], or
- the problem is specified by an external client [see, e.g., 1.8 *Project with a Client*].

Supervision

Supervision on design and build projects varies, depending on what role the project plays in the curriculum. Small, early, design and build projects are used as teaching exercises, and supervision may include explicit teaching as well as strategic, tactical, and technical discussion. The more common, later, larger design and build projects are used to consolidate student knowledge and skills, and supervision tends to take the form of high-level guidance, monitoring and troubleshooting, rather than instruction per se. Late, advanced, integrative, design and build projects are used to confirm students' ability in the domain, and so supervision is limited and strategic, allowing students to "get on with the job".

Whatever the model, supervision usually occurs on a regular basis, usually through weekly classes or meetings. Contact time varies with the level and the intensity of the project, from 15 minutes per week for early projects, to 1 hour per week for later projects. The more advanced the project, the more likely the supervision is to be individual – but the less likely it is to include specific technical input.

Assignment to Groups

Groups may be self-assembled (more usual for advanced projects) or assigned (more usual for early or second-year projects).

Various assignment schemes are employed, e.g.

- arbitrary
- tutorial groups
- demographic dispersal
- range of skills
- affinity (or dis-affinity).

Student Process

The student process derives from the pedagogic focus: the student or team follows a methodology in order to produce and deliver a product. The student process is oriented to product implementation and method documentation. Often the methodology is prescribed, but students may be allowed to choose among established methodologies. Most commonly, design and build projects are group projects, meant to be accomplished collectively.

As with other aspects of these projects, the student process depends on the project's place in the curriculum, and the students' responsibilities reflect supervisory roles. Early design and build projects may be more prescriptive, with the supervisor playing a more directive role, say as project manager. Later design and build projects tend to be self-organizing, with students taking responsibility for their own management, and supervisors providing guidance only. The later in the curriculum, the more student-run these projects tend to be.

Group projects that come late in the curriculum are often there to enable students to work on a big project. The size of the task shapes the nature of the project and the student process. Student roles and project management have greater importance on a larger project, where coordination is harder to "fudge".

Deliverables

Deliverables are often staged to conform to the development life-cycle, for example requiring requirements specification, system design, detailed design, implementation, documentation, and testing and evaluation documentation at appropriate stages.

Assessment:

- completeness, correctness and quality of each deliverable
- group mark, perhaps with an individual adjustment.

Cited Keys to Success:

- getting the scope of the project right
- getting the team dynamics and roles sorted out early in the project, rather than late
- building in review and recovery time.

1.7 Project with Industrial Involvement

○   ○   ○   ○

Individual or group?	can be individual, more often groups of 3–6
year	2, 3, or 4
assessment	industry partner and supervisor, based on deliverables
pedagogic focus	relevant exposure to industry practice and concerns
special characteristics	direct input from industry
key problem	industry priorities must be balanced with academic objectives

Size and Duration

Projects of this sort usually run over one or two terms, i.e. 12–24 weeks. The topic is usually substantial.

Context

The impetus is *relevance:* to provide real-world skills relevant to software engineering and computer science in industry, to make graduates more employable, to respond to recommendation from industrial collaborators and employers that students should be given exposure to practice within the computing industry.

The level of industrial involvement can vary widely, from providing interesting problems (without direct involvement in the project work itself), to providing company personnel to contribute to project management and teaching on campus, to contributing hardware and/or software to support projects.

The industry participant is a computing/IT professional, for example in the computer industry or in the IT department of a large company. Sometimes the industry participant has some connection to the institution (e.g. as an alumnus), sometimes the participant is the "champion" of the linkage, usually the participant has a personal commitment to the participation. The company usually makes the investment through a combination of goodwill and self-interest: any real return is likely to be long-term, in the form of a raised company profile, links to research centers, more employable graduates and possible recruitment. Nevertheless, agreement must be made in advance about who owns the intellectual property rights to whatever the students produce. There is often only one industrial partner, especially where the industry participant takes an active role in project management and becomes involved in meetings or teaching on campus.

Finding the right industrial partner (i.e. one who presents appropriate problems, is accessible and enthusiastic, makes contributions compatible with the department's teaching, and is reliable in the interaction with students) is obviously crucial, particularly if the partner is to contribute to teaching. The partner must have appropriate expectations about outcomes; industry priorities must be balanced with academic objectives.

Objectives/Aims/Pedagogic Focus

The focus is the efficient introduction of real, relevant industrial exposure in order to highlight practical (including non-technical) issues that face software development teams in industry. Industrial linkage aims to provide:

- exposure to working practice in industry
- experience of project management and teamwork as conducted in industry
- exposure to quality assurance issues.

Common objectives arising from those aims include:

- tackling real problems with industrial relevance and currency
- focusing on the whole "business problem" rather than just the technical issues
- learning what methods, rigor and standards are applied in industry (at least in the partner organization) – and conforming to them
- adhering to organizational practice in handling administration, management, reporting, and finance of a project
- completing the project effectively within the practical constraints
- developing professional skills
- developing communication and presentation skills
- gaining insight into individual strengths and weaknesses.

Topics (Allocation)

Topics are provided by the industrial partner. The number of topics varies depending on the nature of the industrial participation; often there is one topic for all students. The topic may be focused or refined through consultation between the industrial partner and the students. Topics usually have genuine commercial value; this is part of their appeal to both students and industrial partner.

Project topics vary in terms of the linkage and the pedagogic aims, but all arise from industry and reflect industry concerns. "Classic" projects in this context have involved computerization of manual tasks, and problems involving legacy software: transferring platform, upgrading, starting over to address same functionality. As the industry has advanced, topics have become more demanding, involving less-routine problems. Students may be asked to investigate new technologies, to address speculative problems that don't fit existing industry budgets, to follow up spin-offs of industry projects, or to research new approaches or demonstrate new techniques.

Supervision

The industrial partner acts more as employer than as client, providing not just the problem but also the work context. The industrial partner may act as project manager, imposing company standards and processes on student work. Students are largely responsible for their own work and, where appropriate, their own team management.

When the industrial partner is actively involved, the supervisor is then separate from the project management role and may provide more "mentoring", giving strategic guidance on time management, team processes, technical issues, and so on. The supervisor also oversees the relationships (between industrial partner and students, within teams), insuring that there are no significant obstacles or problems.

Contact time is usually in the range of ½–1 hour per week per project.

Student Process

Where the industrial partner is actively involved in project management, meetings with them provide structure to the project work. A typical structure might involve:

Initial Phase:

- presentation of the problem by the industry partner, probably to the whole cohort
- meetings and discussions to establish the terms of reference (including expected methodology and standards of practice)
- possible introduction to others in the organization, e.g. those responsible for technical strategy;

Working Phase:

- a few scheduled meetings with partner (additional meetings with supervisor, probably weekly).
- short interim reports with feedback from partner that provide opportunities for clarification of requirements, diagnosis of problems; they may correspond to formal phases in software development

- email communication, at the discretion of the industrial partner;

Final Phase:

- presentation and report
- response from industrial partner; possibly prize giving.

Students manage their own work, in consultation with the supervisor, who may advise about priorities and time allocation. Roles and tasks are usually self-assigned.

Where the industrial partner provides only the problem, the structure comes from the supervisor, and the student process is like that of any other student project.

Deliverables

Depending on the nature of the problem, the students may produce just a written report, or may also produce some form of prototype or practical demonstration. Usually students are expected to make an oral presentation to the industrial partner, possibly to a wider audience. Although this form of project is about exposure to practice, the deliverables tend to focus on the products and outcomes, sometimes augmented with a reflective report for the supervisor.

Some example deliverables, drawn from a project involving a software prototype:

- feasibility report
- requirements specification
- design document
- test report and statistics
- software listing and documentation
- user manual
- demonstration.

Assessment

The assessment usually focuses on the final deliverables, with both the industrial partner and the supervisor contributing to the assessment. The assessment may be criterion based; it will usually take into account the terms of reference set out by the industrial partner.

Cited Keys to Success:

- forming the right partnership between industry and academia, with compatible expectations

- identifying real problems – but ones which are not on the critical path for the industrial partner's immediate plans
- establishing the terms of reference clearly and early enough
- students accept things from industry that they won't accept from academics (e.g. partial information, late answers) and so it is possible to achieve greater realism.

Composite Case Studies

1. 8 Project with a Client

○   ○   ○   ○

Individual or group?	groups of 3–5 (less often individual)
Year	2, 3, or 4
Assessment	group and individual, based on deliverables
Pedagogic focus	developing the professional skills to work as a contractor for a real client within realistic constraints
Special characteristics	external clients who are not computing specialists
Key problem	screening the clients

Size and Duration

Projects are designed to be of feasible scale and scope, and typical teams are small, with 3–5 members.

Projects usually occur within one term (i.e. 12 weeks), with student commitment time varying from 3–12 hours per week.

Context

Projects with clients are designed to provide exposure to working with "real" people who are not computing specialists. In effect, students act as software, IT, or computing consultants to local organizations, developing and possibly maintaining software for clients. Hence, students gain exposure to real problems faced by commerce and industry, and to the interaction of business and technical concerns, i.e. to the complex constraints of a real environment. Classic problems in this context are computerization of existing manual systems, but application-based projects have become increasingly common. It might be possible to devise a divide-and-conquer scheme, where the client presents a substantial problem, and different teams address different aspects, providing components that combine into an overall solution.

Emphasis is given to communication skills; it is not enough for students to have good technical ideas, they must also elicit and comprehend the client's needs, "sell" the proposed solution to the client, and convey the use and usefulness of their implementation. Different attempts are made to increase the realism of these projects. The client may judge the products of competing groups all given the client's brief. In some cases, an explicit company structure is set up, with bank accounts and company records, so that students are responsible for the "business" of development, as well as the product.

Client

There may be one or many clients for a cohort. Often, "best use" will be made of client participation by assigning more than one group to a client and introducing an element of competition. However, there is a limit to the number of teams with which a client can interact, usually noted as 3–6.

Finding "good" clients who meet the needs of the educational program (i.e. those who are cooperative, interested, accessible, informed about their own needs, and have appropriate problems) can be an issue. Clients must be found well in advance of the project – but not so early that the problem is "past" before it is solved. Clients must have appropriate expectations; clients are rarely satisfied if they view these projects as a cheap source of software. What companies generally receive is a better view of the problem, and some input into its solution, rather than a complete software solution.

Scale is of course an issue. With a large number of students, more clients are required, and hence more set-up work and coordination of the whole effort is required.

Skills and Resources

Client projects require students to have sufficient technical knowledge and skill to provide a genuine service to the clients. Therefore, as group projects they are usually situated at the end of the second year or in the fourth year of a B.Eng. Less frequently, they are undertaken as third-year individual projects. Appropriate software tools must be available, so that the students can produce software that the clients can run.

Intellectual Property (IP)

Agreement must be made in advance about who (client, university, student) owns the intellectual property rights and the software copyright. The client must retain the right to use the software and subsequently to modify or develop it.

Maintenance

Agreement must be made about what maintenance is offered; either the client must waive maintenance, or the department must establish a maintenance scheme (this is most easily accomplished in departments which have created viable, ongoing, in-house software consultancies).

Objectives/Aims/Pedagogic Focus

The point of the project with a client is to give students a "taste of the real world" and especially to expose them to the ways in which the business environment impinges on the work of the computing specialist. Hence, the focus is on interacting with a real client, eliciting requirements, developing an effective client/engineer relationship – and on the communication and management skills associated with that interaction.

Objectives include:

- experiencing the responsibility of working as contractors to a real client
- working with people outside the university
- learning to meet and balance varied objectives arising from self, group, client, course
- tackling a real problem with commercial or social relevance
- finding effective and cost-effective solutions within the time limit
- developing professional skills
- developing communication and presentation skills
- exposure to business practice: contracts, record keeping, business reports, consultancy reports
- applying technical knowledge in a realistic environment.

Topics (Allocation)

Topics arise in consultation with clients. Usually, the department has screened the clients in order to insure that their problems are an appropriate vehicle for the educational goals – as well as to insure that the clients have appropriate expectations of the exercise. Topics must have commercial potential, but they may take different forms, e.g.

- IT audits or feasibility studies
- developing IT strategies (e.g. change strategies, with appropriate research and costing)
- product development, application-based development (e.g. spreadsheets, databases, information systems).

The assignment of students to clients (and hence to topics) follows different approaches:

- arbitrary allocation
- "matchmaking" based on skills and interests
- allocation by supervisor which takes account of student bidding systems or "preference voting" (i.e. indicating 1st, 2nd, and 3rd choices)
- client selection of students/teams based on student submissions.

Usually, the topic will be refined during the consultation between students and client. In a sense, the biggest risks lie in topic choice; all parties must have appropriate expectations, students must have appropriate skills and tools, and supervisors must have appropriate control over conditions, if the project is to be successful. Some topics – such as those which are business-critical for the client, those which suffer from too many business constraints, those for which the client expects an finished industrial-strength product, or explorations of new technologies beyond the feasibility stage – are inappropriate for student projects. The aim is for students to meet clients' real requirements, yet to do so within an academic framework.

Supervision

In a sense, it is necessary to supervise the client as well as the students, in order to insure a productive interaction. It is necessary to strike a balance between the client's requirements and the academic objectives. It is necessary to arrive at a stationary target and avoid requirements drift. Much of this will be sorted out in the initial set-up of the project work that is done by supervisors and clients in the months before the project commences. Because of the pre-existing relationship between supervisor and client, supervisors are usually associated with clients and follow the client assignments.

The supervisor may act as line manager: overseeing progress, suggesting strategies, assisting with management, reminding students that there is a client. The development methodology or process might be imposed by the supervisor – rarely by the client. Usually, the supervision is "hands off", to allow students to take responsibility.

Supervision is usually on a weekly basis, sometimes handled per group, sometimes handled as a plenary session. Contact time ranges from 1–3 hours per week per group.

Assignment to Groups

Often, students choose their own groups, usually based on previous experience of working together. But groups may also be assigned, using any of various assignment schemes, e.g.

- arbitrary
- tutorial groups
- demographic distribution
- range of skills
- affinity (or dis-affinity).

Student Process

The client project is intended as a realistic assumption of roles, in which students take responsibility for the client's job. Hence groups usually manage themselves, with some strategic interaction with the supervisor on issues like time management. Project teams need to "normalize" early, perhaps by deciding key roles such as team leader (who interacts with the client) and financial controller (who monitors costs and keeps business records), perhaps through the negotiation and agreement of the solution strategy.

Initially, the client presents the requirements to the students. When the client serves more than one team, presentation is usually on campus, and the initial briefings may be plenary meetings. When there is a different client for each team, requirements elicitation may take place at the client's site.

After the initial requirements capture, the team leader continues to liaise with the client on a regular basis, refining the specification, demonstrating prototypes, or testing. Regular meetings may be scheduled on campus, but student visits to the workplace may also be used (e.g. for testing or usability evaluations). Some remote contact may be allowed (for example, via email), at the client's discretion.

Students present the completed project to client, with documentation. This is often on campus, with all teams presenting their projects "publicly". Students also submit a project report, which meets academic requirements.

Finally, the client tests and assesses the product. In competitive schemes, the client may be asked to choose a "winner" and to give a prize.

Deliverables

In a sense, students are serving two masters: the client and the department – and they must deliver material to each.

Client Deliverables:

- requirements specification
- prototype(s)
- software product
- software documentation, including installation and user manuals
- test records and reliability assessment.

Additional Academic Deliverables:

- design report: requirements, analysis, design, testing
- process report: reflections on experience, documentation of team working, etc.
- acceptance testing.

The academic deliverables may augment group reports with individual reports.

Assessment

Assessment usually encompasses both client and academic perspectives. The client usually contributes to the marking, often using a marking scheme or form. In competitive arrangements (where more than one student or group works for a client), the client chooses a "winner" or winners. The supervisor is the principal marker, again usually working within a criterion-based scheme, perhaps with a marking scheme that specifies how marks should be distributed among aspects of the project work.

Assessment usually encompasses a variety of factors, including communication, development process, business process, team working, the product itself. Since there are usually interim products as part of the team-client interaction, continuous assessment is feasible, but usually assessment is summative, based on final deliverables and reports.

Assessment is usually group marking, since it is based substantially on the work of the group, although assessment may be adjusted in terms of individual contributions.

Cited Keys to Success:

- good clients with clear contracts and appropriate problems
- having more students on a team than is strictly necessary (to accommodate attrition)
- having extra clients available (to accommodate attrition)
- good time management by students.

Composite Case Studies

1.9 Process-based Project

○   ○   ○   ○

Individual or group?	group (typically 3–6, up to 20 possible)
Year	2 or 3
Assessment	cumulative, involving interim, non-technical products
Pedagogic focus	the process of project work and professional activity
Special characteristics	emphasis on process
Key problem	getting the students to see the point rather than just go through the motions

Size and Duration

Two weeks to one term, 3–6 students per team is typical, but large teams of up to 20 have also been reported.

The scope and duration of process-based projects are related to their place in the curriculum. Projects occurring earlier (in the second year) tend to be smaller and shorter, with some lasting only a week or two. Those which occur late (in the final year) tend to be longer, run over one or two terms.

Context

Software engineering puts the emphasis on the development process, rather than focusing exclusively on products. Hence the "products" of software engineering are not just the actual code, but also the documents that reveal the development process and that support the development and maintenance of the software. Process-based projects attempt to give attention to non-technical issues in software development and to turn students' attention to the interdependencies of project phases and to issues beyond implementation.

The process-based project takes different roles in different parts of the curriculum. One is often placed early in a degree program, to bring home relevant ideas early. It can be used as a gentle introduction to project work, introducing some of the lessons of project life-cycles, record keeping, and other process issues in preparation for more intensive, more advanced project work later. Alternatively, it is often placed late in a degree program as a culminating activity of more substantial scale and with an attempt at greater realism. In such cases, there is often significant industry involvement, in order to relate student experiences to industry practices and processes.

Objectives/Aims/Pedagogic Focus:

- introduction to team work and to industry practice
- attention to non-technical aspects of project work
- stressing the importance of reflection on practice.

Topics (Allocation)

Topics are usually assigned, since the topic (hence the technical or problem-solving focus) is important primarily in its demands for due process, rather than its technical interest for the students. Topics may be generated by industry collaborators or drawn from "real" examples in order to insure the richness necessary to illustrate the advantages of good process.

Supervision

Supervision is usually in groups, because the emphasis is on the team rather than the individual. Supervision is usually on a weekly basis, of the order of 10–60 minutes per group. Particular arrangements vary from scheduled meetings between a team (or its project leader) and the supervisor, to "visiting" arrangements in which the supervisor attends a scheduled team meeting, to supervision on a whole-class basis, with intervals for each team.

Process-based projects are often embedded in software engineering or project management courses and are often accompanied by teaching about relevant processes and practices. Often such lectures or seminars are staged to coincide with particular phases of the project – a sort of "just in time" teaching. Sometimes outside expertise, particularly in the form of practitioners from industry, is brought in for the teaching.

Those projects which occur early in a degree program are usually more constrained and more controlled than those which occur later; early process-oriented projects tend to be introductory, whereas later ones tend to aim for more intensive and realistic experience of the software development process. Supervisors' roles therefore relate to the project's place in the curriculum. In early projects, supervisors may act as project leaders or clients, as well as teachers and technical gurus.

In later projects, supervisors tend to stay out of project management, acting primarily as advisors. Sometimes the supervisor is available on a technical advisory basis, but more often students are encouraged to seek information elsewhere. Supervision may be augmented with technical surgeries. Other roles may be provided by other staff or by external partners, such as industry collaborators who may act as project managers, or local business people who may act as clients.

Assignment to Groups

Because of the emphasis on team process, groups are most frequently assigned with the intention of assembling mixed, "balanced" groups. Ability is most often the primary factor (especially in interdisciplinary or mixed-skills cohorts), but demographic distribution and personal characteristics are also often taken into account. Yet other mechanisms are used, including self-selection.

Student Process

Student roles in the team are likely to be formalized, for example using a rotation system (which is common) to give students the opportunity to experience key roles, or choosing roles through an election. Sometimes roles are assigned; this is more common in earlier projects. Less frequently, roles are determined through negotiation with the supervisor.

Process-based projects are usually structured with fixed interim milestones associated with different phases of development, usually based on a particular development model. Usually some deliverable is associated with each milestone, so that for example, the first milestone might be a requirements specification, the next a design document, and so on, culminating with testing strategies and outputs, and usability analysis.

The emphasis on reflection and critique is often embodied in activities such as individual project journals or (less frequently) coursework. These activities are usually mandatory, but they are often not assessed. Evaluation of both process and outcomes is common. Peer- and self-assessment is often incorporated into the project work as a device for reflection, for example in the form of critiques of one team's product or presentation by another, or in peer- and self-evaluation among teammates. Handover of components between teams may be included in order to promote critical appraisal and communication. Sometimes uncertainties, such as fuzzy specifications, are introduced into the project structure, in order to force students into negotiation and decision making. Sometimes students are required to choose among options, for example to choose among interface designs or software components.

Some form of teaching or preparation is usually incorporated into the process, either in advance of the project or in tandem with it, in order to help students in performing their roles well. This includes not just technical preparation and introduction to the software development method to be adopted, but also introduction to the relevant forms of record keeping, to presentation skills, and to reflective and critical activity.

Sometimes, "perturbations" are introduced into the process, such as system shut-downs or reshuffling of personnel, to simulate the problems and obstacles that arise in real practice.

Deliverables

There are usually technical deliverables associated with stages in the development process, such as requirements specifications, design documents, interface proto-types, the final software, user documentation, testing harnesses and test data, and usability studies.

Process-oriented deliverables are typical, including minutes of team meetings, weekly records, task breakdowns and work plans, and version control documen-tation. Many of these will have had regular submission schedules. Sometimes teams are required to maintain a team portfolio with up-to-date documentation.

In projects framed in a business context, business and customer records are usually required.

Reflection-oriented products, such as project journals, reflective summaries, and peer- and self-assessment forms, are common deliverables, although not all of these are assessed.

Assessment

Assessment is often cumulative, including substantial amounts of formative assess-ment, and using products (like journals) that must be created over the whole life of the project. It is the student's own reflection that is significant, more than "deliv-erables success". Students' work as members of the group is significant, i.e. their ability to fulfill their own roles and support others in fulfilling theirs. The process-based project often includes student assessment as a component of the final mark.

Cited Keys to Success:

- staff commitment
- choosing topics that are large enough to require collaboration but easy enough to de-emphasize the product
- an intensive period of project work
- good preparation for non-technical tasks.

Composite Case Studies

1.10 Integrative or "Capstone" Project

○   ○   ○   ○

Individual or group?	individual
Year	final
Assessment	summative, final-product-oriented
Pedagogic focus	to integrate and demonstrate the skills and knowledge acquired previously
Special characteristics	not just using information learned in disparate courses/modules, but also pulling it together into a coherent body
Key problem	needs a problem that allows demonstration of skills; and needs the students to have those skills to demonstrate

Size and Duration

The "capstone" integrative project is usually substantial, similar in size and duration to other final-year projects, cast as either a full-time project during the last or penultimate term, or as a part-time effort extended over two terms. Expected student hours per week depend on the intensity of the arrangement, ranging from 6–35.

Context

The capstone project is the culminating project, demonstrating knowledge and skills acquired during a degree program. The name "capstone" refers to the coping stone that completes a wall and ties together the final layer of the structure. The capstone project usually has as prerequisites the "core" of traditional computer science teaching: courses such as data structures, communication networks, operating systems, compiler design, software engineering. It aims both to culminate the degree program with a practical demonstration by the student confirming their ability in the domain, and to make learning "real" by integrating theory and practice through authentic problems, processes and deliverables. Ideally, these projects are learning experiences, giving students a sense of what they have learned as an integrated "whole". Capstone work is usually designed to be intensive and extensive. Often, the capstone project course will be the sole activity in a term without lectures or examinations, so that students can focus on it exclusively.

Beyond this, capstone projects can vary enormously in their form, running as isolated design and build projects, projects with clients, projects with a handover, or projects set in "real business" contexts. Hence, although the capstone is usually an individual project, designed for an individual demonstration of "know how", it can be run as a group project (e.g. (Tuttle, 2000)). But even then students are normally assessed individually.

The capstone emphasis arises from the realization that the engineering aspects of software development are difficult to address in the curriculum. The relationship between process and product must be illustrated and made relevant to students and a concrete experience that requires the integration of the different subjects, methods, and techniques in the pursuit of a solution to a realistically large and complex problem is a way to convey its importance. Putting learning into practice is also a way of rounding off the course, giving students a reason to revisit previous material and reflect on their education as a whole.

Capstone projects are typically final-year projects, but projects may be used to integrate preceding work at any time in the curriculum. Integrative projects earlier in the curriculum tend to have a smaller scope, their role being to integrate a specific portion of the degree material, say that covered in a particular course such as operating systems.

Objectives/Aims/Pedagogic Focus:

- to integrate, consolidate and demonstrate technical knowledge and skills acquired over the whole of the degree studies (and thereby potentially acquire new knowledge)
- to apply computer science theory and methods to solving authentic problems and making engineering decisions
- to confirm the student's ability in computer science
- to demonstrate both constituent and management skills through the whole software development process
- to bring home to students that their formal education is incomplete without an ability to put hardware and software knowledge into use in solving problems.

Topics (Allocation)

The topic is of importance, because it must require a range of knowledge and skills emphasized in the degree program. Often, it will be a substantial software engineering topic which is technically demanding and admits a variety of solutions. Although a variety of allocation mechanisms are possible, topics are often assigned, in order to ensure appropriate coverage and complexity, and usually the same topic is assigned to all students.

Supervision

Supervision is limited and strategic, allowing students to "get on with the job". Supervisors may act as consultants, providing advice on request but rarely intervening. Weekly individual supervision meetings are common, but other arrangements, such as weekly meetings with a number of students, are also used.

Student Process

Integrative projects are largely student run; students are given a chance to "show what they can do", from managing the project to addressing its technical challenges. Students are expected not only to draw on what they've learned before, but also to combine it productively. Everything students learned previously becomes a resource to solve the problem, but excellence demands that students consolidate their prior learning into an interrelated whole, so that solutions benefit from new combinations of knowledge.

Although the integrative project can be cast as a group, more often it is presented as individual work, and students are discouraged from collaborating.

Project structures may vary; for example, students may be expected to exchange interim products part way through the project.

Deliverables

The integrative project is a summative exercise, and the focus is on final products. Projects are product-oriented, with an emphasis on technical deliverables.

Assessment

Assessment of integrative projects is commonly summative, although some interim assessment may be taken into account.

Cited Keys to Success:

- success comes when students have real knowledge and skill to bring to the project from their previous education
- rich enough project topics, which require students to draw on material from different courses, and which allow both "vanilla" demonstration of skills and also admit exceptional or insightful solutions which exceed previous teaching

- often works better when students have done previous project work, so that the focus is not distracted by the mechanics of project work but can remain with the technical challenge of solving the problem.

Reference

Tuttle, S. M. (2000) *SIGCSE Bulletin. Proceedings of SIGCSE Symposium (Austin, March)*, **32**, 265–269

Composite Case Studies

1.11 The Professional Bodies' View

○   ○   ○   ○

Individual or group?	individual
Year	3
Assessment	usually product-based, perhaps with attention to professional process and issues
Pedagogic focus	demonstration of sufficient professional technical skill
Special characteristics	accreditation is based on practical, problem-solving projects
Key problem	identifying projects of sufficient depth and breadth to meet the accreditation criteria

Size and Duration

Around 100–150 hours of work by each individual, depending on the level of accreditation. Can be arranged as part-time work over two or more terms, or as full-time work in one term.

Context

Both the BCS's and the IEE's view of computer science education in the UK is shaped by the Engineering Council's "Standards and Routes to Registration" (SARTOR) third edition (1997). The SARTOR definitions pertinent to project work are those for the first two (of four) levels of "Engineering Applications" given in the SARTOR policy statement (IEE, 1997):

- EA1: "An introduction to good engineering practice and the properties, behaviour, fabrication and use of relevant materials and components" (which the IEE interprets as: "EA1 will introduce engineering students to good engineering practices, including the need to formulate and satisfy specifications to meet market and other needs and in particular to the use of materials and tools relevant to the branch of engineering in which they intend to practice . . .")

- EA2: "Application of scientific and engineering principles to the solution of practical problems of engineering systems and processes. Emphasis on the relevance of theory and analysis, including the ability to develop and use theoretical models from which the behaviour of the physical world can be predicted. Each course should embody and integrate theoretical, practical and project work commensurate with the level of study being pursued."

Based on the definitions given in SARTOR, the professional bodies provide a framework within which to consider accreditation of degree programs. The IEE requires that EA1 and EA2 must be included as integral parts of an accredited course, with the principle that EA2 should pervade the whole course, so that students have many opportunities to apply the skills they acquired, culminating with the final-year project. Hence, two parts of practical work are encompassed:

1. practical experience (throughout degree). This can take many forms, including group work.
2. integrative demonstration of technical skill in application and over the full software life-cycle (final year).

Similarly, the BCS holds "a true engineering perspective" as its theme, requiring that courses develop a high level of technical proficiency and professionalism, underpinned with knowledge of basic principles, including mathematics and engineering science, relevant to the chosen specialism. It demands that technical knowledge be placed in context, in order to develop practical, cost-effective solutions. Hence, project work is a key component of an accredited program, and the final-year project must contribute significantly to the degree classification.

Accreditation is not required of computer science programs, but is sought by those whose aim is to produce marketable computing professionals. The BCS dictates that, "An accredited course should equip students with practical skills essential to begin a professional Information Systems Engineering career". IEE accredited courses are intended to provide ". . . the education and training needed to insure that a Chartered Engineer may demonstrate an acceptable level of competence".

Both bodies propagate the view of engineering as a wealth-creating activity conducted within a market. Each expects project work to encourage sensitivity to the concept of the life-cycle of a product or system. Similarly, "skills" are interpreted by both bodies to include practical skills situated in the marketplace as well as professional and communication skills. "The IEE believes that early contact with the real world of engineering is essential . . ."

Objectives/Aims/Pedagogic Focus

The major project in an accredited course is practical, problem solving, design and build, and integrative; it is the culminating exercise of individual skill. The project should be "real" in the sense that it reflects some attention to a notional marketplace, for example recognizing that the product is for users other than the author. The report should demonstrate an appropriate level of professional competence in the practical development of a suitable application.

The BCS criteria for such projects include that:

- the topic is a practical one involving the production of a piece of software
- the practical work involves a structured engineering approach, including application of skills through all phases of the software life-cycle: analyzing requirements, specification, design, system construction and programming, testing, evaluation, documentation
- the practical work has an integrating role
- it must involve the production of a competent report on the process and the product, including a critical evaluation
- ideally, it must put the problem in context, survey the relevant literature, and must involve some innovation/novelty.

Topics (Allocation)

This view of project work admits any topic allocation mechanism that satisfies the criteria for such projects.

Supervision

The professional bodies stipulate little more than that the practical work is well organized and supported by staff. However, they give attention to the qualifications of the staff doing the supervision, requiring that they are suitably "professional", as indicated, for example, by membership of the appropriate professional body.

A typical interpretation of what satisfies accreditation is the "final-year project" composite, including supervision on a one-to-one basis, with the supervisor nurturing the growth of the student-as-practitioner. Supervision is typically light-handed, providing high-level guidance, especially on project planning and management (see supervisory roles). Supervisory meetings are usually regular, with weekly contact of the order of $\frac{1}{2}$–1 hour. The student-supervisor relationship is usually backed up by some monitoring arrangement and some access to technical support.

Student Process

The student process varies, within the common framework of the student-supervisor relationship. The student works largely independently, drawing on knowledge and skills gathered throughout the degree program, and with guidance from the supervisor and possibly some input from a second supervisor or a technical advisor. The focus is design and build, but other key elements of the process are the experience of the whole software life-cycle, including documentation and presentation. Where possible, the student comes into contact with industry, perhaps as a client, perhaps as a "host" for the project, perhaps through presentation.

Professional elements should be part of the experience, with attention given to how products enter the marketplace, and the use of mechanisms such as external clients can play a role in bringing the "real world" context of software development to life. Finally, the process requires communication in the written and oral presentation of the project.

Deliverables

The BCS specifies that the report on the project should include:

- elucidation of the problem and the objectives of the project
- survey of the context/literature/other similar products
- specification – how the specification of the problem was arrived at, what it is and the initial work schedule; this should include the preparation of an overall project plan with timescale and resources
- design – how the project was designed including design method, design process and outcome; this should include design decisions and trade-offs, such as selection of algorithms, data structures and implementation environments as appropriate
- implementation and testing – description of the production, testing, debugging and proof that the specification had been satisfied, including development aids and how they were used
- critical appraisal of the project, indicating the rationale for design/implementation decisions, lessons learnt during the course of the project, and evaluation (with hindsight) of the product and the process of its production (including a review of the plan and any deviations from it)
- references
- appendices – technical documentation.

Assessment

Assessment is strictly individual, product oriented, and should be in line with stated objectives. Notionally, the project work may be part of a group project, but assessment must clearly identify each individual's personal contribution. This requirement is interpreted strictly enough that group projects are usually considered infeasible for this purpose.

Cited Keys to Success:

- the quality of the learning environment, including learning support, quality assurance, and resources
- the up-to-date expertise of the supervisors, as developed through research, scholarship, and industrial liaison

- quality assurance throughout the degree program, insuring that content, syllabus, and assessment are kept current and provide the skills on which the project work draws

Reference

Institute of Electrical Engineers, *Guidelines for the Engineering Applications Content of IEE Accredited Honours Degree Courses (EA1 and EA2)*, (Membership Brief M12)

2 Mechanisms

2.1 Allocation of Topics to Students (or Teams of Students)

○   ○   ○   ○

Projects have to come from somewhere – someone has to think them up. The generation costs lie in how many projects are needed, how fully projects are specified, and whether they reside in some context (e.g. extending an existing system, requiring particular resources). Scale quickly becomes an issue, with implications not just for how many projects must be generated, but also what sorts of supervisory expertise are required and what range and level of other resources are involved. Also, the problem of project generation must be considered over time; one way of keeping it manageable is to "recycle" projects. Although recycling raises its own concerns (e.g. about the recycling of solutions), it also affords economies over a period of years, and allows the gradual establishment of complex contexts so that projects can be set within a larger area, or students can be allowed to extend previous work.

The key issues in project allocation are mainly to do with who controls the choice of project (student or supervisor), how expertly the project can be supervised, and the trade-off between ease of project management (controlling the number and context of projects) and variety of projects. There are implications for supervision, resources, assessment, and what students might learn from other students' project work.

One Topic for All

All students (individual projects) or teams are given the same topic to address. Using a single topic for multiple projects needn't lead to "cookie cutter" outcomes, how closely the outcomes resemble each other depends in part on how fully the problem and approach are specified. Solutions may differ, interpretations may differ, priorities may differ, and (in group projects) teams may organize the work differently. One variation of this mechanism has each student or team taking on a different approach to a given topic, e.g. using a different development method or solution technique, hence encouraging varied outcomes from a uniform topic.

Advantages: The mechanism is simple and equitable: there is only one topic to generate, and all students are treated the same. Keeping it down to one topic can trade against designing a better topic, writing a better specification, embedding it in a larger system, focusing resources. Students may learn from differences in approach from one individual or team to the next. With only one topic, comparing the level of difficulty is not an issue in assessment.

Disadvantages: Depending on the specificity of the topic, copying may be a potential problem. There is a tendency for students to compare notes and "homogenize" their work. Alternatively, there is the potential for students to think that they will be assessed competitively, and so behave competitively. Topics can become "stale" for supervisors or markers.

Aspects of One Topic

Each student or team takes on one aspect or sub-topic of a large topic (e.g. components or subsystems of a system). Each project may be independent, or the aspects may be intended to interface with each other.

Advantages: Makes it easier for the supervisory team, because all projects have the same context. Students can experience a "taste" of being part of a larger effort, especially if the components are intended to interface properly. Students can discuss the context freely, while still working on separate pieces, so that they can share without fearing to jeopardize their outcomes.

Disadvantages: It's a lot of work up front; an appropriate system has to be identified and analyzed into subsystems of comparable size and complexity. The whole must be coordinated, and, if the subsystems are meant to integrate, the interfaces between the subsystems must be ensured. If it is important that the whole system runs, then it may be necessary to provide model solutions, against the possibility that some student or team does not succeed.

Assigned Individual Projects

Each student or team of students is assigned a different project, chosen by the supervisor or coordinator. Projects are notionally chosen to represent comparable work and complexity. Although the demand for numerous projects can make this mechanism prohibitive in a very large class, the control of projects can be used to advantage in a small class, for example to arrange for coverage of key aspects of the curriculum, or to arrange for coverage of "classic" problem types. Hence, this mechanism is usually associated with group projects, where the number of projects may be significantly smaller than the number of students in the cohort. A variation of this mechanism, which retains the focus on "assignment by supervisor" while reducing the number of projects that must be generated, is the assignment of projects from a given set of topics.

Advantages: Students get to "own" the project. Students can "learn" from other students' presentations of different projects, when there is some common supervision that brings them together. The mechanism provides variety for students and supervisors.

Disadvantages: Supervisors need to find many projects, need to judge comparability of projects (and potentially to deal with perceptions of inequality), and need to find sufficient expertise for supervision. Students may resist the imposition of projects, or find it unfair.

Choice of Set Projects

A number of projects are set by the supervisor(s), usually on the basis of supervisors' interest and expertise, often with an eye to covering particular aspects of the discipline, possibly with an aim of contributing to a program of development or research. The student (or team) chooses one project from the list. Students may be permitted to propose variations on the set projects. Some variations on this mechanism limit the number of projects undertaken, say by limiting choice to one project per supervisor, or to one project per class. Some contingency mechanism may be required to ensure a reasonable distribution of projects or to ration how many students are permitted to undertake a given project, for example first-come-first-served, a bidding system, a lottery, or supervisors' discretion.

Advantages: This mechanism limits the number of projects that must be supervised, focuses the projects on available interest and expertise, and potentially allows both variety of projects and comparison between projects on related projects, so that students can relate to each other's work.

Disadvantages: Supervisors need to think up projects that are comparable in difficulty and scale. Students may be limited by their supervisor's interests. If the mechanism is used in the context of a large class with multiple supervisors, then there may be implications for the allocation of supervisors to students. If supervisor allocation follows project choice, then there is some danger of "clumpiness" (i.e. heavier demand on some supervisors) for which some contingency strategy must be devised. There is an issue of comparability for supervision and marking across projects.

Negotiated Projects Within Constraints

This sort of negotiation of project starts from some context, usually the context of supervisor interests, combined with constraints about "what constitutes an acceptable project". Students can negotiate projects within set constraints about what topic areas are acceptable, what sorts of outcomes are expected, what aspects of the curriculum must be encompassed, level of difficulty or complexity, and so on. In a sense, the topic choice is balanced between supervisor and student, and part of this negotiation process anticipates the supervisory relationship. Negotiation is, in part, about moving from topic to project. The negotiation may be about a range of projects to be undertaken by the cohort (e.g. creating a suite of related projects within a single area), not just about individual projects. Some rationing may apply, so that projects are not oversubscribed. There is usually a deadline structure for the negotiation, and students who do not complete the negotiation in time are assigned projects and supervisors.

Advantages: This mechanism limits the areas that must be supervised and focuses them within the supervisor's interests and expertise. It increases the likelihood of different students or teams working on related topics within a given area, so that each can relate to the other's work and benefit from the broader coverage of the area, and students can benefit from exchange of ideas without jeopardizing the distinctiveness of their work.

Disadvantages: The negotiation process can be time consuming and problematic. Supervisors must judge the appropriateness and comparability of projects and must balance the difficulty of different projects – or make accommodation in assessment – in order to ensure fairness. There are potential problems in the distribution of students among supervisors, if some area is fashionable or some supervisor is popular.

Externally-provided (or Negotiated) Topics

Topics are set by an external collaborator, either an industrial partner (e.g. as used in 3.1 *Large-scale Group Project*), or a client (e.g. 3.3 *Creating a Real Company*). Topics offered by external sources have real-world credibility and currency, as well as a business context – but they may also have real-world ambiguity and incomplete specification. Such topics must be shaped into projects (usually in collaboration with the external partner) to fit the educational context, in terms of pedagogic goals, as well as scale and complexity. Sometimes this is conducted as a three-way negotiation between the student, the supervisor, and the external party (perhaps a client or an industrial collaborator), with the aim of using the external party's knowledge to identify an authentic topic relevant to current practice, and using the supervisor's knowledge to ensure that the project is also appropriate for and relevant to the pedagogic aims. This negotiation of project topic is distinct from an elicitation of customer requirements.

Advantages: Students may be motivated by "authentic" externally-provided topics, that they tend to perceive as more "real" and more relevant than those set by academics. The source may be able to provide a richer, more realistic, more complex context for the topic than it would be possible to invent, which can introduce students to some of the bigger issues. Students and staff benefit from external exposure and collaboration. In negotiation, students may benefit from discussion between the other two parties, if it helps them to reflect on the purpose and nature of the choice.

Disadvantages: Externally-provided topics must be groomed for educational use. There may be problematic discrepancies between what an external party wants as a topic, and what the university requires as a project for learning and assessment. Finding a topic of the right size and complexity and setting it up as a project may require much work and negotiation. The constraints (and contradictions) of the real-world context may prove intractable for students. Access to the topic's source may be limited. Many real-world topics are actually quite mundane and routine.

Students Propose Topics

This mechanism is student oriented; it starts from student's interests. Students must not only come up with the topic, but also find someone willing to make it into a project and to supervise it. There is usually a deadline structure for the negotiation, and students who do not complete the negotiation in time are given projects and supervisors.

Advantages: Students "own" topics and can follow their strengths and interests. Supervisors may be "surprised" by novel topics or approaches. Supervisors needn't generate lots of projects.

Disadvantages: Places a heavy burden on students, who must figure out what constitutes an appropriate topic, as well as think of one and "sell" it to a supervisor. The negotiation process can be stormy. There is potentially a high demand on supervisors, who must ensure that projects are appropriate (in content and scope) and who may have to supervise outside their expertise. Students may be disadvantaged if their project falls outside supervisors' interests and expertise. Topics may be inappropriate, and good topics may be rejected due to shortage of supervisory expertise. If students are ineffective at finding topics, then supervisors still have to generate projects for them.

Negotiated Across the Cohort

This mechanism is designed to introduce a measure of "democratic choice" of project, while constraining the number of projects to something manageable. The project allocation process becomes a two-stage affair. The topic area is negotiated across the cohort, perhaps using a ballot of student preferences. The negotiation need not be extended, potentially being completed in a single class session. Particular projects are then constrained to that topic area and can be chosen using another mechanism such as students proposing projects, or a set project list.

Advantages: Students have some input into the topic area, allowing them to follow their interests or strengths. Student interests can be taken into account without opening the door to wildly disparate topics. The level of student input into the second stage can be adjusted depending on the nature of the cohort, varying from full control by the supervisor to something largely student led.

Disadvantages: Students whose interests lie elsewhere may feel disenfranchised. It can be problematic if students press for a topic that is inappropriate, resource hungry, or outside the supervisor's expertise. The negotiation process must be managed skilfully. The supervisor may still have to generate particular projects. Issues of comparability among particular topics as projects must be addressed.

Weighted Projects

Projects are set by supervisors/coordinator and are "weighted" in terms of difficulty. The weighting may constrain what final mark is achievable for a given project. This is analogous to diving competitions, in which marks combine a level of difficulty score with the score for performance within the terms of the chosen dive. Supervisors may further constrain who may undertake which project, based on previous performance, so that for example the strongest students are not permitted to undertake the least difficult projects. A variation on this mechanism weights the solution components rather than the project, so that the weighting reflects the difficulty of the interpretation, rather than the project itself.

Advantages: Students can make informed decisions about what they want to achieve, and choose projects appropriate to their aspirations.

Disadvantages: The weighting is difficult to set up, and it may be perceived as unfair. It may be difficult to anticipate how students will interpret a project, making the weightings difficult to predetermine. Students may regret their choices, having chosen above or below what is appropriate for them. Students who have been constrained in their choice may feel that they have been treated unfairly.

2.2 Allocation of Students (or Teams) to Supervisors

○   ○   ○   ○

The student-supervisor relationship is key in project work, and getting a "good fit" can enhance the experience for both student and supervisor, as well as affecting outcomes. But matching people up is a thorny business, and it is crucial to maintain a perception of fairness on both sides. Good matches can be motivating. Poor matches can be demoralizing, and a perception of preferential treatment of someone else can lead to resentment. The business of matchmaking can be highly demanding and hard to implement well, and it can be difficult to make the rationale for allocation "transparent" to supervisors and students. Seeking good, well motivated matches trades off against the need to balance the supervisory load among available staff, both in terms of numbers of projects and in terms of the "real" demands of individual students.

Arbitrary Allocation

Students are assigned arbitrarily to supervisors, with attention being focused on "spreading the load" of supervision. An aspect of this is "whoever is teaching the course", i.e. supervisor allocation is contingent on allocation of staff to modules.

Advantages: The mechanism is straightforward to implement and is fair inasmuch as it treats all students (and supervisors) the same.

Disadvantages: The mechanism does not accommodate individual needs – and takes no advantage from special characteristics of students or supervisors. It spreads the load in terms of numbers, but not necessarily in terms of the demand on supervisors.

Existing Relationships

Students are assigned to supervisors with whom they have existing relationships, tutoring, counseling, or previous work. For example, students might be assigned to their laboratory supervisor from a previous course, or to the lecturer who has met them in tutorials (i.e. their tutor) or problem sessions, or to a lecturer who presented pertinent special topics in earlier teaching.

Advantages: There is an existing relationship (notionally a working relationship). If the existing relationship is based on tutoring, for example, the supervisor is likely to have insight into the student's needs and may therefore be able to give relevant guidance. There is a clear rationale for the allocation.

Disadvantages: Students potentially lose out on a chance to establish a new working relationship with a lecturer. If the existing relationship isn't effective, then the project work can inherit existing problems.

Tutorial Groups

In departments where there is a tutorial system in place (where small groups of students meet a tutor for discussion and problem solving), both student (team or individual) and supervisor assignment may follow current tutorial arrangements, with tutorial group leaders supervising students in their tutorial groups.

Advantages: Assignment is straightforward and has a clear rationale. The load is already balanced among tutors/supervisors. Supervision can build on the existing relationship; the supervisor can draw on the knowledge of the student gained through tutorials to tailor the supervision. Students may feel more confident working with a familiar supervisor.

Disadvantages: The nature of the tutorial relationship may prompt expectations that are not appropriate in a supervisory relationship. The supervisor's role may be different from a tutorial role, for example when the supervisor acts as customer for a design and build project, which may be confusing. Students may feel that the tutorial history colors or even biases their supervision.

Students Choose

Students choose who will supervise their project work, subject to availability. The student governs the choice, and may base it on many factors: personality, topic, previous working relationship, expertise, expected future work, etc. Obviously, some contingency strategy is required, in case the choices are not evenly distributed among available staff.

Advantages: If the students get their choice, then they have less reason to complain about their supervision (supervisory allocation). In an environment with an abundance of popular supervisors this mechanism can work well, and students can feel "in control".

Disadvantages: This can resemble a popularity contest, resulting in "uneven" requests and disappointments. If the supervisory capacity is limited and heavily loaded, then it can be hard to make this process seem fair; students may experience a succession of "rejections" if their choices are popular, and that process may leave them feeling ill-served. "Sour grapes" about a failure of choice can influence the subsequent supervisory relationship. Students' reasons for choosing may not be based on seeking the best education; choices based on "frivolous" reasons may result in poor matches. For shy students, this process can be a nightmare; this mechanism may favor confident extroverts.

Supervisors Invite

Supervisors invite students to work with them, on the basis of mutual interests, abilities, or just affinity. The invitations may be coordinated among supervisors, to ensure that each student or team receives an invitation (and possibly only one invitation).

Advantages: Known difficulties can be avoided (if there aren't too many of them). There is a chance to use and extend existing relationships between supervisors and students, and to take advantage of mutual interests.

Disadvantages: Students may not divide neatly among supervisors in terms of interests or ability – some supervisors might wish only to invite the best or most interesting students to work with them. Students might wish only to work with the best or most interesting supervisors. Students may feel obliged to accept invitations, even if they have other (realistic) preferences. Students who don't fit neatly within the available interests must be accommodated. Students may feel demoralized if invitations are not prompt.

Students Propose, Supervisors Choose

Supervisors choose which students to supervise, on the basis of the project proposals which students submit. Supervisors normally select proposals for topics within their expertise or special interest, but their choice may take account of other factors, such as the quality of the proposal or knowledge about the student. Because project proposals may not be evenly distributed among supervisors' interests, and because supervisors' interests may overlap, there tends to be a negotiation phase among supervisors, in order to balance supervision loads and ensure that all students have appropriate supervision. The process may be overseen by a coordinator.

Advantages: There is a chance to make matches based on mutual interests and on topic expertise. Given a clear deadline structure and cooperation among supervisors, the process can be efficient and the assignments prompt, while still taking account of student interests. Supervisors have input about which students are assigned to them and can both seek best matches and avoid known poor matches. Students have indirect input through their choice of topic.

Disadvantages: Students may see the process as a form of judgement, particularly if they have some notion of a "league table" of "best supervisors". Although it is to the student's benefit to choose a topic of genuine interest, attempts to sway the choice may leave some students with an inappropriate topic and without their preferred supervisor. The assignment may appear arbitrary or unfair to students, especially those disappointed in their preferences. Students who don't fit neatly within the available interests must be accommodated.

Assignment Based on Student Profile

Students are assigned to supervisors on the basis of factors such as ability, experience, skills, previous coursework or other history. The intention is to make a good match, making the most of the strengths of each. Assignment may also take account of personal qualities – such as style, manner, working practice, temperament – again with the aim of making a good match between student and supervisor.

Advantages: This can balance the load on supervisors in terms of student needs as well as numbers. Known mismatches (of style, temperament or skill) may be avoided. A good match can motivate both supervisor and student.

Disadvantages: Someone has to analyze the student profiles and weigh up the factors; this may be done more or less informally. The process may be "opaque" to students, leading to speculation about how assignments are made or to perceptions of unfairness. At worst, this may appear to be a "beauty contest". Some matches will be easier to make than others.

Team Supervision (with Specialist Roles)

Supervisors work in concert, each taking a particular role, for example dividing up according to special knowledge or skills, or taking different roles in a management structure (e.g. project leader, client, technical support).

Advantages: Ideally, supervisors can do what they do best, and students can have the benefit of several supervisors' expertise. The load for any one project is distributed among supervisors, and multiple perspectives can be brought to bear on any problems.

Disadvantages: Team supervision may actually entail more work for supervisors, who probably share responsibility for more projects than they would supervise under an individual supervision scheme – but this may be counterbalanced by the focus on one aspect of the project work. Students may not be clear about "who's boss?". Indeed, the overlap of responsibilities may well be opaque to supervisors as well as students. If the supervisory team is not consistent, students may become confused about expectations.

"Pool" Supervision (Whoever Is Available)

There is no specific assignment of students to supervisors. The burden is on the students, who are expected to seek out the supervision they require, from whoever is available. There is usually some rota system, so that at least one supervisor is "on call" at all reasonable times. There may in addition be a token system or some notion of a "currency" of supervision, with the dual purposes of ensuring fair access for all students and providing some record of what supervision is given. This mechanism may be embedded in a supervisory structure that includes regular meetings, so that student progress can be monitored and problems can be diagnosed promptly.

Advantages: This can be a way to make the most of limited supervisory resources, ensuring the most regular access to some supervision. The mechanism facilitates multiple perspectives on student work and problems, potentially benefiting both the students and the management of the project work. Students gain access to a variety of people, with differing expertise.

Disadvantages: Supervision may be uneven. Different supervisors may give different information, leading to confusion. Students may try to "play" one supervisor against another. Students may form preferences and concentrate on given supervisors, which may unbalance the load. It may be easier for students to "disappear" and have no supervisory input at all. It may be difficult to monitor student progress.

2.3 Allocation of Students to Teams for Group Projects

○   ○   ○   ○

Group projects are often as much concerned with the group process and the development of interpersonal skills as with technical outcomes, and so the composition of the team, and the way it affects interactions, is of key interest. The perceived fairness of allocation is focal, especially when groups are assessed collectively, and as a consequence, assessment has a key role in the dynamics of group projects. Students often find the prospect of group work daunting (if not intimidating) – especially their dependence on other students for success – and so the formation of the team is an emotive issue. Dependent as it is on interpersonal skills, teamwork is sensitive to individual and cultural differences; some students are better prepared for cooperative working and decision making. If teams are to be assigned, then supervisors must be familiar with their students and able to analyze key characteristics.

Self-selection (Affinity)

Students are allowed to form their own teams, which they usually do on the basis of existing relationships. Some contingency strategy is necessary for those who don't find teams for themselves.

Advantages: Most students work with others with whom they have some affinity, which can be motivating. Students often choose on the basis of existing relationships, which can increase the likelihood of early progress. Having been responsible for forming the team, students may feel more responsible for making it work.

Disadvantages: Supervisors don't need to make the assignments, but they may have to cope with the "fallout" from the students' efforts, if the teams are not formed easily. Some students, who do not have effective pre-existing working relationships, may be disadvantaged. For example, there is often a small clutch of students "left over" who are typically formed into a team, often with poor results. Students may be limited by their team choices, since they may not bear any relation to skills requirements. For example, students are often observed to form groups "within culture" (Thorn, 1998). Students may be limited socially in their ability to break away from existing relationships to form teams on the basis of skills or other criteria. Students working within existing relationships may by limited by history and may not have an opportunity to take on new roles and discover new skills.

Thorn, K. (1998) In *Projects in the Computing Curriculum* (Eds, Holcombe, M., Stratton, A., Fincher, S. and Griffiths, G.) Springer-Verlag, London, pp. 217–224.

Dis-affinity

The allocation is designed to split up "affinity groups" such as known friendships or cultural groups, in order to force students to work outside familiar relationships.

Advantages: Students are given the opportunity for new interactions, and the change of social environment may reveal unrecognized strengths and abilities. All students start on an "equal" basis, without the possible differential advantages of familiar working relationships. For example, shy students are not disadvantaged by their difficulty in approaching teams. Students who have experienced this sort of group assignment usually report good experiences afterward, despite early reservations or difficulties.

Disadvantages: Students often resent the imposition of teams, and this can impede their progress early in the project. Supervisors must cope with students' complaints. Students may be teamed with others with whom there is some "negative" history, and coping with this adds to the project load (although the experience can have a positive outcome). Students must work out roles, which may slow early progress – but may be considered as part of the learning process. Supervisors must be sufficiently familiar with the students and "in touch" with student culture to be able to analyze where the affinities lie in order to divide students up fairly.

Allocation by Ability or Skills

Students are allocated to teams based on their previous performance, so that those with comparable abilities, skills, or interests are grouped together.

Advantages: Students work with others of "like" ability and skills, which may facilitate effective interaction within the team. If the allocation is on the basis of skills and interests, then that can be exploited by the project choice, so that students may have the advantage and motivation of working on something they're good at.

Disadvantages: Students may be limited by their past performance and may feel that the outcomes are prejudged. Students lose the benefit of interacting across abilities, both in terms of gaining from those who are stronger and gaining from helping those who are weaker – or the benefit of interacting across skills, fostering inter-reliance.

Allocation Across Ability and Skills

Teams are designed to cut across abilities and skills (both interpersonal and technical), with a comparable distribution across teams, so that teams have roughly the same mix of skills overall. The allocation may also be designed to split up "affinity groups" such as known friendships (see "Dis-affinity").

Advantages: The allocation is notionally fair, with each team composed of a variety of abilities and skills. Students work outside existing relationships and must learn to cope with the differing abilities and skills in the group; this can lead them to learn about relying on others and about assessing their own strengths and weaknesses. The potential for peer learning may be increased, since potentially each student has some skill or knowledge that others lack and that must be shared.

Disadvantages: Someone has to make the assessment of abilities and skills; the supervisor must have sufficient knowledge of the students to make that assessment. It may take time for groups to cohere and for students to find appropriate roles within the team. Students may resent the imposition of groups. The allocation may be perceived as unfair.

Allocation Based on Demographic Distribution

Students are assigned to teams on the basis of factors such as gender, cultural background, geographical origin, age, or school background. Usually, the allocation will seek a distribution across the teams (e.g. dispersing members of a given cultural background). This mechanism arises from teachers' own observations about how their students interrelate, and about how particular demographic factors have influenced the performance of past groups.

Advantages: The allocation is notionally fair, with a distribution of "types" across teams. In situations where students of a similar background tend to stick together, a demographic distribution can widen their experience; students working outside existing relationships can learn new ways of interacting and have cause to reflect on their own performance.

Disadvantages: The demographic distribution may not correspond to the skills and abilities distribution, which means yet another set of factors to consider in aiming for comparable teams. Any process that takes into account explicitly, factors such as cultural background may be misunderstood and may lead to controversy. Students may resent the imposition of groups, particularly if the allocation splits up "affinity groups".

Allocation by Tutorial Group

In programs involving a tutorial process, in which small groups of students meet a tutor for discussion and problem solving, allocation may follow the existing tutorial group assignments, either using small groups "as is", or subdividing the tutorial group into project groups.

Advantages: The mechanism is simple to implement and can be considered fair inasmuch as the assignment to tutorial groups is fair. It can build on existing relationships within the group, and this may facilitate early progress. Supervisors can use their prior knowledge of students to add value to project supervision.

Disadvantages: Assignment to tutorial groups is often arbitrary, and so all the disadvantages of arbitrary assignment apply. Students miss an opportunity to interact with unfamiliar students. Problems or prejudices in the tutorial group may be carried into the project.

Arbitrary

Students are allocated arbitrarily to groups.

Advantages: The mechanism is simple to implement and can be represented as fair inasmuch as it treats all students the same.

Disadvantages: The process is seen to be arbitrary and may thus be perceived as unfair. Groups may be of uneven composition in terms of ability and skill. Groups may be of uneven composition in terms of existing relationships or other affinity, giving some groups an advantage.

2.4 Supervisor's Roles

○ ○ ○ ○

The student-supervisor interaction is crucial to project work. Supervision is the focus for teaching within project work, for structuring, diagnosis and management of student work, and for assessment. Supervisors may assume various roles, or vary their roles during the course of project work. The involvement of the supervisor with the detailed project work trades off against the independence of student work, and the roles taken may reflect assumptions about student "maturity". The expectation of students' abilities (both technical and organizational) will depend on the stage of their development at which the project takes place, varying from a point where project goals and process are set and managed explicitly by the supervisor, to a point where students are largely self-reliant, learning new material and techniques on their own initiative and putting them into practice. This is most clear in the differences between undergraduate and research-postgraduate project work. The roles that supervisors assume, and particularly the input they have into project work, have an impact on assessment. The effectiveness of supervision may hinge upon the credibility of supervisors' assumption of roles.

Observer/Commentator

The supervisor is largely a monitor of the project work, rather than a participant in it. The students run the project for themselves, sometimes in the presence of the supervisor. The supervisor observes from their actions (and any required documentation) the roles that they have taken, and the success with which they are implementing these roles. The supervisor may suggest lines of attack or potential solutions to problems, but will not, in general, require that the students adopt them.

Advantages: Gives students maximum freedom to show what they can do. Students must rely on their own decisions. If the supervisor isn't making specific suggestions, then students have no obligation to follow a particular line or view. Most appropriate for more advanced projects, when students have necessary skills.

Disadvantages: Students must cope with little guidance, and some students may founder without a more substantial "scaffold". Students may find it hard to interpret general advice or to relate it to specific techniques.

Project Leader

The supervisor directs the project, maintaining close oversight of and interaction with the project work, down to a tactical level. The supervisor is involved in project decisions, contributing material or ideas to the mix. The supervisor may further act as coordinator, record-keeper, and interface to the rest of the world. This is the traditional "science" model of project supervision, where (typically) a small aspect of the supervisor's research project or interest is marked off as the students' project, to be integrated on completion. The supervisor has a particular interest in the success of the students' project, and will guide them to that end, allocating sub-tasks and directing progress.

Advantages: Simulates industrial practice. The group can benefit from the supervisor's experience, while retaining responsibility for detailed decisions. Students can benefit from supervisor's interest and enthusiasm. The close interaction can facilitate early diagnosis of problems. Pitfalls that can scupper a project can be avoided.

Disadvantages: Students often don't find academics "credible" in their representation of industry. The supervisor can "overshadow" the project, with the result that students don't enter into their own roles fully. An overbearing supervisor can limit students' decision making. Students may be hindered from pursuing alternatives, when they are in conflict with the supervisor's opinions. The supervisor is normally an assessor, which makes students reluctant to disagree with the supervisor's advice. The more proactive the supervision, the harder to factor out the supervisor's impact on the project during assessment. The closeness of the interaction can make the supervisor "blind" to problems. Students may not get the full learning experience of managing the project themselves, and some problems may be bypassed without the students recognising them or benefiting from solving them. This role takes even more time than more light-handed roles such as project manager or observer.

Project Manager/Line Manager

The supervisor has input to the project but is more remote than a project leader. The supervisor is not involved in day-to-day decisions. The students manage and implement the project, but they report to the supervisor who tracks progress and contributes to strategy but not tactics. The supervisor gives broad guidance, perhaps dictating key points, such as approach taken, form of documentation, or similar matters, if they are not already specified.

Advantages: Can speed up group processes, "leveraging" off the experience of the supervisor, while keeping the supervisor "at a remove" from the project. Supervisor has enough contact with the project to diagnose the major problems early enough to intervene.

Disadvantages: Some students may need more than broad guidance. Other students may not do as much as they might, waiting instead on the supervisor's input.

Conflicts of decision or opinion between students and supervisor may impair progress, especially given the supervisor's role as assessor (i.e. the students may be inhibited in exploring alternatives, and the supervisor may be influenced in the assessment).

Client

The supervisor acts as a client, from whom specification must be elicited, whose requirement must be satisfied, and whose viewpoint may not marry comfortably with the students' aspirations. The client portrayed may not be a computing professional; for example, the supervisor may play the role of a small businessman who has an information systems requirement but no technical expertise. The students retain technical responsibility and propose (or "sell") solutions to meet the client's requirement. The students manage and implement the project, but may discuss strategy with the supervisor/client.

Advantages: Simulates an aspect of "real world" practice and introduces a key vector of unpredictability. Allows students to work on developing key skills in a "safe" environment.

Disadvantages: The supervisor may not make a convincing client, particularly in combination with other advisory or troubleshooting roles the supervisor may take. The supervisor may not know enough about the topic domain. The arrangement may appear so artificial to students that they don't take it seriously.

Teacher/Lecturer

The supervisor provides explicit teaching of skills, teamwork, processes, etc. in lectures or group sessions. In a sense, there is a "project work curriculum" that runs in parallel with the actual project work ("just-in-time" lectures), and there may be tasks specifically associated with that curriculum in the requirements for the projects.

Advantages: Students understand the teacher-student relationship. Relevant information can be delivered as it is needed and at a time when direct experience has made students ready to receive it.

Disadvantages: Students may become confused about which information is "useful" and which is "required to be used". This role may not integrate well with other, less familiar roles (e.g. client), since it places the supervisor in a position of knowledge and authority.

Mentor

Mentoring focuses on realising the students' potential and guiding the students' learning. The supervisor shapes the tasks and strategies undertaken by the students, often subtly, and provides additional skills and ideas to extend the students'. The supervisor uses the students' own work as the focus for teaching (introducing concepts, approaches and strategies), guiding strategy, or promoting improvement.

Advantages: Supervision is tailored to students' learning. Students who comprehend the mentoring relationship can benefit profoundly from the tailored interaction, helping to shape it and to draw information from the supervisor.

Disadvantages: Supervisor-intensive, requiring both significant time and significant attention. Mentoring is hard to do well; supervisors must be excellent diagnosticians in order to mentor effectively. The close interaction may make assessment difficult. Requires a "readiness" in the student, who must be receptive and responsive to the guidance offered. Mentoring depends on the rapport between student and supervisor, which may vary with individuals, resulting in uneven treatment of students.

Master

The supervisor takes on the traditional "apprentice master" role, with the supervisor passing on skills and advising the student on the approach to be taken to tasks. The supervisor is "in charge".

Advantages: Some students like to be told what to do; the clarity of this relationship can provide an effective structure within which students can practice the techniques and skills they have been taught. Some supervisors like to be "in charge".

Disadvantages: Students may be daunted by this relationship, which can be more one-way than interactive. This relationship may be at odds with other types of staff-student relationship. Supervisor input into the project may be hard to assess. The nature of the relationship can be burdensome to supervisors, who must provide the energy and momentum of the work. It can also "blind" supervisors to alternatives. Not appropriate in projects whose pedagogic aims include students taking charge, solving problems independently, and being responsible for maintaining progress.

Technical Guru

The supervisor provides technical expertise: helping with problems, making suggestions about techniques or technologies, introducing tools. In effect, the supervisor acts as a consultant, to whom students come with questions and needs, rather than as a manager or auditor.

Advantages: Students get help with technical problems. Technical help can be a way to teach.

Disadvantages: Supervisor may not have the necessary expertise. May be hard to balance the technical help against the project learning objectives, i.e. to give only just enough information. Taking the supervisor's input into account in assessment may be problematic. Different students may get different amounts of help. May place undue demands on supervisor time. Technical help works best when it takes the form of teaching; handing students the answer may defeat the pedagogical aims of the project.

2.5 Meeting Composition: Attendance and Focus

○ ○ ○ ○

Who attends meetings has an impact on where the meeting is likely to focus; whether on the individual, the group, or on issues beyond the students' own projects. There are advantages in models that foster individual development and in models that encourage comparison between different students' experience and learning. How the meeting is composed favors different educational objectives. Each of the models affords potential for monitoring student progress. The biggest cost is in time required, especially of supervisors, and some of the most "nurturing" meeting models may be prohibitive in their supervisory demands, particularly for large classes.

Individual Meetings

Each student meets the supervisor individually, so that meetings focus solely on a single student. This may be most appropriate where students doing individual projects take different topics and the supervisor : student ratio is high. It is also appropriate, when the purpose of the supervisory session is the personal development of the student: the individual meeting provides an opportunity to tutor the student and advance his or her reasoning, as well as to address practical issues in the project work. Similarly, individual meetings suit a research model, where the student's project work is set within a broader research agenda, and the meetings can be used to develop the research thinking.

Advantages: The focus of meetings is clear, and the supervisor can ensure that each student is heard. Students receive individual attention. Each project comes under regular, individual scrutiny.

Disadvantages: Consumes substantial supervisor time. The trade-off may be that meetings are kept short, and so there may not be time to discuss issues fully.

Whole-group Supervision Meetings (Group Projects)

For group projects, each team meets the supervisor separately, so that meetings focus on a single project but include the whole team.

Advantages: All the voices on the team can be heard, making it easier for the meetings to address group dynamics as well as technical progress. Separate meetings can encourage students to discuss project progress freely, without concern for how other teams perceive them.

Disadvantages: Can consume substantial supervisor time, depending on the number of projects per supervisor. Some team members may tend to dominate meetings.

Collective Meetings, More than One Project

All students doing projects (or all students of a given supervisor) meet for sessions with the supervisor, so that more than one project is discussed during a session. This may be particularly appropriate where all projects cover the same topic, so that information is provided uniformly to all projects. Similarly, it can be appropriate where all projects cover related topics, for example under a research model when students are researching different aspects of an agenda, and students can benefit from a discussion of the ideas across the area. Where collective meetings are implemented in group projects, it may be *delegates* who meet, rather than the whole group (and rather than the project leaders). The meetings can be used as more than problem sessions, for example as a way to identify overriding issues of project work or to draw collective lessons. They can be used as teaching sessions, giving instruction in project work techniques, tactics, or technical issues.

Advantages: Students can benefit from each other's experience, including obstacles and tricks for overcoming them. Students can be reassured about their progress compared to other students' progress. Can be cost-effective, eliminating repetition of common problems while giving students the broadest exposure to how projects proceed.

Disadvantages: Individual voices may not be heard, and individual problems may not be detected.

Meetings for Project Leaders (Group Projects)

All supervision is funnelled through the student project leader, who relays information to and from the team. This mechanism can simulate how some projects work "in real life", with the project leader providing the interface to management and clients. It fits best within a software engineering model, where the objective is to experience a process comparable to that encountered in industry, or within a product development model, where the primary objective is a successful product.

Advantages: Gives a focus to supervision, requiring students to pool information and plan for supervision meetings in advance, and giving the supervisor one student to concentrate on.

Disadvantages: The value of the supervision hinges on the communication skills of the project leader; this puts additional pressure on those students who take the role. Individual voices may be suppressed, if their questions or concerns are not conveyed to the supervisor. Other students may feel excluded from access to key resources, or penalised by an under-skilled project leader. There may be assessment implications for those taking on such a large role.

2.6 Time for Meetings

○ ○ ○ ○

Meetings with supervisors (and external participants in projects such as industry managers or clients) can provide structure for project work, a series of "checkpoints" at which students are required to communicate about their projects to someone else. The fundamental issue is: how much access is the right amount, both in terms of preserving students' independence and in terms of efficient use of limited supervisory/managerial resources. Many set-ups combine mechanisms, augmenting a backbone of regular scheduled meetings with some form of "at need" access.

Students may not take advantage of "office hours" arrangements. Even in arrangements where students are expected to attend regular meetings, some students don't. Departments (or individual supervisors) may have ways of keeping track of contact, so students can't "hide" from the process.

Prescribed

Meetings occur at regular, prescribed intervals, usually within designated time slots. A common example is the weekly supervisory meeting, ranging in time from 15 minutes (for example, individual meetings dealing mainly with "issues arising", usually used when each supervisor has many individual students or teams) to an hour (for example, group meetings that cover multiple projects or individual meetings that allow for a more comprehensive progress discussion and more supervisor input). Obviously, the amount of time allowed and the attendance at the meeting shape the purpose of the meeting, and vice versa. Regular meetings allow routine monitoring and are often mandatory. They may include diagnosis of project problems, provision of technical or other information (for example, "updates" on available resources or recent system problems), general progress discussions, strategic guidance about project process, clarification about deadlines and deliverables, teaching about techniques or process, and so on. Other examples of prescribed meetings include scheduled meetings with an industry partner or external client, for example, at say four times during the course of the project – such meetings may be in addition to supervisory meetings. Groups will typically schedule their own team meetings, when they gather face-to-face to coordinate work, discuss strategy and problems arising, and push the project forward.

Advantages: Prescribed supervisory or management meetings can provide a structure to the project course and provide "checkpoints" for students. Regular meetings can facilitate monitoring. They can be an efficient use of scarce supervisor or external participant time. Prescribed meetings give students regular access to the supervisor or external participant, without requiring the students to take initiative in seeking them out.

Disadvantages: Regular prescribed meetings can give the impression of communication without actually achieving it, if students do not bring information to the meeting. Prescribed meetings may not coincide with project needs. Allowing time for prescribed meetings may reduce accessibility of supervisory and management resources at other times.

Office Hours

Supervisors are available for consultation in their offices or otherwise "on call" during published hours. (This mechanism can be used for external participants, such as industry partners or clients, but it is usually associated with supervisory meetings.) Students either drop in during office hours, or sign up for portions of that time. The office hours may be "virtual", for example providing times when email is answered immediately or when a supervisor will be on-line to a conference. This mechanism is also common for technical support, under a "help desk" arrangement that provides for some technical assistance to be available during specified times.

Advantages: Ensures regular accessibility of supervisor to students.

Disadvantages: Ties up the supervisor's time, whether students come for consultation or not. The load may be uneven, providing inadequate access during key periods. Office hours may reduce the supervisor's accessibility overall, especially if office hours are limited or are inconvenient for students. Time for individual meetings within the office hours may be limited, depending on how many students seek contact. Under sign-up schemes, students must plan ahead, and so the system is not responsive to "matters arising". This mechanism requires students to take initiative in coming to the supervisor.

Appointments Only

Meetings occur only by appointment, at times that must be negotiated. This mechanism applies mainly to meetings of "consultation". For example, this is most common in projects where there is an external participant (such as an external client) who does not make regular appearances at the university, or whose visits are infrequent. It may also be the norm for seeking technical advice or consulting someone not usually involved in the project work (such as a local expert in a specialist topic). It is less common for supervisory meetings, but may also be used in that context. One variation is to prescribe the number of meetings, but not the schedule, so that meetings are "regular" but times must be negotiated.

Advantages: Ensures that those consulted spend time in meetings only when needed.

Disadvantages: This mechanism offers no guarantee of regular contact with students, and some students may get much more access than others (some "token" or "quota" system may be required). Waiting on requests makes it difficult to plan ahead, since the demands for access may vary widely over the duration of a project. Students may find access difficult, depending on the availability of the supervisor or other party, and may feel frustrated. Students must take the initiative and must plan ahead, making it difficult for supervision to be proactive.

Catch-as-catch-can

Nothing is prescribed, but students seek out supervisor or other participant opportunistically. This encompasses all forms of ad hoc supervisory meetings, whether opportunistic or by appointment. Combined with prescribed meetings, this can be used as a way to emulate practice in industry, where teams interact with management opportunistically, for example catching a busy manager at the coffee machine.

Advantages: If used intelligently, this mechanism may maximize access at key times. Students seeking to exploit small "windows" may be encouraged to focus their requests efficiently. Equally, supervisors may "casually" walk through a lab at a time they know students will be working.

Disadvantages: The mechanism does not facilitate monitoring. The outcome can be haphazard, with no assurance that contact is achieved when it is required, and no assurance that all students get fair access or equal contact. Students may feel frustrated if they have trouble "catching" the supervisor. Alternatively, if supervisors are normally accessible, they may feel beleaguered by student requests, particularly if students seek contact before they think through their objectives for the meeting.

2.7 Roles in Groups

○   ○   ○   ○

It is in the nature of group projects that students must rely on each other, dividing up work and management among the team. Most teams adopt (by direction or election) a team leader, who has a focal role in decision making, progress monitoring, and information flow, but other team structures are possible.

Rotating

Students rotate through management and other roles over the life the project, for example each acting as team leader for a week or a fortnight. This mechanism works most smoothly when the project is substantial enough and divides into a sequence of sub-projects, so that each manager is responsible for one coherent unit.

Advantages: Each student gets to experience each role. Students experience handover of roles. This mechanism can help keep domineering students from taking over the project management. Students can learn from other students' experience, and themselves experience a variety of management styles. The rotation through roles can help expose individuals' strengths (and weaknesses).

Disadvantages: It may be hard to achieve consistency under a continual change of management. Students may not have time to "settle in" to roles or may not take them seriously, knowing that they will rotate out of the role shortly. Students must carry the overheads of learning new roles as well as doing the project work.

Self-organizing

The group sorts out its own roles. The process may be more or less formal. For example, roles may be sorted out informally by self-proposal, or by discussion. Alternatively, members of the team may elect one of their number as team leader. They may, further, elect students to other roles, such as "chief coder", "documentation officer" or "librarian".

Advantages: Students feel "in control" of the selection. An elected team leader has a democratic mandate.

Disadvantages: Students may not choose the most able student; popularity and ability do not necessarily coincide. Students may be forced into a role by virtue of particular aptitude (ace coders, for example) when they would rather take on something different. The process of discussion or election may be divisive. Some mechanism may be required for resolving a split vote.

Supervisor-appointed

The supervisor appoints the team leader. The supervisor or the team leader may then appoint students to other roles, such as secretary/librarian. This parallels common practice in industry, where project leaders are normally chosen by management based on previous performance, aptitude, and seniority.

Advantages: Supervisor can play to students' strengths or needs, for example ensuring that the "best qualified" student is chosen, or that a student who might not normally be elected to such a role is given a chance to assume it.

Disadvantages: Students may resent the imposition. The student appointed team leader (or, indeed, those not appointed) might feel unfairly treated.

Negotiated

The structure of the team, and the roles within it, are negotiated within the team and between the team and supervisor. Through this mechanism, students may choose to adopt an alternative team structure (for example, forming a partnership to share team leadership, or dividing different management functions among team members).

Advantages: Students may be able to structure their teams to "play to their strengths". Students get to "play out" the consequences of their management design, potentially learning the reasons for existing structures.

Disadvantages: The negotiation process is an additional overhead on project work. Under this mechanism, every team can be an experiment, and project progress can suffer while students sort things out. Supervisors may have to stand back and allow projects to founder under inadequate structures, in order for students to have a chance to recognise their errors. Students are often inexperienced in team-work and so cannot necessarily anticipate what roles involve, or what the implications of an eccentric division of labor might be.

2.8 Motivation

○　○　○　○

Student motivation (indeed, supervisor motivation) may make the difference between a salutary project experience and a dismal one. The obvious points for motivating are at the beginning, middle and end, i.e. the set-up of expectations, project work structures that support progress and give students a sense of "where they stand" with respect to the goals and to other students' progress, and goals and incentives. Individual differences loom large in this area: what one student finds challenging, another may find daunting; or what one finds reassuring, another may find overbearing. The key issue is balance: providing inspiration and momentum while allowing students to learn the lessons of self-management. The mechanism of motivation shouldn't swamp the educational goal.

Choices about What Is Compulsory, What Is Assessed

Students are engaged in defining the project work, in specifying deliverables and targets, and in setting assessment criteria. Usually, this negotiation is subject to some constraints, for example some fixed points in the assessment, or some compulsory deliverables, but students may be given considerable latitude in defining their work.

Advantages: Students "own" the project that they've helped define; they are less likely to complain about targets they helped to set. Students learn the lessons of trying to meet their own targets. Assessment criteria are discussed in advance and agreed.

Disadvantages: The negotiation can be problematic. Students may be ill prepared to set realistic and appropriate targets. Supervisors may be ill prepared to guide students through the negotiation. Students may perceive the different agreements for different projects as unfair. Consistency of assessment may be problematic.

Pace

The way in which project work is structured and "paced" affects motivation. Too slow a project loses student interest. Too intensive a project may "burn them out". Too structured a project can stultify. Too "loose" a project can leave students floundering. The trick is to present a project at a pace that provides challenge but allows students to recover from slips and to assimilate lessons along the way. A variety of devices are used to provide "pace", including: revealing project goals in stages; "just in time" delivery of key information or "just in time" teaching of techniques; presentation of strategic changes or obstacles; industrial involvement with limited access to the industrial partner; and staged deliverables such as design documents, interim reports, and prototypes.

Advantages: A well-paced project provides continuing challenge and fosters regular progress.

Disadvantages: Pacing takes planning. Pacing is influenced by the individuals and the topics; what worked with one contingent may fail with another. Different students respond to different paces and structures; it is difficult to identify and accommodate the different needs.

Competition

Competition (see also 1.4 *Software Hut*) can provide challenge and pace, giving students something to pit themselves against, and giving them a basis for comparing their progress. The motivation is in the comparison: students strive to stand out as the special one among the many, to "win". Competition is conducted at various points in the process, from tendering for a project, to competing to "buy" or "sell" components, to competing for product acceptance. Competition is conducted in a variety of ways, from student-judged efforts, to department-wide exhibitions, to externally judged or public competitions. Prizes can be project related (e.g. publication or display, industrial adoption of a prototype for development, job placement) or not (e.g. cash, books, toys, holidays).

Advantages: Competition can be enlivening and focusing; students often report afterward that competition intensified their project work experience and made them work harder. Competition can reduce copying. Competitions can bring status to project work, including external recognition. Competitions can be a basis for collaboration with industry.

Disadvantages: Competition can be intimidating and divisive to students. Not all students respond to competition. Competition can divert students from the educational goal. Failure to "win" can be demoralizing. External judging "exposes" the department to external scrutiny. Prizes that are disproportionate or unrelated to the project work may be seen as inappropriate or unethical. Judging is not always perceived as "fair"; judges and students may not share the same criteria.

Incentives

Students tend to be goal oriented. They often work disproportionately hard for bonus points of relatively little impact overall. Incentives aim to use that orientation to motivate project work. Incentives can be offered in any scheme, and most incentives are individual: the student "reaches for the carrot". Incentives are not inherently competitive, since there are usually enough carrots for every student, but some incentives, particularly prizes, are associated with competitive arrangements. Incentives are usually course related, e.g. points, access to resources.

Advantages: Incentives and prizes can add "spice" to the effort. They can be relatively "cheap" to implement. Incentives can focus student attention on important aspects of work. Incentives are optional; students need not feel pressured into participating.

Disadvantages: Incentives can distort student goals.

External Visibility

Publishing student work, for example by establishing project work websites, or by inviting an external audience to project work exhibitions, can confer status to student projects and motivate students to produce something that is "worth exposing". Work usually has to "pass muster" to merit exhibition, thereby protecting both university and students from embarrassment, and adding to the prestige of the exhibition. Making work public may be a way to invite comment, so that students receive external feedback.

Advantages: Project work can be a point of contact between students and potential employers. Showing student work can bring prestige to both students and university, particularly if the work is of good quality. Exposing work to a wider audience can bring comment and insights that adds to the students' experience.

Disadvantages: Making weak work public may be undesirable; some "filtering" mechanism may be required. The prospect of "public exposure" may be daunting to some students.

Peer Encouragement

Students can be terrific motivators, providing a bridge between educational objectives and what matters to students. Students working together often "get a buzz" from each other, sometimes just by example, showing other students how to learn through their own learning, sometimes by contagion, infecting other students with their own enthusiasm. Students can often provide subtle insights into each other's work that draw on their "mindsets" – on what they know, on what they're unsure of, on what matters to them. Students can boost each other past obstacles through their interaction and collaboration. Project work can exploit peer learning implicitly (simply through the nature of teamwork) or can be structured to foster it. Peer reviews, exchanges of software components, role play, cooperative coding techniques, critiques of others' projects are all devices to encourage students to reflect on each others' work.

Advantages: Students draw on their own resources to teach and learn from each other. If students support each other, they can reduce the demand on lecturers.

Disadvantages: It depends on the students. Students can misinform as well as inform.

2.9 (i) Nature of Assessment

○　○　○　○

Continuous Assessment

Continuous assessment is based on intermediate products, so that the mark accumulates over the life of the project. Continuous assessment may incorporate a variety of assessment and marking mechanisms; usually it is structured around clearly specified milestones and deliverables, which may include evidence of "process" as well as interim products.

Advantages: Students receive intermediate feedback, so that they can adjust their work accordingly and have an impression of the likely outcome they're heading for. Assessment can take account of interim successes, even if the final product is disappointing. Continuous assessment may favour ways of working, for example distinguishing between those who work steadily and those who leave everything to the end. Spreading the assessment over time may make each assessment stage easier to handle.

Disadvantages: Continuous assessment requires continual attention from the markers. It may involve more assessment than a summary mechanism, if more material is examined. If the feedback is to feed into subsequent work, it needs to be prompt, which puts a heavy periodic load on the markers.

Summary Assessment

Summary (or summative) assessment is based on final products only, characteristic deliverables are a final report, code, a presentation. No account is taken of other material; if something is pertinent, it must be represented in the final products.

Advantages: It is clear what is assessed, what material is taken into account. The assessment is focused and happens once per project, limiting the load on assessors. Students have time to recover from earlier problems, possibly without penalty.

Disadvantages: Students need to pace their work, maintaining progress without external milestones. Depending on the final products, it may be difficult to assess aspects of the project such as process – the assessment is limited to the material in the final products.

Formative Assessment

Formative assessment occurs during the course of the project, with the aim of giving constructive feedback to students so that they can, if necessary, adjust their activity. It is based on interim products and reports, usually giving particular attention to items such as project journals or logs, which allow the assessor to comment on the students' process, as well as their progress. Formative assessment is often qualitative, rather than quantitative, perhaps taking the form of comment rather than a mark. Indeed, it may not contribute to the final mark.

Advantages: Students receive feedback early enough to adjust their work accordingly. Students receive an impression of their progress. The assessor receives more information about the students' process, on which to base comments.

Disadvantages: Formative assessment is demanding, adding to the assessor's load. Depending on what materials it uses, it may also increase the students' load. Students may resent the extra scrutiny, especially if they do not see a benefit. Students who are outcome-oriented may not take it seriously if it does not contribute to the final mark. If the final mark differs from the expectations raised by the formative assessment, then students may feel unfairly treated. The quality of feedback that can be given depends on the quality of the students' reporting, and so it may be hardest to diagnose the weakest projects in detail.

2.9 (ii) Group Assessment

○   ○   ○   ○

In group projects, there is an overriding strategic issue: whether groups are assessed together (and get one mark) or whether they are assessed separately and so get individual marks. The decision reflects choices about the nature of the group project, about its aims and focus. Of course the options are not mutually exclusive, for example a project whose products are assessed on a group basis can include an element of individual reflection.

Individual Deliverables

Individual deliverables focus on the individual's contribution to the project, in terms of production and/or teamwork, and on the individual's experience of the project.

Advantages: Individual deliverables gives students a chance to document their role in the team and may promote reflection about the project experience. The collection of individual submissions may give the assessor a more accurate profile of the group. Individual voices may make it easier to compensate for an unbalanced team, or one with a lazy member.

Disadvantages: Individual deliverables may require students to divide up attribution, which may be difficult in true team working. Knowledge of the assessment scheme may inhibit true team working, if team members are working to maximise their individual marks. There are more deliverables to assess, and hence a greater load for assessors.

Group Deliverables

Group deliverables focus on the collective effort, emphasising the importance of effective teamwork. Individual contributions are not demarcated.

Advantages: This approach makes clear that the group must work as a team, and students often pull together as a result. Students must learn how to collaborate, how to compromise, how to delegate, etc. They must resolve any differences about style, expectations, presentation and so on, in order to arrive at mutually acceptable products. Hence, this approach may support non-technical pedagogic goals. Group deliverables can be economical of assessors' effort.

Disadvantages: Students may resent being lumped together and may feel anxious about having their mark rely on others' performance, particularly at the start of the project. Students tend to find group assessment stressful. Students may feel that they are held back by the group. Alternatively, students may let others "carry" them. Students must resolve any differences about style, expectations, presentation and so on, which may be problematic.

2.9 (iii) Basis of Assessment: Deliverables

○ ○ ○ ○

Deliverables vary enormously, potentially covering any aspect of the software engineering process as well as the learning process. A common deliverables package
includes design documentation, software demonstration and documentation,
together with a reflective final report. Deliverables may be "staged", with interim
deadlines throughout the project to provide checkpoints and milestones. (Similarly,
assessment of deliverables may be staged.) The "minimal" deliverable is the
summary report. Final reports vary as much as deliverables lists – indeed, they
are often collections of other deliverables with a small reflective component or
even just a brief overview and table of contents. The list presented here indicates
some of the range of deliverables associated with different aspects of projects
(although where they fall is a matter of interpretation).

Initial Problem Capture:

- project brief or description document (commonly 500–1000 words)
- survey of theoretical background and literature
- annotated bibliography
- proposal for practical investigation or implementation.

Analysis and Specification Documents:

- feasibility study
- risk assessment
- requirements specification (ranging from 2–5 pages to 10–20 pages)
- formal specification (commonly 5 pages)
- flow charts
- entity relationship diagrams.

Design Documents:

- design description
- block diagrams
- entity relationship diagrams.

Project Plan

(commonly 1000–3000 words).

- implementation plan
- timeline or schedule of work
- Gantt chart
- Pert chart
- quality assurance plan
- configuration plan.

Progress Reports:

- interim reports, sometimes weekly, giving work-to-date
- changes to plan
- timesheets.

Process Documents:

- meeting plans, agenda, minutes
- configuration management documents
- project log.

Software

(commonly 1,500–4,000 lines of code, but ranging from 500–10,000).

Product Documentation:

- maintenance or technical manual
- user manual
- advertizing brochure
- quality assurance document
- quality control plan

- peer inspection report
- code walkthrough
- test documentation
- test plan
- test sets and outputs, possibly outputs from prescribed tasks
- installation test report
- user evaluation
- client feedback, formal (e.g. using a marking scheme) or informal
- usability testing
- sales/purchase strategies.

Assessment Products:

- final report 10–100 pages or 10,000–40,000 words (these are often specified separately), depending on the scale and duration of the project and on what other deliverables it encompasses
- reflective "post-mortem" reviewing progress, reflecting on process or performance, identifying of group working and technical problems, and so on
- group and/or individual components
- presentation/demonstration
- scheduled talk (10 minutes–1 hour; usually longer for group presentations and interviews)
- "trade stand" (10–20 minutes)
- poster display
- oral examination or project interview (45–50 minutes, including demonstration).

2.9 (iv) Assessment: Who Marks?

○ ○ ○ ○

The main issues in assessment are fairness, consistency and accountability. Students wish to know who decides their grades and on what basis. They wish to receive feedback promptly. Assessment may value different aspects of project work and may admit different points of view, but the more perspectives it takes into account, the more complex it becomes. Consistency and calibration of marking (both between projects and between supervisors) may be problematic, especially as scale increases. The mechanisms for maintaining quality of assessment may be costly (usually relying on additional assessors or monitors) or they may be constraining (if they focus assessment on particular aspects or confine it to close interpretations of fixed criteria). Assessment may be formative (influencing the learning process) or summative (based on final products), and the nature of assessment itself may encourage reflection by students on their own work.

Supervisor Marks

The supervisor is solely responsible for marking the project, often in terms of criteria or a marking scheme. Where more than one supervisor is involved in project work, the marking scheme or criteria may be used as a way of providing consistency, and the scheme may have been agreed among the supervisors, or determined by the coordinator or department. This mechanism fits comfortably in a small class, especially where there is only one supervisor responsible for all projects.

Advantages: The responsibility is clear, and there are no overheads for communicating or reconciling grades between multiple markers. The supervisor should be well informed about the project, what input was received and what obstacles were encountered, and so should be well placed to mark fairly.

Disadvantages: There is no "calibration"; the grading is not moderated or monitored, and the students may not perceive the supervisor as accountable for the marks assigned. If more than one supervisor is involved, this can lead to inconsistencies between supervisors that disadvantage some students. If the student is at odds with the supervisor, then there could be a perception that personal feelings have influenced the grade.

Supervisor Plus Another

There are a variety of "supervisor plus another" mechanisms, and most projects use one of them. The "other" may be an internal or an external examiner, usually someone whose experience of the project work is strictly through the deliverables, possibly only through the final report and the deliverables directly associated with it. In this way, there are at least two opinions given on the project work, one from the supervisor most familiar with the student and with the detailed progress of the work, the other from an examiner who judges the products in the absence other information. (Of course, members of staff may play more than one "role", operating as supervisor for some projects and internal examiner for others.) Usually there is some mechanism (e.g. see Moderator mechanism) for handling serious disagreements between the two markers.

Advantages: Responsibility for marking is shared. Collaboration can have advantages for staff development, both as a way of introducing new staff and as a way of sharing or giving new perspectives. Having two markers can be perceived as fairer than just one, and working out disagreements in the marking can not only reveal things about individual projects but can also reveal weaknesses or ambiguities in the marking scheme. Students benefit from an "insider's view" and an "outsider's view" of their work, so that individual factors can be taken into account but need not cloud the assessment.

Disadvantages: The load on markers is doubled. Some arbitration scheme is necessary, even if only a discussion between markers.

Moderator

The normal marking mechanism is supported by monitoring or moderation, providing an extra opinion and thereby a "safety layer" and additional quality assurance. The moderator may take different roles: monitor, arbitrator, or mentor. In the "monitor" role, the moderator looks at all marking to ensure consistency and guard against misunderstandings. In the "arbitrator" role, the moderator intervenes in the case of disputes. For example, in a "supervisor plus another" set-up, the moderator may provide a third, casting opinion if the first two markers' opinions differed substantially.

In the "mentor" role, the moderator inducts new supervisors into the scheme, giving advice and assisting with interpretations. For example, the moderator may be consulted about how marks should be adjusted if a student has received substantial supervisor input. The moderator may view the whole process from a different perspective, taking an overview and ensuring department standards.

Advantages: Someone is acquainted with the marking overall and can assess consistency. Supervisors have an informed party to consult about marking, if necessary. The mechanism provides a "safety layer" for students and makes the accountability of the marking visible. The overview the moderator acquires can feed back into improving the marking or monitoring mechanisms.

Disadvantages: Someone has to act as moderator, and usually this requires an experienced lecturer who is familiar with supervision and examination of project work, and the local conditions under which these are conducted. Moderation may require significant effort dealing with those who don't follow rules, who won't conform to the project, supervision, and assessment structures. If the class is large, then the task of reviewing all projects – even cursorily – can be unwieldy. The process of multiple marking can take time, delaying the arrival of the assessment in the students' hands. Substantial time may be spent just on administration, for example chasing people who don't submit their paperwork on time.

Self Assessment

Students assess their own work. This is usually done within some published terms of reference. The self assessment may be quantitative, for example paralleling an overall marking scheme, or it may be descriptive, or both. The self assessment is usually a component of the mark, rather than the whole. When used as part of a group project, self assessment can contribute to the assessment of individual contributions (for example to apportion credit), or it can be used "to salve peer assessment".

Advantages: If done well, self assessment can foster reflection and can extend the learning process. Self assessment can give students a chance to present mitigating circumstances that might otherwise not be revealed.

Disadvantages: The mechanism relies on students acting in good faith. Individual differences can be expressed as discrepancies in self assessment. Students are not equally able to reflect on their own work, and students are not equally critical. Supervisors report that many students are unnecessarily critical of their own work. If the self assessment is discursive, then it needs to be read and "assessed" along with the other material.

Peer Assessment

Students sometimes contribute to each other's assessment. Peer assessment normally applies within group work, when students assess each other's contribution to the team. In such a case, it may be used to apportion credit among students. But peer assessment is possible in other contexts, for example, students (individually or in groups) may take the role of "critic" of another's project. Peer assessment may be used as a reflective tool, so that students are asked to consider performance in terms of set criteria or outcomes. Peer assessment is usually only a contributory part of an assessment strategy, used in combination with other mechanisms. The form it takes may vary, from individual assessment of another's work or of other team members, to collective assessment of others' work, to a negotiation apportioning credit among a team. Alternatively (and less frequently), peer assessment can form the major part of assessment, with students working from published criteria to mark each other's work. In this case, it may be subject to vetting by the supervisor.

Advantages: Students take some responsibility for assessment and can express their judgement of outcomes. Peer assessment can show students that they are account-able to the rest of their team. Peer assessment in group work can be a way to take into account differences of contribution to the team and the project's success.

Disadvantages: The mechanism relies on students acting with goodwill; otherwise, it may be seen to be unfair or spiteful. Individual differences may show up as assessment discrepancies that can be difficult to normalize. The process may be divisive.

Moderation of Team Marks by Student Peer and Self Assessment

Combining assessment mechanisms can be a way to use one's strengths to coun-teract another's deficiencies. In group work, there is often concern that the team mark will not reflect accurately an individual's contribution: students often worry about being "brought down" by a weak or lazy team member. Peer- and/or self-assessment can be used to address that concern, giving students a chance to contribute to the grade and potentially to express issues that are not represented in the products of the product. The contribution can be made in different ways, for example as a portion of the marks, as an adjustment on the grade, as a way of apportioning credit among team members. The significance of the moderation may be more symbolic than actual; use of peer- and/or self-assessment may be a way to signal that students are responsible for their outcomes.

Advantages: The team mark may be moderated to take individual contribution into account. Students take some responsibility for assessment and can express their judgement concretely. Marking accommodates more points of view: the supervisor's, the examiner's, the individual student, and the other team members.

Disadvantages: This sort of moderation adds complexity to marking, since the additional marks must be factored in to the final grade. The weight given to the peer- and self-assessment must be judged. May be emotive and divisive, if students are not perceived to be acting in goodwill.

Industrial Partner or Client Marks

Assessment may draw on external partners, such as industrial collaborators or clients. External party assessment is usually contributory, giving students an impression of how their work might be viewed "in the real world". Usually, the external party completes a pro-forma or checklist that sets out the criteria for assessment. Alternatively, the external party may be invited to articulate their own criteria, in order to highlight distinctions between academic and industry values. This approach may be associated with competition, for example providing the basis for award giving, or determining which of alternative solutions is to be adopted or to be developed further.

Advantages: Increases the "stakes" in a way that can be motivating to students. Makes students' work visible outside the university. Can give a perspective on industry practice and values.

Disadvantages: In a competitive system, only one project wins, and the rest may consider themselves "losers". External views may not be based on university criteria. May be difficult to maintain consistency and keep "under control", given industry pressures and expectations.

2.10 Marking Schemes

○   ○   ○   ○

Marking schemes vary enormously, although they tend to follow a few common patterns. They are one of the mechanisms often "tweaked" in successive presentations of project work. Two thorny issues that must be taken into account are non-student input (from supervisor or technical support) and level of difficulty of the topic (relevant whenever students undertake different topics or different approaches). Students are usually appraised of the marking scheme, or at least of the broad categories and criteria, in advance, in the hope that they will know what to expect, will be able to plan their work accordingly, and will perceive the outcome as fair. Marking mechanisms may serve either summary assessment or continuous assessment. The big trade-off is between consistency and flexibility: highly specified schemes encourage consistency, but at the expense of flexibility in dealing with particular cases.

Unweighted Criteria

Criteria (or categories) are established or suggested for what will be assessed, but the relative value of the those criteria is not stated. Criteria may be many or few, although they commonly cover about half a dozen categories. Criteria may cover any aspect of product or process; some schemes are strictly product oriented, while others give equal attention to the student's conduct of the project or to the student's comprehension and learning.

Example:

- "conduct
- comprehension
- approach, method and design
- implementation
- results and evaluation
- presentation and organization".

Example:

- "We look for theory, design, build, testing, report writing".

Example:

- supervisor's technical and managerial input to the project
- student's application of an appropriate process, i.e. the extent to which an appropriate life-cycle was specified, followed and documented:

"For the project as a whole ...

- the quality of the problem analysis and solution design delivered
- the quality of the documentation, hardware and software delivered
- the complexity of the task attempted and the extent to which the students understood the domain and necessary tools at the outset of the project.

For each student on a project ...

- the value and "degree of difficulty" of the individual student's contribution to the project
- the extent to which the student has critically evaluated their technical work and their working processes
- the student's contribution to the working of the group."

Advantages: Focus of assessment is stated in advance, so that students are given an indication of what is to be assessed, while assessors retain flexibility in assigning marks.

Disadvantages: Although criteria are stated, relative importance is not, and students may feel unsure of what's important. Uncertainty may lead students to feel unfairly treated: "Why didn't they tell us that so-and-so would matter so much?" Loose specification may make it difficult to maintain consistency among multiple markers.

Weighted Criteria

Specific weightings (i.e. percentages or numbers of points) are allocated to specific parts of the project work (i.e. criteria and/or deliverables). The allocation may be more or less specific. Often broad weightings are specified and the finer detail is left to the marker. Sometimes the mechanism is refined into strict scheme (often embodied in a pro-forma).
    Example:

- interim reports (15%)
- requirements specification (15%)
- design (15%)
- implementation (25%)
- evaluation and testing (15%)
- presentation (10%)
- conclusions (5%).

Example:

- seminar (10%), subcategories: organization, communication, visuals, technical impression

- demonstration (10%)
- report (15%), subcategories: organization, literacy, presentation, diagrams
- quality of work (55%)
- technical impression from report (10%).

Advantages: If the criteria are published in advance, then they provide a way for students to assess what contributes to the grade and hence to plan their work accordingly. In this way, supervisors can influence where students put their attention. The stricter the scheme, the easier (notionally) to maintain consistency in marking by a variety of assessors.

Disadvantages: Not all learning objectives may be represented as specific weightings or criteria, and students may be given a distorted sense of what's important. If the criteria are too broad, they are open to interpretation and hence to inconsistency or to perceptions of unfairness. On the other hand, a strict scheme may not easily accommodate special circumstances.

Negotiated Criteria or Negotiated Weightings

Criteria – and/or weightings of marks for criteria – may be negotiated by students at the outset of the project, with marking against the agreed criteria. In this way, students and supervisor can set individual priorities for the project work and can shape the project (though the marking) to focus on and value the particular interests or needs of the students.

Advantages: Students have a role in determining priorities for the project work. Students have clear knowledge of the marking scheme in advance.

Disadvantages: The process of negotiation may be awkward and time consuming. If negotiation doesn't go as students hope, there may be ill feeling. It may be difficult to maintain consistency among projects. Differential treatment may lead to feelings of unfairness.

Comparison Against Models

Student work is compared to models of "exemplary" and "average" performance. Models may be drawn from previous work or written by the supervisor.

Advantages: Models provide concrete examples of how student work is interpreted against standards. Models are sometimes available as part of the history of the course or of the course approval or accreditation process.

Disadvantages: Models can be difficult to generate. The "judgement of similarity" to a model may be a variable business, with different markers attending to different aspects of the work. New staff must abstract "what makes this exemplary" or "what makes this average" from the examples. Students can find this sort of comparison opaque (and hence may perceive it as unfair).

List of Typical Attributes

Criteria are expressed as a list or table of attributes typical of projects within a given degree class.

Example

"To fall in a class, a project has to satisfy the relevant criteria, which are as follows:

Original Contribution – Prize-Worthy

Range of references including journal articles
Considerable intellectual challenge
Mathematical proof/analysis
Very well written and structured report
Worthy of publication/use
Good review of related work
Evidence of original thinking

Exceptional Features – First Class

Decent references
Mention of related work
Evidence of intellectual challenge
Would/will use the end result
Well written and structured report
Possibly worthy of publication and worth using
Well tested
Very well designed and engineered

A Solid Product – Upper Second

References to material used
Some intellectual challenge
Well written and structured report
Student worked well, planning and managing the work
Possibly worth using
Robust
Systematic testing
Well engineered/designed

Close to Project Brief – Lower Second

Adequate background reading
Less challenging project or intellectual challenge not fully addressed

Student worked steadily, needing guidance
Evidence of proper testing
Adequate design and engineering

Slow Progress – Third Class

Some background reading
Misjudged size of problem, needing guidance
Some inappropriate material in report
Loss of morale and initiative
Insufficient time to do full testing
Some weaknesses in design or engineering
One or more major features not implemented

Some Evidence of Progress – Pass

Little evidence of background reading
References missing
Needed considerable supervision
Poorly written and structured report
Partial fulfilment of the brief
Little evidence of testing

Little Evidence of Progress – Fail

Advantages: Expressed in this way the marking scheme gives a fairly clear indication to students of what they must achieve – how all the components fit together – in order to earn a particular grade. The description within grade bands emphasises what distinguishes one grade from another.

Disadvantages: The scheme must be accompanied by some notion about "sufficiency" (i.e. how many of the characteristics must be met to the grade standard), in order to accommodate projects that don't fit neatly into any one band of attributes but have different levels of virtue in different aspects. Attribute descriptions tend to be qualitative and must be interpreted: how much is "adequate" or "considerable" must be quantified or made concrete. No indication is given of the relative importance of different aspects, nor of other factors that may be taken into account.

Banded Constraints or Performance Thresholds

The marking scheme specifies performance thresholds. These can be tasks captured in an audit checklist or product standards according to given metrics or criteria. These threshold criteria constrain the bands that correspond to grades. The achievement of the performance criteria ensures entry into the band, i.e. ensures a minimum mark. This is in a sense a different perspective on the "List of typical attributes" mechanism; here the attributes are operationalized as tasks to accomplish or standards to achieve.

Example:

"to achieve 40–50%, demonstrate adequate solution to problem
to achieve 50–60%, above plus demonstrate disciplined approach
to achieve 60–70%, above plus appreciation and application of best practice
to achieve 70% plus, above plus originality, flair, imagination, even novelty or scholarship"

Advantages: The criteria are expressed in a concrete and grade-related way that should make clear the relationship between work and assessment. If the bands and constraints are well expressed, then marking is fairly unambiguous, and students should be able to predict their grades.

Disadvantages: Making attributes concrete and stating them as clear constraints sounds appealing but can be difficult. It can be difficult to use the full range of marks (0–100%).

Mixed Marking

Some schemes may use a combination of mechanisms, drawing marks from different sources, or applying different schemes for different aspects of the work. Marking may combine numeric and qualitative components.

Example:

"weighted marks for deliverables, plus qualitative assessment of what the student has learned with regard to group working, project planning, software engineering, and their general conclusions on the project as a whole"

Example:

"mark produced by client, analysis report based on strict marking scheme, criterion-based assessment marked on e.g. a 5-point scale"

Advantages: Can give flexibility to handle different aspects of project work. Allows some latitude to give credit for "intangibles", aspects of project work that are difficult to characterize in a marking scheme.

Disadvantages: Adds complexity to the already messy business of marking. May be confusing. May be open to interpretation, and hence may make it difficult to maintain consistency among markers. Students may consider a qualitative element to be "a fix".

2.11 Overseeing, Moderation and Quality Assurance (QA)

○ ○ ○ ○

Whenever there is more than one person involved in supervision and assessment, there is potential for disagreement or discrepancy, and so there is a need for moderation, and there is a need to ensure standards and consistency. Some mechanisms (e.g. moderation) are reactive, used only at need, whereas others (e.g. monitoring and coordination) are regular overheads. Often the QA and moderation mechanisms can feed back into practice.

Coordination Structures for Supervision

At some point in the evolution of project work, usually when it scales up beyond the capacity of a small group of dedicated supervisors, the structures and procedures for supervision are codified. This articulation and documentation clarifies what is expected of each of the participants (students and staff), describing what constitutes an acceptable project, how projects are assessed, what is expected of supervisors, how supervisory efforts are coordinated, how quality is maintained. Because the codification is usually a reaction to issues of scale and quality assurance, it sets out roles for primary supervision, for backup supervision, for moderation between supervisors and for coordination and overseeing of all supervision. It also provides structures for communication, mechanisms for resolving discrepancies or disputes and methods for maintaining quality. For example, the common "supervisor plus another" arrangement (that covers most supervision and assessment) is usually backed up by some routine monitoring (to ensure standards and consistency) by a third-opinion mechanism (for moderating or arbitrating disagreements), and by a mechanism for auditing (to examine the nature and quality of supervision overall).

Advantages: Codifying structures and procedures can provide clarity for all concerned. Having explicit coordination structures makes it clear where to turn for help and supports the induction of new supervisors. Mechanisms for monitoring and coordination can improve consistency, fairness, accountability and quality.

Disadvantages: Coordination takes time and attention. Any form of monitoring, auditing, or third opinion involves additional staff and additional overheads. Over-specified coordination structures can be hindering, rather than helping.

Supervisor Teams, Meetings

Often, whenever there is more than one person supervising project work, supervisors meet to agree supervisory practice and to address matters arising in the actual supervision. Many supervisory arrangements are closely coordinated, with supervisors meeting regularly, often treating supervision as teamwork and addressing any difficulties collectively.

Advantages: Provides support and calibration for supervisors. Regular meetings contribute to a collective vision of goals and procedures, to identification of gaps or discrepancies, and to sharing of ideas and resources. Provides "induction" for new staff. Problems arising from the set-up can be detected early.

Disadvantages: Meetings take time. Where there are philosophical disagreements about aims, or where there are perceived inequities in workloads, meetings may provide fuel rather than resolution.

Consistency Quality Assurance (QA)

Whenever there is more than one supervisor, consistency is an issue. Sometimes quality assurance is implicit, for example in small, closely-knit supervisor teams, where quality assurance arises from normal discussion of supervision and procedures. Larger numbers of supervisors may require more explicit mechanisms for ensuring consistency, for example codification of the supervisor role, assessment procedures and marking schemes, monitoring arrangements in which an experienced overseer reviews supervision and assessment practice. Project work coordination structures may incorporate a variety of mechanisms for QA.

Advantages: Monitoring or QA arrangements can improve consistency and can detect problems with the set-up or with individual practice. QA can provide additional support to supervisors.

Disadvantages: Any QA is an additional overhead. The greater the scale of the project work in a department, the greater the need for QA, and the greater the challenge and cost. QA must be tolerant of appropriate variation, allowing some leeway for individual differences, and allowing exploitation of particular expertise – the balance between consistency and variation can be a hard balance to strike. Given all the demands and difficulties in doing project work well, QA can be a rod for the department's own back.

There is a crossover of QA with supervisor role, supervisory input and assessment.

Arbitration, Moderation (Assessment)

Moderation usually takes the form of "the extra opinion", often used in supervisor-plus-another schemes. The extra opinion is a straightforward moderation mechanism that can short-circuit elaborate discussions between dissenting assessors by providing the "casting vote". The extra opinion may be provided by an experienced individual, or by a small panel, for example those coordinating the project work in a large program. The extra opinion can also contribute to the formulation of practice, generalizing from the lessons of individual cases to clarify or elaborate how project work is done – hence, moderation can feed back into the supervision process in a way that reduces future need for moderation.

Advantages: Efficient use of the extra, experienced resource. Can feed back into practice. Can help inform supervisors.

Disadvantages: Takes a third person reviewing the work.

2.12 Staff Deployment

○ ○ ○ ○

The management and supervision of project work is a resource-hungry business. Even in cases where projects are small enough or involve few enough students to be the sole responsibility of a single teacher, supervision "consumes" the time and attention of that teacher – and hence not everyone may want to supervise project work. When project work numbers or expectations are scaled up, then providing and coordinating supervisors becomes an issue of department-level resource management – often becoming the department's single greatest resource "sink". Larger numbers of supervisors highlight the issues of fairness, consistency, and quality of supervision, emphasising the need to codify quality assurance procedures.

Everyone Supervises

When there are many students undertaking substantial projects, it is not uncommon for all available members of staff to supervise some projects.

Advantages: The deployment is "fair" in the sense that everyone does it. Full deployment means access to the complete range of expertise in the staff. A consequence of the management issues may be that procedures, structures and expectations are more fully worked out and documented in advance, which can make the integration of new staff easier and can make the whole process clearer for all concerned. Involving everyone may increase the status of project work in the department, since everyone has first-hand experience of the work involved in supervision.

Disadvantages: More supervisors means that more coordination required, with quality assurance issues at the fore, and of course greater management overheads. The issue of "matchmaking" between student and supervisor is amplified. Differences in supervisory skill may become manifest. If everyone supervises, then no one gets a "break" from supervision, and over time staff may grow "stale". If not everyone supervises – given absences, excuses – then staff may perceive unfair loads, raising clashes and political issues in the department.

Concentrating Supervision Within a Small Group of Staff

Supervision is undertaken by a small group of staff. Such groups usually work closely together as a collective that meets regularly to agree procedures, resolve any difficulties, and coordinate work through discussion. Alternatively, the group may be constrained in number simply by requirements for particular expertise (e.g. for supervision of research projects).

Advantages: Smaller numbers of staff can make it easier to ensure tight supervision procedures, with the supervisors working together closely to maintain a strong collective view of what is expected and to support each other. The small group and tight coordination can provide clarity and confidence for students.

Disadvantages: Loading the intensive work of project supervision on a few members of staff can be perceived as an unfair burden and can exclude them from other work.

Supervision Beyond the Department

Supervisory staff are drawn from other departments to work in tandem with Computer Science staff as a way of incorporating additional expertise. Joint supervision can be a mechanism for making "hybrid" projects possible, for example joint Business and IT projects that draw on both disciplines and may be assessed in both.

Advantages: "Looking outside" can be a way to add expertise, fresh views, and fresh energy to supervision. The chance for collaboration beyond the department can be exciting to both students and staff. It can broaden the possibilities for what projects can be undertaken, and in joint programs it can make the integration of disciplines more concrete.

Disadvantages: Drawing on external resources requires inter-departmental negotiation about resources (both staffing and funding) and expectations – and hence may involve inter-departmental politics or may attract university-level overheads. Staff crossing borders may be "pulled in two directions" if the arrangements (e.g. funding, time allocation, educational goals, and assessment) are not fully worked out.

"Pulling in the Bodies"

Supervisory staff are drawn from outside the department just as a way of providing sufficient teaching power by drawing extra resource from non-faculty staff. This may include research assistants and technical support staff, as well as academics from other departments. This approach is strictly about coping with numbers.

Advantages: Supervisory demands can be met. Students and staff might both benefit from the fresh expertise and perspectives brought in. The management demands may necessitate that procedures, structures and expectations are more fully planned and articulated, which can make the integration of new staff easier and can make the whole process clearer for all concerned. Students may view non-faculty staff with higher esteem.

Disadvantages: Seeking non-faculty staff can be problematic, raising issues about job specifications, funding, overheads, and so on. The staff "pulled in" may suffer in the crossfire between managers. Non-faculty staff must be inducted into supervision, incurring both the induction costs and the overhead of articulating processes and expectations.

Graduate Students as Supervisors

In many larger departments, graduate students (i.e. teaching assistants) provide the project work supervision, under the coordination of a member of staff. This arrangement is comparable to laboratory supervision, where the structure and preparation are provided by the lecturer, but the graduate student assistants provide the one-to-one guidance needed in the labs. In the same way, graduate students may be deployed to play particular roles in project work supervision.

Advantages: Graduate students are often "close" to student work, especially when they are also deployed in marking and laboratories. Their own studies and research often give them particular expertise (particularly technical expertise) that can be advantageous. Students may perceive them as more approachable than lecturers. Using graduate students for the labor-intensive business of supervision frees lecturers for other, more strategic roles.

Disadvantages: As with any inexperienced supervisors, graduate students may be ill-prepared for ensuring fairness and consistency in supervision. Involvement may be hard to judge. If they are conscientious, they may be drawn into giving disproportionate attention to project work supervision, or becoming too much involved in the students' work. Alternatively, graduate students may be "off-hand" about students' work and may not give consistent or progressive guidance.

Industrial Involvement

In projects with industrial involvement, the industrial partners may be drawn into supervision, sometimes taking substantial responsibility, sometimes playing particular roles in supervision (e.g. project manager, client), usually coordinating closely with teaching staff. Attention must be paid to industry/academic partner needs in setting the project, with an understanding of mutual expectations.

Advantages: Students get all the advantages of outside expertise grounded in "real-world practice". Students get exposure to industrial practice and industrial thinking. Industrial supervisors can have a "credibility" which contributes significantly to the students' experience of the project work.

Disadvantages: Industrial supervisors have other work to do, and industrial priorities may not always fit well with those of the university – contingency plans are required in case the collaboration breaks down. Industrial supervisors must be introduced to teaching expectations, and their efforts must be integrated into the teaching, so that the projects don't take on a divergent life of their own. Initiating, integrating, and orchestrating industrial involvement entails additional overheads for teaching staff, rather than diminishing their work. There may be a tendency for industrial partners to want to vet (or rewrite) any documents produced, thereby compromising assessment.

Supervision by Subject Area

Access to particular expertise such as technical knowledge can be problematic where expertise is concentrated in a few people, but supervisory roles are generic. This is a mechanism for deploying staff in roles that best exploit their expertise. Supervisors and/or supporting staff are designated as specialists. Students seek help as needed, for example getting database or programming language help by going to the "database guru" or the "Java guru". Depending on local circumstances, this help may be offered by an individual (a "guru") or by a group (in a surgery or at a specialist help desk). Where expertise resides in groups, which individual the student consults is typically a matter of the luck of the rota.

Advantages: Technical help is explicitly recognized as a specialist resource. Students must do at least enough self-diagnosis to identify the right specialist to consult. Expertise is used as appropriately as possible, and students can expect to consult the most appropriate person.

Disadvantages: Demand may be uneven, with some specialisms receiving the brunt of the enquiries. In group arrangements, students may feel a lack of continuity or even consistency between different advisors. Students may be frustrated if their problems "fall between two stools" and resolving them requires them to "ping-pong" between specialists.

3 Specific Case Studies

3.1   Large-scale Group Project (University of York, UK)

3.2   Project Managed by Negotiation (University of Teesside, UK)

3.3   Creating a Real Company (University of Sheffield, UK)

3.4   Third Year Students Supervising First Year Groups (University of Leeds, UK)

3.5   Emphasis on Personal Transferable Skills (University of Exeter, UK)

3.6   International Group Project (Uppsala University, Sweden and Grand Valley State University, US)

3.7   Computing History Projects (Metropolitan State College of Denver, US)

Specific Case Studies

Introduction

○   ○   ○   ○

These are included as real examples of good practice, with some element of novelty, special interest, or innovation. They display choices in concert and in context – and thereby illustrate the importance of context in shaping the project form. In effect, each is characterized by a "theme", and each shows how one theme (i.e. one choice about a key mechanism or a pedagogic focus) has an impact on other aspects of the project form.

Although the origins of many of these projects can be located in mundane or pragmatic choices – perhaps finding sources of project topics, or finding a way to provide suitable supervision with limited staff resources – what emerges as the example matures is practice driven by the pedagogic objectives. Perhaps this is inevitable as practice grows over time. As people other than the originators are involved, they no longer know (or care) what the situation was when the project was defined, but engage in the evolved form for its own merits. Hence, each of the examples is illustrative of a particular aspect of project work, identified by its characteristic objectives.

Specific Case Studies

3.1 Large-scale Group Project (University of York, UK)

○   ○   ○   ○

Individual or group?	group (20)
Year	2
Duration	9 weeks
Contact time	weekly lab class
Assessment	group mark for deliverables
Pedagogic focus	activity beyond the individual
Special characteristics	multiple, mutually-dependent subgroups
Key problem	topic division that produces a balanced set of activities

Size and Duration

Twenty-five percent of 9 weeks within one term in the 2nd year.

Laboratory class 3 hours per week, plus about 9–10 hours of independent time per week.

Context

The large-scale project was first run in 1977 with Computing (CS) students. The early focus was on implementation. Subsequently, specification and formal methods came to the fore and took prominence in the project.

The "IT, Business Management & Language" (ITBML) course began in 1994. As a result, the project for this group broadened out and became more interdisciplinary. The focus shifted to developing a software artifact in the context of a business/linguistic problem, for example perhaps with foreign language input.

In 1997 or 1998, the department began a business link with *Marks and Spencer*, which provides real business problems for students to solve as well as input into the project work.

Hence this model has had two incarnations:

- CS (large teams),

- ITBML (smaller teams, business context, business client providing real topics).

A typical cohort for CS would be 60 students, divided into 3 teams of 20, each subdivided into 5 teams of 4. A typical cohort for ITBML would be 20–24 students of varying backgrounds, divided into 3 teams of 7–8.

The students and staff enjoyed most the business-management-related projects: they found them more rounded, varied, and interesting.

Objectives/Aims/Pedagogic Focus

- Experience of group work: interacting with other people, in principle to produce something more than they could produce on their own (not necessarily so in practice, although the interconnectedness of the project tended to break up efforts to "go solo")
- exposing students to how things work in the real world
- giving students a project experience in which technical performance doesn't really matter.

Topics (Allocation)

The topic is assigned and must be selected and shaped to be suitable for large group work. At the core is a technical topic that will divide into a number of chunks (4 or 5), so that the technical content can be decomposed into sub-topics suitable for an individual or a team. The decomposition must have two key characteristics: 1) the sub-topics must be interrelated, and 2) the decomposition must not imply a time sequence for solution; the parts must be do-able in parallel. The aim is to achieve a decomposition that requires interaction both ways between sub-topics, i.e. that requires discussion between groups.

Topics are usually artifact building, e.g. a database, a program for formatting reports. A typical topic would include data structures (good things for students to have to agree on) and some associated human–computer interaction (HCI). Strongly algorithmic topics are avoided. Anything too algorithmic tends to mean that one group becomes isolated, working intensively on the algorithm.

In the context of ITBML, broader topics are used: artifact plus business plus financial planning. Hence the artifact sits within the business and cultural context, for example using a spreadsheet, responding to a cultural context, working with an existing business. In the recent collaboration with *Marks and Spencer*, one topic was to determine the feasibility of a franchise operation in Cyprus. This required the students to demonstrate company understanding and to interact with *Marks and Spencer*, in order to produce spreadsheets for financial analysis and forecasting. The business-based topics need careful setting up with the partner, giving opportunities for interaction.

Supervision

In CS:

One supervisor for the whole cohort, supported by hand-picked laboratory assistants. The main supervision was provided in a laboratory class for the whole cohort, 3 hours per week. Students could also raise individual queries at need.

In ITBML:

The project involved different specialities. Supervision was undertaken by four members of staff who took different roles as directors in an artificial company:

IT director
Personnel director
Finance director
Technical director.

Students were not told which staff member played which role; all interaction was via email to the job title. Hence there was a division between technical advice (via email only) and general guidance (which might happen in the corridor in a conversation with any of the supervisors).

There was also a weekly laboratory class for the whole cohort.

When the *Marks and Spencer* link was established, all questions were emailed to the single point of contact at the company.

Assignment to Groups

For Large Teams (CS):

The allocation of the cohort into the large teams of 20 was "neutral" or arbitrary. The allocation of the large teams into sub-teams of 4–5 was aimed at achieving a spread of ability. The class list was ranked, based on performance in the previous year, and students were allocated to sub-teams strictly by rank. No attention was given to other factors. Sub-topics were allocated to the sub-teams by the supervisor.

For Multidisciplinary Teams (ITBML):

Assignment to teams observed specialisms, so that each group has mixed skills.

Student Process

Students do some "running around" initially, with two focal issues:

1. Group and subgroup organization
   For this, students are left alone, in the hope that natural leaders will emerge

and the groups will all sort themselves out. Roles and management are left to the students to determine. No management advice is given. This process can be frustrating to the students, who are up to that point used to being directed. The groups take about three weeks to stabilize, i.e. until the first deliverable deadline.

2. Technical issues

   For technical issues, advice is given, including pointers to other expertise. The project relies on the use of good teaching and laboratory assistants.

Students are given a timetable, designating tasks week by week. Projects usually divide into phases, e.g.

specification due end of week 3 (of 9-week projects)
design due end of week 5
implementation due end of week 8.

Obstacles can be introduced, for example taking a team with only one programmer and removing the programmer – what happens? Students come up with novel solutions, like "subcontracting", which in this context is considered a good business solution.

Deliverables

Deliverables are defined for the students and include a mix of group and individual work:

- groupwork, 60%: specification, design, software artifact, report of testing
- individual, 40%: A reflection on their experience in the form of giving good advice for students following the next year, e.g. what went well, what went badly, why, and how it could be avoided or fixed.

A good reflective essay shows:

- an appreciation of the software engineering process, and the way the various parts fit together
- an appreciation of the way parts relate to the activities of individuals and are made to fit together
- an ability to stand back and observe what they've done, and what they should have done, i.e. analysis, software engineering, and teamwork.

In practice essays often say: "It was a disaster because . . . and this is what we should have done." Failure to produce a deliverable can be as valuable a learning experience as producing one.

Assessment

Group work is given a group mark. Assessment is based on the deliverables for the major technical phases: specification, design, testing. There is no formal demonstration, although the supervisor will usually have seen it working at some point in the laboratory. There is no mark for presentation, because a certain number of "rough edges" are expected and accepted.

Cited Keys to Success

For the Project Work:

- a topic that produces a balanced set of activities between individuals
- the topic must result in some product that is deliverable, so that students feel they succeed in some way.

For Students:

- ability to reflect on individual strengths and weaknesses in order to combine into an effective team
- keeping records (e.g. minutes of meetings, managing process); they provide a mechanism for resolving disputes, for referring back to decisions.

Acknowledgements

This case study was written based on an interview with Keith Mander.

3.2 Project Managed by Negotiation (University of Teesside, UK)

○   ○   ○   ○

Individual or group?	group (5–6)
Year	2
Duration	26 weeks (2 semesters)
Contact time	1 hour per week per project
Assessment	formative and summative, according to negotiated criteria checklists
Pedagogic focus	developing learning autonomy and encouraging process improvement
Special characteristics	most project aspects are a mix of prescription and negotiation
Key problem	students and tutors must be coached in the techniques and attitudes required for negotiation

Size and Duration

Usually 5–6 students per team, occasionally 3–4 (attrition). Expected to spend at least 3 hours per week on project work. Two semesters of 13 weeks each (plus 2 weeks for assessment).

Context

The detailed objectives, management processes and assessment criteria are a mix of prescription and negotiation. Negotiated learning was used to develop learning autonomy and to encourage process improvement. The integration of learning contracts and existing software engineering management techniques has enabled teams to define and reflect effectively on systems development and learning processes. Evaluations have indicated that teams can become more actively engaged in learning and can develop reflective skills in a structured manner by exploiting mechanisms for negotiation.

The original context was a 30-week team project course, part of the second year of a four-year sandwich course in Software Engineering. This was adapted in 1993 to two 1-semester modules. It precedes the industrial placement year.

Team projects in software engineering started at Teesside in 1987. At this early stage, significant attention was paid to process issues with, for example, teams required to give presentations at specification and design meetings. However, the presentation format often masked poor individual performances, and there was little opportunity for formative assessment of products.

Around 1989, quality management techniques were introduced to identify individual contributions, the demarcation of individual responsibilities, and to produce a clear definition of goals for each project. Standards for quality plans, products, and processes were produced, and audits were used to test compliance with these standards. By September 1991, it had become apparent that the production of quality plans had become too time consuming, to the detriment of product development processes.

In 1991, teams were given partially complete quality plans (to establish consistency and comparability between teams), with some critical parts left for the teams to complete (so that they retained responsibility for assigning roles and deciding how progress and contributions would be documented). However, the expectation of prescription by the students, and the lack of an appropriate framework for consistent negotiation between teams and supervisors led to significant problems in defining and describing processes and products.

During 1992–1994, a negotiation framework was evolved, with published, prescribed learning objectives augmented by subsidiary learning objectives that are wholly negotiable between the students and supervisor. The degree of prescription versus negotiation varies depending on circumstances, e.g. the willingness of teams to negotiate. In general, the work required to pass (i.e. to achieve 40%) is prescribed; the rest is subject to negotiation. The identification of the deliverables and of individual responsibilities and grades were captured in a matrix. Deliverables were required to have associated standards against which they were to be assessed, and these were captured in assessment checklists. In addition, every key process enacted by a team had an associated definition. Hence, the product and process contract matrix captured the detailed individual responsibilities, team organization, assessment arrangements, and the relationships between processes and products. Audits are used to check teams for compliance with the process definitions referred to in the quality plan. Inspections were used to assess deliverables.

Overall class size up to 35, with 7–8 team projects running at one time.

Consistency is maintained through scrutiny by the project coordinator. All outcomes of negotiation are scrutinized and authorized by the coordinator.

The hardware platforms are networked UNIX workstations, PCs and text-based terminals with standard software. Programming languages have been constrained to C and C++. No other constraints have been applied, with the condition that options chosen must be available to all members of the team.

The scheme was evaluated during 1994–1996. Overall, the evaluations concluded that negotiation of learning contracts solved some significant problems associated with the development of learning autonomy, motivation, and individual assessment. It is clearly a feasible approach given that tutors are committed to a student-centred philosophy. However, there is an investment of time needed to coach students and tutors in the techniques and attitudes required initially.

Objectives/Aims/Pedagogic Focus

The overall aims are to develop learning autonomy within the constraints of inter-dependence on other people (hence enabling the future engineer to work cooper-atively with peers and clients) and to develop software engineering practice.
    The objectives as stated in the course documentation are:

- "to gain experience in the application of software development methods and tools
- to develop the basis of skills in evaluating methods and tools
- to develop skills in the definition of objectives and the management of progress in teams
- to develop scheduling and time management skills
- to develop skills and knowledge in quality management
- to gain experience in the application of software development methods and tools for requirements definition and specification
- to gain experience in the application of software development methods and tools for design and implementation
- to develop management plans and progress monitoring techniques for the team
- to engage in, and gain knowledge of, client negotiations."

Topics (Allocation)

The application domains of the projects are prescribed by the project coordinator and always involve the use of a distributed database, graphical user interface and communications facilities. The topics are always beyond the capability of an indi-vidual or team, given the resource constraints. This is to encourage teams to negotiate the scope of deliverables and to prevent one team member doing all the work.

Supervision

A range of 1–4 supervisors in any presentation so far.
    Each team has a single supervisor who is a full-time member of staff (not a research student or associate). Early in the project, supervisors provide strong direction, but this is relaxed as teams take responsibility for their own learning through negotiation. Supervisors facilitate learning by offering expertise, advice, and technical support when required.

Allocation to Groups

The means of selecting individual students for teams varied over the years. Initially teams were either selected at random, or allowed to form themselves. This led to the problems of "clustering" and teams strongly polarized into weak teams and strong teams.

The technique that produced fewest problems was a selection based on the following criteria:

- the course background of the individual, e.g. Higher National Diploma (HND) transferees were clustered in the same teams
- academic background – teams of mixed ability were sought
- students were not placed in teams where there were students they had stated they did not want to work with (they were given the possibility of confidentially naming one student that they would not work with)
- students were placed in teams that included two students they had named as people they wanted to work with.

It was unusual for the team to satisfy all these criteria. The "best fit" was sought. This process seemed to minimize problems and to satisfy, at least partially, the needs of the students and the needs of the course. The HND transfer students are usually placed in the same team(s) as it was found that they lacked confidence due to the heavily prescribed nature of the HND courses in the past. They also lacked confidence in their own abilities and easily became passive when mixed with degree students in a team. It was also unlikely that they knew any of the degree students.

Student Process

The reliance on negotiation and self-direction assumes a fair degree of autonomy on the part of the student – which requires motivation, encouragement, and development by the supervisor.

The life-cycle to be employed is negotiable, as long as the processes of specification, design and validation are evident. No methods are prescribed, but recognizable methods are expected to be negotiated by the teams, in accordance with the team organization and the nature of the project.

Deliverables

Detailed composition of deliverables is negotiated between the supervisor and the team. A basic requirement of specification, design, implementation (including code), and testing is made, but the particular requirements, including scale, are subject to negotiation.

Deliverables are of two types:

- product deliverables consist of those documents pertinent to the development phase (e.g. specification, design)

- process deliverables consist of those documents necessary to demonstrate progress visibility (e.g. plans, agenda, minutes), configuration management (e.g. library records), and quality control (e.g. peer inspection records).

Assessment

The topics are judged (or adjusted) by the coordinator to be comparable before the projects start and are hence regarded as being of the same level of difficulty.

Assessment criteria associated with negotiated objectives are wholly negotiable and are scrutinized by the project coordinator for comparability. The overall learning objectives as stated in the course documents are tested using broad criteria that make heavy use of the outcome of negotiations. All product and process documentation is made available for both formative and summative assessment.

Assessment criteria are defined and made explicit to the teams before they start work. The project has three phases of assessment covering marks bands 0–40%, 41–60%, 61–100%. Each band has products and processes associated with it.

An assessment checklist is produced for every product and process deliverable. If the deliverable meets every item on the checklist, then it receives the marks negotiated for the delivery of that item or the successful enactment of that process. If the product is incomplete or the process not wholly effective, then the supervisor has discretion on the marks to be awarded, within the negotiated constraints. The supervisor does all the marking for the summative assessment within the constraints negotiated with the team and the assessment framework.

Formative peer assessment using formal inspections is used as part of a quality control process. Summative peer assessment has been used in the past but was found to consume too much staff time.

Cited Keys to Success

- Individual assessment was enhanced by including processes for the visibility and traceability of contributions in the negotiation process
- it was found that negotiation had to be introduced fairly assertively in order to convince students that it was valuable activity in itself and not simply an overhead on the project
- integration with existing quality management techniques provides credibility in the student's perception and adds value to their learning experience
- successful negotiation was found to be dependent on a strong commitment to the development of learning autonomy by tutors
- there is a need for a strong coordinating role in order to ensure comparability of outcomes between teams.

References

Birtle, M. and Jones, A. (1989) An Individual Assessment Technique for Group Projects, *Software Engineering Journal*, **4(4)**, July 1989, 226–232

Birtle, M. (1994) Contract Learning in Software Engineering Projects In Finkelstein, A. and Useibeh, B. (Eds) *Proc. ACM/IEEE International Workshop on Software Engineering Education*

Birtle, M. (1997) Process Modelling in Software Engineering Team Projects In: *Proceedings Of the Fifth Conference on Information Systems Teaching in Practice*

Birtle, M. (1998) *Negotiated Learning Contracts in Team Projects* Annals of Software Engineering, **6**, 323–341

Birtle, M (1998) HEFCE EPCOS Project: Towards a Framework for Transferable Negotiated Learning Practices in Team Projects In: Holcombe et al. (Eds) *Projects in the Computing Curriculum*. Springer-Verlag, 129–142

University of Teesside, School of Computing and Mathematics Team Project Handbook

Acknowledgements

This case study was written drawing on documents by Malcolm Birtle.

3.3 Creating a Real Company
(University of Sheffield, UK)

○   ○   ○   ○

Individual or group?	group (4–6)
Year	4
Duration	2 semesters
Contact time	variable, and divided between lecturers and clients; a minimum of one hour per week
Assessment	based on deliverables and on input from other parties
Pedagogic focus	preparing students for business by getting them to run real businesses
Special characteristics	real companies, real clients
Key problem	improving teamwork and management skills

Size and Duration

A range of 4–6 students per team. Forty credits (1/3 of the total load) run over two semesters. Nominally 400 hours per student, 1600–2400 hours per team based on 100 hours for 10 credits.

Context

This project module, *Setting up and running your own IT company*, involves students forming and running companies that offer IT consultancy and software development services to outside organizations. The emphasis of the work will be on learning how small IT companies are created and managed, the legal and financial frameworks within which such companies operate, the practical management of the companies and their successful trading. Students will involve themselves in the following activities:

- researching market opportunities for software products
- carrying out IT audits on behalf of local organizations and preparing appropriate IT strategies
- acting as software/computing consultants to local organizations
- developing software for clients
- maintaining software for clients.

During the course of the module students will keep company records, prepare company reports as well as developing analysis and design reports and other consultancy reports for clients. (Holcombe and Stratton, 1998)

The project module was designed for fourth year M. Eng. and M. Comp.[1] students seeking what are described as "prestige degrees", with high entry requirements and a mid-degree performance threshold. The module and degrees are aimed at C. Eng. accreditation, following the requirements of SARTOR. The module has a number of prerequisites, with the dual aims of ensuring that students have a broad grounding and that entry is restricted to an appropriately accomplished cohort. The curriculum leading up to this module includes:

- a "software hut" project [see 1.4] in the second year with attention on business processes and interactions with a client
- a technical third-year program
- a major individual project
- a software engineering seminar which reviews the "state of the art", and
- in initial years students took seminars about aspects of setting up companies, organized by the Sheffield Training and Enterprise Centre in conjunction with the National Westminster Bank. These were later discontinued (as the student reviews did not find them that helpful) and replaced by own material on setting up a company covering legal, managerial, marketing, etc.

Potential clients, from various retail, manufacturing, and service companies, were identified prior to the course. The Sheffield experience is that there is no shortage of clients, and, if clients and topics are properly vetted in advance, that there is no withdrawal of clients. It is estimated that one person-week per semester is required to recruit and screen the needed clients. (Parker and Holcombe, 1999)

The model implemented in the first year of presentation involved three divisions (or companies) operating concurrently: software development, software consultancy, and software training. Each division (or company) had two officers: a chairman and a finance director. Each student in the group had a role in each division, and each student was an officer in one division, with roles changed in the second semester so that each student took both chairman and finance director roles. This was later revised with less emphasis on the finance director (since money flows in rather infrequently). What has become more important is the appointment of two systems administrators from amongst the students.

The module has been run over several years. In the first year, six students participated, with two additional M.Sc. students joining the company during the summer to carry out projects of their own within the company. In the second year, 16 students participated. There are some questions about whether increasing student numbers will create management problems. After the first year, when the course

---

1 M.Eng and M.Comp are four-year undergraduate Master's programs

was offered at 20 units, it was decided that 20 units were insufficient to reflect the work required, and the module was doubled to 40 units.

Objectives/Aims/Pedagogic Focus

- Helping students to understand the context, processes and constraints that apply to modern businesses – by setting up real companies and trading with real clients
- providing valuable, challenging, and relevant experience
- preparing students for work
- providing an education that is real, enterprise-oriented, and enjoyable.

Topics (Allocation)

The topics are based on client needs. In the first year, topics included:

- constructing a web-based database to enable hospital consultants to access and submit details of medical cases and treatments on an on-going basis
- extending an existing sales/stock control system for a philately company
- a consultancy with a local technology transfer organization
- developing a simple training package to enable personnel in a local organization to use new email and Web facilities effectively
- developing a training course to teach the use of Access database packages
- installing a videoconferencing system to enable remote communication with future clients.

More recent topics have been:

- web-based international management game
- e-business site for an antiquarian bookshop
- website maintenance tool for a specific client
- database for a scientific laboratory
- rota planning tool for a chain of public houses
- planning tool for a university nursing department.

Supervision

Supervision is in the form of guidance; responsibility for the company and projects lies substantially with the students. Lecturers help students make contact with clients. They help with planning and discuss issues such as process, project management, and quality assurance. They monitor students' progress through weekly meetings with the company as well as reading the monthly documentation. They monitor individual students' contributions.

Supervisors contribute about 30 hours each, and each client is asked to commit to a minimum of 25 hours.

Student Process

Although there were regular discussions about project management issues, procedures were not prescribed. The experience has been that students changed their attitudes through the project, recognizing that they needed to formalize procedures. Students held private weekly business meetings, which they minuted.

Companies had full responsibility for setting up their own facilities, including their systems and network, backup procedures, financial packages, management and planning systems, and videoconferencing. Students had to establish their methods for identifying, distributing, and monitoring work. They chose reporting methods, quality control methods, and costing methods, including the "virtual" costing of labor.

Deliverables

Monthly Documentation:

1. monthly real accounts
2. monthly virtual accounts, including notional labor costs
3. monthly report identifying work achieved in the current month, targets reached, problems or delays experienced, and an updated plan including a schedule and deliverables for the coming month
4. any deliverables completed in the previous month, e.g. requirements documents, design documents, implementations, documentation, etc.

Assessment

Assessment is apportioned among principle headings:

- customer satisfaction, as indicated by client questionnaires at the time of product delivery
- administrative procedures, as indicated by the deliverables
- quality control, as indicated by elements of the deliverables
- profitability, based on the annual virtual accounts, and based on the Bank's assessment of the viability of the business plan.

Cited Keys to Success

- Real clients. "The mechanisms for managing projects, reviewing the quality of their output, and delivering on time have been given a new dimension now since it is they who are seeking client satisfaction now. The clients are *their* clients."
- students had full responsibility for setting up and administering their company infrastructure, including computer and financial systems. "The fact

that they were responsible for their own facilities helped to engender a much more mature and professional approach than one might have expected."

References

Holcombe, M. and Stratton, A. (1998) VICI: experiences in introducing student-run software companies into the curriculum. In: Holcombe et al. (Eds) *Projects in the Computing Curriculum.* Springer-Verlag. 103–116.
Parker, H.E.D. and Holcombe, W.M.L. (1999) Campus-based industrial software projects: risks and rewards. Manuscript.
Parker, H.E.D. and Holcombe, W.M.L. (1999) Keeping our Clients Happy: Myths and Management Issues in "Client-led" Student Software projects. Computer Science Education, 9 (3), 230–241.

Acknowledgements

This case study was written drawing on documents and talks given by Mike Holcombe and Helen Parker.

3.4 Third Year Students Supervising First Year Groups (University of Leeds, UK)

○   ○   ○   ○

Individual or group?	individual 3rd year per group of 1st years (4)
Year	1 and 3
Duration	5–6 weeks
Contact time	variable, as needed
Assessment	1st years: 65% group deliverables, 35% peer assessment 3rd years: based on deliverables
Pedagogic focus	demonstration of sufficient professional skill
Special characteristics	3rd years provide nearly all supervision of 1st years
Key problem	synchronization of modules, with one person in charge

Size and Duration

First Years:

First semester; 25% of the module, 10–15 hours per student per week (although with the usual high variance) over 5–6 weeks.

Third Years:

Thirty percent of their module, roughly 20–30 hours (although sometimes considerably more).

Context

The project runs in the context of concurrent third- and first-year modules, with one individual having control over both. The first-year module, in the first semester, is on professional development: cooperative skills, delivery, and timing. A typical cohort has 160 students, divided into 40 groups. The third-year module is also on professional development: personnel skills, motivating others, management. A typical cohort has 100 students, of whom some 80 volunteer for this project supervision, of whom only 40 take part. Selection is based on a letter of application, written to given guidelines. Unfortunately, there tends to be bad feeling among those refused.

The initial motivation was to set up an exercise for the third year students. Although it was not a project exercise in the first instance, that aspect turned out to be successful. The success of the arrangement is most evident when those who participated in their first year subsequently supervise in their third. One student wrote in his experience log, "I was amazed to observe how much I learned in two years".

The arrangement was developed and run for three years by a single supervisor. It was "staggeringly successful in the first year". In the fourth year, the project was taken over by a different member of staff, with some assistance from the originator. They found it "hard to transplant into someone else's custody". When staff were cycled, the arrangement began to struggle, and the symmetry disappeared.

Objectives/Aims/Pedagogic Focus

First Years:

Providing experience:

- first experience of group work
- first experience of a longer term (5–6 week) project with intermediate deliverables
- introduction to university-level, large-scale activity
- some work with packages like text processors and graphics.

Third Years:

- first experience of personnel management
- reflection on their own achievements and abilities
- experience motivating others.

Topics (Allocation)

First Years:

All groups are assigned the same topic, with two topics used in alternate years:

- develop a product to assist academic staff in automating compilation and analysis of end-of-term feedback
- develop a library catalog interface.

Supervision

Of First Years:

Third year supervisors are assigned one to a project. Supervision is specified as advisory, not technical. Supervisors are expected to meet their group at least once a week to check progress and give guidance as they see fit. Different supervisors interpret this differently, some providing disciplinary management, others developing "matey" relationships, and so on. "There is always one that's a catastrophe."

Input from the lecturer into first year supervision is negligible, by design. There is a briefing session for all first years which includes the Belbin questionnaire on group roles, which is taken into account in assigning groups. (Belbin, 1981) There is a "gelling" session once groups are assigned which includes some practical exercise like Lego building or eggs in parachutes, so that students get acquainted with their team mates.

There are established mechanisms (e.g. programming classes, bulletin boards) for technical help.

Of Third Years:

Supervision of the 3rd year supervisors occurs in "surgeries", providing hand holding and guidance. Surgery is mostly electronic on an as-needed basis, but there are also 2–3 plenary face-to-face sessions per term. Reports the lecturer: "Problem for me is that it takes loads and loads of time to organize."

Assignment to groups

First years:

Groups are somewhat arbitrary, although attention is given to achieving a balance based on the Belbin questionnaire (Belbin, 1981), and an effort is made to ensure that students within a group are not familiar with each other (fairly straightforward in the first semester of the first year). No attention is given to skill; the natural skill mix tends to be pretty good.

Third Years:

Assignment of supervisors to groups is largely arbitrary, except where there is a known problem to avoid.

Student Process

First Years:

Clear partitioning of tasks. Clear schedule of staged deliverables. Groups tend to stabilize quickly, usually at or after the gelling session. Most groups work face to face.

Groups are assigned names of rugby teams at outset, which they can change. Most groups adopt their own team names; some build a sophisticated identity, including logos and business cards.

Projects culminate in demonstration days (two days, with 20 demonstrations per day).

Third Years:

Supervisors are not required to attend the demonstration days, but most do.

Deliverables

First Years:

- software
- advertizing brochure
- costing
- demonstration
- write-up.

The deliverables are staged, according to a given schedule.

Third Years:

- record of meetings
- personnel profile of each group member (e.g. strengths and weaknesses, contribution)
- experience log, completely unspecified ("marvellous observations", "reams in the first meeting").

Assessment

First Years:

Group work 65%. This assessment is based on 4 deliverables, worth 25% each:

- software
- demonstration
- advertizing brochure
- user manual.

Students are marked as a group, but there is a peer-assessment component in which a group can elect uniform or differential treatment (most go for uniform assessment, but this mechanism reveals the slackers.)

Projects culminate in demonstration days (two days, with 20 demonstrations per day). Each group, in consultation with its supervisor, develops its own criteria for assessing other projects. Groups presenting on day 1 mark those demonstrating on day 2, and vice versa. Results of the student assessments are compiled and contribute 35% of the overall grade.

Third Years:

Assessment is based on the three deliverables, apportioned as follows:

- record of meetings: 10%
- personnel profiles: 35%
- experience log: 55%.

Cited Keys to Success

"It really worked because the 3rd years took to it big league."
"Really enjoyed it."
"Got lots out of it."
"Later, they return from job interviews, and this was all they talked about."
One person with oversight of both groups – and significant motivation.
Discipline by lecturer to read everything the third years produce. This is a major assessment load.

3.5 Emphasis on Personal Transferable Skills (University of Exeter, UK)

○   ○   ○   ○

Individual or group?	4–5
Year	1 and 2
Duration	2 terms
Contact time	10–15 minutes per week
Assessment	based on deliverables and self-assessment questionnaires
Pedagogic focus	demonstration of sufficient professional skill
Special characteristics	integration between 1st and 2nd year project work
Key problem	choosing the right topic

Size and Duration

First Year Project

15 credits (preceded by an associated 15-credit programming module). The module includes 10 hours of lectures; the rest (during a 6–7 week period) is project work. Cohort of 55–60. Teams of 5 (or 4).

Second Year Project

Thirty credits (of 120 credits for the year). Cohort of 55–60. Teams of 5 (or 4).

Context

Exeter's attention to personal transferable skills (PTS) is integrated throughout the degree program. The emphasis is on drawing students' attention to non-technical issues. Both the teaching and the assessment pertaining to PTS draw on research by Liz Dunne (1996), which distinguishes four broad areas and identifies associated skills:

- management of self (time management, listening, independence, autonomy, self-confidence)
- management of information (presentations, report writing, documentation, technical English, using media, oral skills)
- management of task (problem analysis, creative problem solving, project management, objective setting, project evaluation)
- management of others (decision making, cooperation, teamwork, leadership, influencing, assertiveness, negotiation).

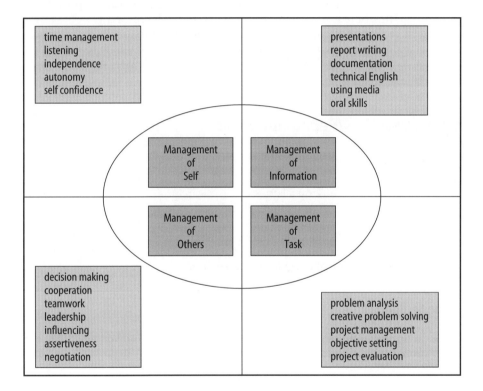

PTS attention begins in the first year, when a one-semester Java course is followed by a team project in the second semester. During the team project implementation, the emphasis is on PTS; students are told that the process is more important than the product. Two- to three-hour training sessions on project management, general teamwork skills, and presentation techniques are run by trainers from outside companies. Peer- and self-assessment forms giving attention to non-technical issues have substantial weight in the assessment.

The same orientation is carried into the second year "Design and Method" module, a software engineering module that spans the whole year and is structured around the second-year project. The project topic always includes some sort of permanent data storage feature and a user interface, and uses a "front-end/back-end" development method.

The second-year project is divided into stages:

1. decide user task
2. prototype front end
3. define back end – engine – in VDM (Vienna Definition Method)
4. implement back end
5. put the two halves together.

All stages except the front-end prototype are conducted as teams; the front-end prototype is considered individualistic.

Peer- and self-assessment forms related to those in the first year are used in the second year, this time to moderate the team marks. In the second year, the forms have equal sections covering non-technical and technical issues. In order to help students to do this assessment well, the careers service is brought in to run a "how to assess" exercise (using the Belbin questionnaire (Belbin, 1981)) during the time the team is running.

Objectives/Aims/Pedagogic Focus

In the First Year:

- to learn how to work on a large-scale software project in teams using appropriate tools (e.g. students must all develop code and must all use tools for collaborative development)
- to learn the skills for collaborative development
- to understand the whole process of team working
- to learn how to make technical presentations.

In the Second Year:

- to understand the reasons for having a development method which has the front-end/back-end split
- to implement using that method
- to continue to develop their personal transferable skills.

Topics (Allocation)

In the First Year

All teams undertake the same assigned topic. The topic is meant to be not too demanding (in order to avoid emphasizing the product) but to be too large for one student to complete alone. The topic varies from year to year, but is always characterized by having a fairly tight specification for about 80%, and a deliberately fuzzy specification for the remainder. For example, one topic was the creation of an estate agent's system. The specification was tight except that it gave no information on the algorithm for selecting good houses for customer wishes (i.e. on matching the two databases).

In the Second Year

One topic is assigned; everyone does the same. The topic always has the front-end/back-end aspect; it always includes some sort of permanent data storage feature and a user interface, e.g. a library system for maintaining the department's collection of manuals, an alternative electronic mail reader.

Supervision

In the First Year:

Three members of staff are involved in the module: one coordinates the lectures, set-up and general running; the other two act as project managers (one per team) and do the assessment. Teams meet as often as they need or wish to. Project managers visit each team once a week, during a scheduled two-hour meeting period; each team is visited for roughly 10–15 minutes per week. Java surgeries are run. Otherwise, students are told that staff are not a resource. They are given a clear specification; if they require technical information, they are expected to use the library resources.

In the Second Year

Three members of staff run the module and act as project managers, one to a team. Students are expected, during the time of team working, to organise as many team meetings per week as they need, with the stipulation that at least one meeting is arranged when the supervisor can visit the team. This is usually a specified time, e.g. Thursday mornings. Students must also come at stated times with stated deliverables.

Assignment to Groups

In the First Year

Groups are assigned on the basis of skills, with the aim of mixing ability and skill across the groups and providing balanced groups. The lecturer's knowledge about personal dynamics among students may be taken into account.

In the Second Year

Groups are assigned on the basis of their first year performance; again, the aim is to mix ability.

Student Process

In the First Year

Teams are largely self organizing. At the outset, students are given a folder with templates for:

- minutes of team meetings
- weekly report of progress and outstanding problems (to be handed in each week)
- work breakdown structure: what tasks, who is responsible for each task, task start and finish dates
- version control for deliverables.

The contents of the folder are how students show their process.

The project is given structure by four checkpoints (three interim checkpoints, and one final check before the final presentation). For each checkpoint, a key product is required to be included in the team folder by the deadline:

- team breakdown work plan
- finalized requirements
- design for system
- complete prototype and test schedule.

In the Second Year

Teams are largely self organizing. Their structure is of their own choosing, and various structures have been observed: sometimes there is a leader, sometimes not; sometimes the group is "democratic"; sometimes the structure evolves throughout the project; sometimes a leader is elected, etc.

The project is organized in stages, with deliverables at each stage. This gives structure and tempo to the work. In addition to the deliverables associated with each stage, students are required to maintain a project log. Students are given the same team folder as in the first year; the aim is that, having been familiarised with the folder in the first year, students can "jump right in".

Deliverables

Deliverables in the first year are designed to show the process:

- the team folder, including the key products
- the code itself, with identification of who wrote which segments

- the self and peer assessments (mandatory)
- presentation of the project to another team and the project manager.

Deliverables for the second year project follow the project stages:

1. decide user task: students produce a task analysis and conceptual design (team)
2. prototype front end (individual):

   - documentation and prototype in Jbuilder
   - demonstration to the rest of the team and the supervisor

3. define back end – engine – in VDM: the VDM is the product
4. implement back end:

   - code
   - define and implement a testing strategy
   - test harness, testing strategy, test results
   - design document which justifies how the code relates to the VDM

5. put the two halves together:

   - demonstration of the total system to the rest of the team and the supervisor (one hour per team, 10 minutes per student)
   - "proper" user evaluation scenario: how to plan and run an evaluation, tasks, measures.

In addition, in the second year, students are required to maintain a reflective journal, which is mandatory but not assessed.

Assessment

In the First Year

Assessment focuses almost entirely on PTS and process. Two major components are assessed:

1. The final presentation: for this each team is assessed by another team and by the project manager, who are the audience to the presentation.
2. The technical and process performance of the team: project managers determine an overall team mark, based on three inputs:

   - notes on process quality made by the project manager during each of the team visits (these are compiled into a profile for a team mark on overall project management)
   - an examination of the products in the team folder
   - a check on the code to examine the quality and amount produced by each team member.

These are compiled into a profile giving a team mark for the main areas (e.g. requirements specification, program development, testing), plus an individual adjustment for each team member on each area.

The project managers also compile the students' self- and peer-assessment forms, detailed questionnaires that reflect on individual contribution to the process. Student assessments are given roughly equal weight to the team mark. Although the peer-assessment adjustment is not reported in detail to the students, an abstract of what the others have said is given as a note on the assessment.

In the Second Year

Assessment is based on the deliverables, with the grade adjusted by the PTS mark. Technical skills are assessed by normal means: marks are given on the basis of the demonstrated quality of the implemented system. Because it's teamwork, the lecturers want a way of trying to find out who did what, not just technically, but also in terms of who led, who was "just a sheep". For this, they use the self- and peer-assessment forms to moderate percentages generated from the technical work. The ratings on the form are compiled into a single figure for each student. Those "scores" are examined across the team. If they indicate differential input, then the lecturers can make up to a +/- 5% adjustment on the marks, shuffling percentages among the team members. Hence, the self- and peer-assessment forms have no impact for balanced teams, but provide adjustment for imbalanced teams. Assessment relies on two other inputs for backup to this process: students' own (optional) comments on the form, and the reflective journals.

Cited Keys to Success

- Integration between the years, made possible by the link between people who teach the different years; "Brian is important"
- preparation of students through seminars
- team teaching
- "If you choose a project that the students can really relate to, something practical (not tediously academic) . . . if we get that right, we get something more successful."
- industrial input to first year training
- fairly intensive first experience of teamwork in the first year.

References

Belbin, R.M. (1981) *Management teams: why they succeed or fail.* Butterworth-Heinemann.
Dunne, L. (1996) University of Exeter Internal Report

Acknowledgements

This case study was written based on interviews with Wendy Milne and Brian Lings.

3.6 International Group Project (Uppsala University, Sweden and Grand Valley State University, US)

○ ○ ○ ○

Individual or group?	group (5–8)
Year	3 or 4
Assessment	based on deliverables
Pedagogic focus	experience of international collaboration
Special characteristics	remote group work
Key problem	students have different knowledge, different "starting states", different expectations

Size and Duration

These are group projects typically involving 5–8 students per team (half of the students Swedish and half American). The cohort in each institution is roughly 25 students (i.e. 50 overall).

The project time period is 5–10 weeks per project (notionally 100–120 hours per student), embedded in a longer course.

Context

This example is embedded in a research project *Runestone* whose primary aim is to introduce real international experience into undergraduate Computer Science education in a way that has value for all participants. The project has three-year funding from the Swedish government, but it is driven by the personal commitment of the faculty at the two institutions whose students are involved: Uppsala University and Grand Valley State University. *Runestone's* secondary aim is to identify effective support structures for remote international collaboration, encompassing strategies for communication, management, and technology use. The project has a subsidiary goal of cutting project costs (especially staff time) without compromising quality.

The research collaboration involves personnel from a number of universities, and it supports a number of sub-projects covering different perspectives – both practical and theoretical – including: feasibility, educational outcomes, technical issues and support structures, costs, teacher preparation, assessment, peer learning, the nature of the interaction within teams.

The project component is designed to fit into distinct courses. The courses at the separate institutions do not "match" in terms of size, assessment practice, or technical content. There is no requirement for them to do so, as the linking feature is the project work itself. Students must have sufficient background to be able to contribute, but not every student needs to have equal knowledge or expertise in all areas. The intention is that the model should be easy to implement as a context-independent component in any combination of institutions and local conditions.

Within the *Runestone* project, the institutional contexts were different in a number of respects.

	Sweden	US
Year	3rd year (of four and a half)	4th and final year
Courses within which project was situated	Computer Systems II (networks, real-time systems and distributed systems)	Capstone project
Notional hours to be spent on project component (per student)	120 hours	100 hours
Course time period	September to March	January to May (condensed for practical purposes)
Assessment	The grading scheme for the whole course was on a scale, Fail, 3, 4 and 5. However the project component was pass/fail. There was an option to undertake a set of additional assignments within the project for extra credit in the course.	The grading scheme was Fail, D, C, B and A.
Grading	Group	Individual

The Swedish students are highly competent English speakers (with 8–9 years of study and English usage required in many university courses), although they are not necessarily fully confident.

Because the students come from different specializations (all computing majors), they begin the project in different "starting states", with different knowledge (down to the level of different programming language knowledge). Because the project is incorporated into different courses at the two sites, it is associated with different expectations. The two national groups had different profiles, in terms of educational background, age (the Swedes being older: 23–24 vs. 20), and external obligations (the Americans having job and family obligations, and some of the Swedish students choosing to undertake consultancy work). Some frustration has arisen because of discrepancies between the two groups of students, in terms of expectations, sense of urgency, time available, local cohesion (and hence local group dynamics), technical skill, and access to resources.

Because of the differences between presentations, it has been found necessary to incorporate a technical and project management briefing in order to achieve a quick and appropriately structured project start, to make clear suggestions about targets and milestones, and to recommend a team management structure.

Objectives/Aims/Pedagogic Focus

The primary aim is to give students genuine international experience. These students will collaborate closely with their foreign counterparts using appropriate communications and computing technology to solve a given problem. Because the students come from different specializations, they have different knowledge to contribute to the project and must rely on their collaborators to bolster their weaknesses.

The stated project aims are to:

- give students international contacts and experience with teamwork with people from a foreign culture
- give students experience of collaboration with a group having a different educational background
- encourage learning through peer teaching
- give students experience with the use of IT in problem solving
- prepare students for the possibility of working in a foreign culture
- use the foreign experience to aid students in producing a superior product locally.

Topics (Allocation)

All groups have the same topic, designed to require a variety of technical knowledge (covering all backgrounds), to draw on the specialist studies of the different student bodies, and to be complex enough to require cooperation. The problem specified was fairly advanced, involving study areas such as real-time systems, networking, and distributed systems.

In the initial years, the problem was to navigate a steel ball through a wooden maze by tilting the maze in two dimensions with stepper motors. The user, working through a Web interface, submits a navigation algorithm, defines a path for the ball to follow, requests the server to execute the algorithm, then waits for access to the game. When the user gains access, the game server resets the ball in the maze, executes the user's navigation algorithm, then provides feedback to the user on the result of the run. Feedback includes information on how the navigation code executed, and a graphical display of the path which the ball traced through the maze. The input to the navigation algorithm is the position of the ball. The output is the rotational positions of the motors as a function of time. Video images of the maze and ball are available from a black and white digital video camera.

Supervision

Supervision is led by two lecturers: one in Uppsala, and one in Michigan. Supervision is constrained, in order to provide equality of access to supervisors for all students. Each team is assigned to one of the two supervisors. Supervisors are available for student questions via email or other electronic communication during supervisory meetings in "office hours".

Each supervisor holds hour-long weekly meetings with all local groups in which general project and progress issues are discussed. Of course, much of the discussion is technical, but issues of staged deliverables, communication and collaboration may be raised.

Assignment to Groups

Students choose their own local partners and are then paired with international counterparts.

Student Process

Students control their own process. Each group elects a team leader who coordinates communication. International communication is typically via email, Web pages, and Internet Relay Chat (IRC), although other facilities are sometimes tried. Local teams meet to discuss work; communications often summarise these discussions for the remote counterparts. Each team is expected to hold weekly team meetings, in addition to individual correspondence.

Because of the research "envelope", meetings and correspondence were recorded. Class meetings contained a short "debriefing" component structured in terms of a loose script. For each team meeting, students were asked to complete short questionnaires about the organization of the meeting, the outcomes (decisions, learning, conflict resolution, clarification, etc.), and the students' satisfaction with the proceedings, both overall and in terms of their own role in the meeting. Students were also asked to keep individual project logs.

Deliverables

Students write a final report, incorporating their code, and demonstrate their projects to the rest of the students and an invited forum of faculty.

The project logs, communication records, and questionnaires are required, but they are not otherwise considered as deliverables.

Assessment

The same piece of work, produced by a single transnational group, is assessed under two separate assessment systems, one in Sweden and one in the US. It is therefore possible that the same piece of work will get different grades for different students, calling into question the parity and equity of assessment schemes – this is an unresolved problem with this example. The Swedish students undertake the project on a pass/fail basis (as one component of a graded course) and are assessed as a group, whereas the American students are given individual grades.

Cited Keys to Success

The early experience with these projects noted a number of factors contributing to success:

- genuine commitment by the faculty involved to international collaboration
- the international factor, and the novelty of the arrangement with respect to other studies (particularly the inability of any individual to control all factors)
- challenge: the students enjoyed the chance to show their ability in a new realm
- the scrutiny the students have been under as part of the research.

All of these contributed to student motivation.

Acknowledgements

This case study was written drawing on correspondence with Mats Daniels of Uppsala University and on papers by *Runestone* project members.

3.7 Computing History Projects
(Metropolitan State College of Denver, US)

○   ○   ○   ○

Individual or group?	group (3–5)
Year	4
Duration	15 weeks
Contact time	60 hours
Assessment	half based on deliverables; half based on peer evaluation
Pedagogic focus	demonstrating and developing knowledge of software engineering and computing principles through simulation of computers and computing of historical interest
Special characteristics	simulation of historic machines or programs
Key problem	synchronizing development effort with progress of course

Size and Duration

These are group projects with 3–5 students per team, 4–6 teams per term. Project duration is the entire 15-week term and requires approximately 120–150 hours per student. More complex projects have taken 250 hours and more for some students.

Context

The computing history projects are part of the Software Engineering capstone course, a four-credit-hour course covering two semesters. The first semester is primarily a lecture course that emphasizes software engineering principles which are applied to a very limited project. In the first term each student is a member of two teams: users and developers. User teams define the first term projects. These user teams perform all the actions that would normally be expected of real users.

This gives the students an opportunity to experience a software development project from the user's point of view. In addition, each student serves on a developer team that applies software engineering principles to the solution of the user's problems. The student developers do everything on the project except the actual programming.

The second term is devoted entirely to the development of a project that is related to computing history. The history-based projects arose as a way to address one of the most vexing problems for software engineering instructors: selecting projects of proper scope (both instructive and possible to complete in a given term) and then of defining user requirements that are realistic. The choice of computer simulation greatly simplified this process. The original manuals for the target machines became the user requirements, and proper guidance during the requirements definition stage kept the students from becoming over enthusiastic and committing themselves to more than they could do in the time available.

The choice of history-based topics had other advantages, too. Prior to adopting the computing history projects, it was noted that many students actually had no idea of how a computer works. They could explain the "fetch/execute" cycle, describe what registers are and what they can be used for, and give an in-depth explanation of how various types of virtual memories worked, but they had no deep understanding of how a computer really operates. These projects were chosen to enable the students to have realistic and doable projects that also taught more than just software engineering. The computers chosen were fairly simple machines that had some impact on the evolution of computing and for which documentation was available. In some cases, they were just simple machines, in others, they were widely used machines.

The choice also helped to address the omission of computing history and evolution from the curriculum. "Everything that we teach is built upon the evolution of computers and computing over the past fifty plus years . . ." (Howerton, 1998) Yet it was observed that, although computer architecture and organization are usually well addressed, those courses "tend to focus on computing as it is today and ignore how it was". In researching and creating their simulations, the students gain an experience of computing history and some insight into how and why systems have evolved as they have. In addition to each team getting the benefit of its own research, all of the other teams were also informed by way of the formal presentations made in class. This way all of the students in each class were exposed to the operational details and internals of several computers.

"Since publishing the list of proposed historic computing projects, students have been forming teams and voluntarily starting the research on their chosen simulations between the terms. This has resulted in some projects that are almost beyond belief in their scope and presentation." (Howerton, 1998)

Objectives/Aims/Pedagogic Focus

These projects teach not only software engineering, but also some of the history on which computer science is based. The projects are capstone projects, intended to demonstrate and reinforce the skills and foundational knowledge which students have learned previously. They are software engineering projects, giving attention to the software engineering process and the dependencies among different phases in that process. Finally, they are intended to reinforce the current popular programming paradigm.

Topics (Allocation)

Each student team selects a topic from a provided list. The instructor created a list of every computer that was considered to be significant in the evolution of computing. This list contained many of the earlier computers in the IBM product line as well as computers that were built by Burroughs, Univac, Control Data, Minneapolis-Honeywell, General Electric, Digital Equipment, Altair, Apple, and others. In addition, the list of projects included language processors and operating systems for virtual machines used in a organization and architecture course and reconstructions of well known and much loved software like Dartmouth BASIC, and the original LISP, and SNOBOL processors. Further, the list included language processors and operating systems for the virtual computers used in teaching the Computer Organization and Assembly Language course (COALP).

The only constraints specified were that the software had to be built in Java and be usable over the Internet, and that the simulations had to be operational and run just like their originals. The scope of the projects is determined by the instructor, occasionally with some negotiation with the students.

Examples actually executed by student teams include:

- simulator of an IBM-1401
- simulator of a DEC PDP-8.
- simulator of the Altair 8080
- a Dartmouth BASIC processor capable of loading and running simple BASIC programs
- a small C compiler for the VM3 virtual machine.

Supervision

Supervision is approximately equivalent to what the teams would get in an industrial environment, which is to say as little as possible. Weekly informal progress reports are given in class, and more formal bi-weekly deliverable presentations are made during class time as well. Careful monitoring in an unobtrusive way usually provides adequate information for the instructor to maintain control.

Assignment to Groups

In principle, teams are self selected, subject to instructor approval. Most teams from the first term continue together for the second term. This is not mandatory, and there has been some rearrangement where necessary to accommodate student wishes. In the first term, teams are created in a semi-random process to prevent groups of "hot shots" from ganging up to form teams. Experience has shown that teams made up of "hot shots" almost always fail to deliver because the team members are unable to agree among themselves on what to do and how to do it.

Student Process

The second term is conducted as a seminar in software engineering management in order to give the student teams as much team meeting time during normal class hours as possible. During class time, they can also consult the instructor. In addition to work on the project, each student is expected to make two or three short presentations from the readings and to lead a discussion on the topic. Approximately every two weeks, the teams make presentations of the current status of their projects. They are expected to adhere to a strict schedule to ensure completion by the end of the term.

Deliverables

Each team must deliver the following software engineering artifacts:

- requirements analysis
- specifications
- design
- code
- test plan
- user manual.

These products are delivered on a predefined schedule throughout the term. The final submission must reflect all cumulative changes that have been incorporated during the development process.

The code should be a working simulation written in Java and usable over the Internet. Part of the final delivery is a demonstration that the simulation runs exactly as the original. Examples include:

- IBM-1401 Simulator. This simulator included a graphical representation of a functional front panel in which every switch and indicator performed exactly as the original. Three relatively simple programs were hand-coded and translated into 1401 machine language and run to demonstrate the functionality of the simulation. The simulator is initiated with a bootstrap loader that was extracted from a 1401 manual that one of the students got from IBM.
- DEC PDP-8 Simulation. Like the 1401 simulator, the DEC PDP-8 had a completely functional graphical representation of the front panel with all indicators and switches operational. Original DEC PDP-8 programs were downloaded from an Internet site in Wyoming and run on the simulator.
- Altair 8800 Simulation. Like the others, this simulation had a completely functional graphical representation of the front panel. To show that their simulation was exactly precise, one of the team members brought in an Altair that he had hand-wired as part of his work on the project. Programs

were run on the simulation and the real computer simultaneously to demonstrate compliance with the specifications.

Assessment

The instructor evaluates the submitted project against the user requirements for compliance, and against the software engineering deliverables defined in the first semester course. It is not mandatory that the simulation works completely, as long as all of the deliverables have been properly developed. If the simulation does not work, the students are expected to describe in detail why it does not work and to identify what remains to be done in order to complete the work.

In addition, the team-mates evaluate each other in a "secret" process. They are given a form that identifies six factors for evaluation:

- attendance
- participation
- timeliness
- quantity of work
- quality of work
- overall performance.

The rating process requires the rater to use a Likert scale for each factor. The Likert scale ranges from "awesome" to "yuk". In addition, raters are encouraged to provide written comments that support their ratings. These ratings are submitted to the instructor and are never seen by the rated team-mates.

Half of the project grade comes from the instructor's evaluation and the other half comes from an interpretation of the team-mate evaluations.

Cited Keys to Success

- The single most important key to success is *good internal team management* on the part of the students. The team project in the principles course should have prepared them for proper management of human resources. The instructor is dependent on the students to report any problems within the team. If problems are reported early enough, it is usually possible to rectify the problem. If the students delay reporting problems too long, it is usually impossible to recover. This makes evaluation more difficult.
- the students seem to really enjoy the history projects because the scope is so well defined at the start. They teach themselves the history as a by-product of developing their projects.
- *the scope of the projects must be very carefully defined.* For a computer simulation, the hardware operations manual and the assembly language programmers reference manual must be readily available. For the programming languages course, a good reference manual or programmers guide is required and an ANSI Language Specification is highly desirable.

References

Howerton, C.P. (1998) Software engineering projects that teach more than software engineering practices, *Journal of Computing in Small Colleges*, 14 (1), 245–249.

Acknowledgements

This case study was co-authored with Charles Howerton.

One aspect of our work was data collection, synthesis and analysis; that has been presented in Part One. The other aspect was concerned with transfer, about how to effect the dissemination of "best practices" and how to ensure that those practices transferred from one context to another. Each partner institution packaged a piece of "best practice" for transfer to another institution and also imported a piece of practice that had been packaged by someone else. Each dyadic transfer had a third party, an "observer", and all parties evaluated the activity. In this way we hoped to find out what influenced the likely success of transfer. Part Two is a result of what we learned in this process.

Part

Background

We have come to believe that activities labeled *Transfer of good practice* and *Dissemination of teaching and learning* are both more subtle and more complex than the common rhetoric suggests. Our understanding has grown from our twin viewpoints, acting both as disseminators (facilitating the transfer of materials/practices) and as practitioners (wanting better solutions to persistent problems) and the interaction between these roles.

Transfer Expects Transformation

Evaluating success in transfers is not easy:

> ... whether a transfer is good or bad is contingent: it has to be judged on the merits of a particular situation. Ideally, one would perform a full cost-benefit analysis on every case of transfer or transfer failure to say if it was appropriate. In practice, this can be very problematic because costs and benefits are delayed, hidden and not quantifiable with confidence. (Busby, 1998)

In particular, in our evaluations, we encountered something unexpected: nothing emerged the same as it went in. No practice was "transferred" in the sense that the importing institution replicated the practice as it was undertaken in the exporting institution. There were recurrent phrases in the evaluations concerned with the changes that were made. "[They] had to implement a version of the bundle themselves", "Any materials used would have to be modified for local conditions so I was not looking for directly transferable materials" and, "As the package provided was sketchy there was plenty of scope for putting our own stamp and interpretation on it" (EPCoS).

At first we regarded this as "transfer failure" but, as it occurred so often, we started to think of it as a characteristic, and came to the view that if a practice had not been adapted or otherwise changed in the process of adoption then "transfer" had probably not taken place. We came to believe that the question "How have you changed this?" was a metric for transfer success. If the question could not be answered, then there was no transformation; without transformation there was no transfer. Our view changed so that for us "transfer" was not essentially concerned with the exchange of ideas and materials but with transfer of the *ownership* of those ideas and materials.

Although surprising to us, these behaviors have been previously documented:

> Diffusion of skill and knowledge from one community to its neighbours and neighbours' neighbours constitutes the central process of human history. Ever since significant differences in skills arose among separate human groups, borrowing back and forth has taken place whenever someone saw a real or apparent advantage

in doing so. Borrowing nearly always involved modifying what was borrowed to make it fit smoothly into a different set of skills and customs

and

In real situations, borrowing provokes invention, when the new does not quite fit what was on the spot already; and invention provokes borrowing, whenever what has been invented proves attractive or threatening to others. (McNeill, 1988)

In the transfers we observed we found that importers were keen to choose only that which was going to advantage their own situation and were careful and cautious in their choices. Secondly, we observed the *borrowing provokes invention* activity in almost every exchange. "It will be used in the context of individual third-year rather than second-year group projects", "If the idea is good it will be adopted and adapted to cope with local constraints", and "The benefits of teaching practices are always oversold. The bundle allowed me to focus on the problem and to gain some improvements but has not provided the total solution it offered. But I did not believe it would to start with (no silver bullets)" (EPCoS).

This act of "tailoring" a piece of practice (which had *already* been abstracted for transfer) seemed to be integral to the process of transfer, and created part of its value. There are *borrowing provokes invention* practices evident in Part Two. The attentive reader will note that some bundles, packaged for different aims and appearing in different sections, are actually different aspects of the same piece of practice. We have kept these in because we recognize the value of the process that they represent.

There are two implications from this formulation of transfer. The first is that you should expect to change anything that you import. The second is that, as an exporter, you have to "let go" and abrogate your ownership of the practice. This is not necessarily easy, especially in an academic environment, where reputation rests on claiming ownership of ideas and practices, but it seems to be the way effective transfer works.

Focusing on Solutions

In undertaking transfers you have to be aware of the pressures on practitioners and the limited enthusiasm they may have for changing their practice. This has been succinctly described with regard to medical doctors and their adoption (or not) of evidence-based medicine, where

. . . the emphasis on the need for evidence in medicine, and better transmission of information, needs to be balanced by a recognition that most general practitioners are *pragmatic, averse to innovation, and already feel overwhelmed with information* [emphasis added] (Salisbury et al., 1998).

Educational practitioners, too, are resistant to prescription and may be "averse to innovate" in the face of explicit expectations that they import "best practices" in teaching and learning from elsewhere. So you have to find a form, a "packaging", for transfer materials which does not prescribe or patronize and equally does not "overwhelm with information".

We use a form that emphasizes what is good and advantageous, addresses real needs and provides sufficient detail without being prescriptive. We were influenced in our choice of "packaging" by the work on patterns and pattern languages

(Alexander et al., 1977; Fincher, 1999), and we devised a pattern-like form which is solution-focused, allowing you to assess the benefits of the practice and to decide whether it would be useful for you to adopt it. This form also allows us to describe a real implementation of the ideas and materials without second guessing whether they would be appropriate in your context.[1]

Dealing with Context

To identify a need for change is to identify only half the problem. Practitioners do not exist in isolation nor work in identical circumstances. For transfer to occur, not only must you want to change your practice but you must also be able to do so. Your context has to permit you to change.

We found context to be a very big problem indeed. Practices for transfer are not recipes, not some set of instructions which you can follow to obtain a guaranteed result, precisely because of context. Context is a difficult thing to grasp, to pin down, but it can wreck many otherwise well-intentioned efforts at transfer. In the same way that it is unhelpful to say that *Wine should be as cheap in England as it is in France* without accompanying the statement with a substantial investigation into the reasons why it is not – reasons of history, geography, taxation regimes, and culture – it is unhelpful to say *You should do projects in this way* without considering all the details of context on which they rest.

And yet, how can that context be adequately described? It is comparatively easy to say "this came from a prestigious research-oriented department" or "this came from a teaching university with large class sizes" but that sort of information is insufficient (and at the wrong scale) when what you want to change is how you do projects. What does it depend on? Smart kids? Small classes? Or something which the original teachers didn't even consider? "We do it this way because years ago we tried it another way and it didn't work" or, "This fits because it builds on something I know my colleague does in a previous class – but only because I used to teach on that course". For effective transfer it is necessary that your chosen pieces of practice are not only fit for purpose, but fit for the culture.

Initially, we tried to list everything, at every level, which impacted on the practice we were describing. However, the unpicking and uncovering of these dependencies proved to be, in practice, not particularly valuable. We were not the first to discover the twin horns of this particular dilemma:

> . . . we tried to give a point-by-point analysis of all these 'real-world' problems, in an effort to show, one by one, how they could be solved . . . But somehow, no matter how we wrote [it], it always seemed thin. Either the solutions we proposed were too concrete and specific, or, in other versions, too vague and general. Somehow, however we wrote this chapter, it never seemed entirely convincing, even though it actually gave detailed answers to all the the specific points which might arise. (Alexander et al., 1985)

We believe the reason which underlies our version of this dilemma is that context is evolutionary. By this we do not mean that it develops over time in a series of

---

The form is "pattern-like" but bundles are not patterns. A pattern specifically describes an invariant quality which has been abstracted from many different examples. Our form inverts this to describe a specific piece of practice, which is inevitably transient.

very small incremental changes (although that, too, is true) but that the final product (which is a piece of practice) is uniquely designed in synergy with the contextual niche in which it was created. Equally, evolutionary products cannot be reverse-engineered. You cannot look at a thing and say, "Oh, OK, we'll grow one just like that too" and then recreate the particular combination of environment and forces which produced it. On the other hand, with project work we are talking about a very small section of products – perhaps (to extend the analogy) just fish, or just birds. Whilst these are very different from one place to another, they still share characteristics by which we know them to be fish, or birds. As one practitioner said of our first attempt of preparing transfer materials, "There is too much unnecessary detail . . . I need ideas, experience and examples of practice" (EPCoS).

So, we have left the practice we describe as context-implicit. After all, practitioners know the particularities of their context very well, so it will be immediately obvious if some solution is not useful – because it will contradict quality assurance procedures, or because they do not run projects very early in the program, or some other specific detail. We also believe that this approach is context-respectful. Context-respectful means presenting solutions, not problems – and it appears to be quite rare. (To take a mundane example, certain shampoos will be advertised as "for fine & fly-away hair". That identifies a problem, not a solution: it tells me what I have, not what it will do for me, and I know very well what I already have). Everyone is an expert on their own context and the problems that they're facing. What they don't have is solutions. If it's not obvious that a given solution will solve their problem, then it's probably not a good solution. "I know the constraints in my own environment and how they will impact on some practice to be adopted. Knowing the constraints in the exporting environment is of no interest. If the idea is good it will be adopted and adapted to cope with local constraints" (EPCoS).

Transfer Checklist

Part Two, therefore, has been constructed to maximize the chances of transfer of practice, taking into account the both the "disseminator-push" and the "practitioner-pull" against three rules of thumb.

1. Look to transfer small pieces of practice. Anything too large will infringe local context and be broken down into smaller things anyway.
2. Focus on the solution, not the problem.
3. Describe the practice as you do it – not in the way you think someone else should.

References

Alexander, C., Davis, H., Martinez, J. and Corner, D. (1985) *The Production of Houses*, Oxford University Press, New York.

Alexander, C., Ishikawa, S. and Silverstein, M. (1977) *A Pattern Language: Towns, Buildings, Constructions*, Oxford University Press, New York.

Busby, J. S. (1998) *Research in Engineering Design*, 178–188.

EPCoS (1999) *Internal Evaluation Comments*

Fincher, S. (1999) *Journal of Computers in Mathematics and Science Teaching*, **18**, 331–346.

McNeill, W. H. (1988) In *The Transfer and Transformation of Ideas and Material Culture* Hugill, P. J. and Dickson, D. B. (Eds), Texas A&M University Press, 75–90.

Salisbury, C., Bosanquet, N., Wilkinson, E., Bosanquet, A. and Hasler, J. (1998) The implementation of evidence-based medicine in general practice prescribing, *British Journal of General Practice*, **48**, 1849–1851.

Introduction

Six Thematic Sections

We have divided Part Two into six thematic sections. The structure of Part Two reflects:

- what we think project work involves
- why we think these are the important aspects.

For example, we have no section on "deliverables". We believe that, if you get these six aspects right, then you get deliverables "for free". That is to say that technical objectives are easily achieved if the project work experience is correctly (and appropriately) structured. The sections are:

Allocation
When undertaking projects, unlike lecture courses, there is usually an element of choice (for both staff and students) which must be managed by a departmental process. How that choice is exercised, and how allocations are made, can drastically affect the outcomes of projects.

Supervision
There are many ways to act as a supervisor for a project. However, in the vast majority of cases, the supervisory role constitutes the primary point of contact between the student(s) and the department. It is crucial that this role is figured in such a way as to maximize the benefit for all parties.

Assessment
It is difficult to transfer familiar models of assessment (constructed in relation to small pieces of coursework and exams) to projects. Partly this is because, with projects, not everyone undertakes the same piece of work to the same deadlines, and partly because they produce a wide range of types of "product" all of which potentially can be assessed. Careful thought has to be expended on appropriate, reliable, and scalable assessment regimes.

Reflection
Students learn not only by delivering the outputs of a project, but also from the *process* of doing a project. This is not always transparent to them. Building in opportunities for reflection on the value of the activity they are undertaking can enhance their experience.

Team or Group Projects
When students work in teams to produce a project, some of the existing problems with project work are multiplied. Other problems occur only as a result of working

with others. Equally some of the benefits of teamwork are not obvious and not obviously predictable.

Motivation

In computing, students are frequently accustomed to lectures as the dominant form of teaching. This often leads them to have certain expectations about the amount of structure and guidance they will receive. The scale and lack of detailed guidance in project work can make motivation an issue. It is important to pay attention to the motivational background of the students and the potential "baggage" they may bring to working on projects.

Each of these sections has been overseen by a different person. Almost always, these individuals are the ones who have worked on the same theme throughout. Each section is structured in the same way, with an introduction to the important issues followed by a set of specific practices which have been prepared for transfer (we call these bundles). More than in any other part of the book, the prefatory pieces outlining the issues are the work of one person, each written in their own "voice". The style throughout Part Two is therefore not even, but intentionally so.

What Is a Bundle?

A bundle captures a piece of practice that we think is in some way "good". It might be the best way we have seen for addressing a particular problem, it might be the *only* way we have seen to address a particular problem. In any case, the practices that bundles encapsulate are real; they have all been used in at least one institution. What we have done is to identify the core elements of the practice and put them ("bundled" them) into a format that makes them accessible. From reading a bundle you should (if your context matches the original) be able to adopt the practice easily, and find no "nasty surprises" of scale, scope or applicability; nor that any essential detail of implementation is missing.

Here is what each bundle looks like:

1. Problem Statement
Each bundle starts with a formulation of a *general* problem to which the body of the bundle is a specific solution.

2. Body
The body of each bundle is presented in a format that shares certain formulaic phrases. These are:

This bundle	A phrase which captures the essence of the practice
The way it works is	A description of what is involved (this may be quite short, or many paragraphs long; occasionally it will be many pages, sometimes including detailed documentation)
It works better if	Key criteria for success
It doesn't work if	Watchpoints for unsuitable (or undesirable) situations.

Every bundle has these. Additionally, they may be supplemented by

It doesn't work unless	Points which are absolutely required
You'll know it's worked if	Ways to check that the desired result has been achieved
Variations	Other ways this might work (mostly, but not always, we have observed these "in real life").

3. Solution Statement

Following the body of the bundle is a *general* solution which refers back to the initial problem statement. (The solution statement, of course, captures the aim of the body too, because a bundle is itself a specific instance of the general solution.)

If you read the problem statement and find that it does not apply to you then you can skip the rest if you want. However, if the problem is applicable but the body of the bundle will not fit your context, then the generalized solution statement should tell you what you have to do – if not specifically how to do it.

4 Allocation

Allocation

The allocation process usually results in a many-to-one mapping from students to supervisors; associated with each link is a defined project. There are many ways of conducting this process, but it should be self-evident that as numbers increase, so does complexity. This brings with it concomitant opportunities for error and dissatisfaction.

Allocation is a many-faceted process – it may be construed as:

- the allocation of students to supervisors (who then define a project), or
- the allocation of projects to students (with an implicit supervisor), or
- the allocation of a student-supervisor pair to a project.

Which of these constructions is applied is an issue of local management, and may operate under any number of personnel and resource constraints. It is not uncommon to see satisfactory mechanisms develop serious tensions over time as staff and student profiles change, resulting in a major change to the allocation mechanism.

It Is Important Not only that Justice Is Done, but also that Justice Is Seen To Be Done

The consequences of getting allocation wrong, either wholesale or just for unlucky individuals, are usually very bad, particularly for the students. Misallocation (actual or perceived) can be extraordinarily demotivating, and the consequences of this, given the characteristic weight of projects, are severe. Misallocation can lead to, inter alia, misunderstanding of the project, or supervisor, or dislike of the supervisor (or, unprofessionally, supervisor's dislike of the student). The day the allocation list is published – usually an open and public event, well advertised in advance – there is often much distress and complaint. This is probably unavoidable, but it is important that students perceive the allocation process as largely "fair", since this will dilute resentment. There is often an understandable, and sometime accurate, suspicion that staff will cherry-pick their "favorites", and all steps should be taken to prevent this happening, and demonstrate publicly that it doesn't happen.

Beware the Beauty Competition

It is natural behavior among many students, given free will, to queue up in front of the "popular" members of staff, howsoever judged; this "beauty competition" is often going to be at variance with best academic advice. Since it is common practice to spread the supervision load across the whole staff, it is highly likely that some supervisors will be quite unknown in name and face to students, which is clearly intimidating. This is especially the case when non-academic staff (research fellows or support staff), or staff in other departments are drafted in to supervise [see 2.12 *Pulling in the Bodies* and *Graduate Students as Supervisors*]. This important fact is often forgotten.

Equally, many staff will be unaware what drives student choice; it might be expected that the topic (especially for research-focused staff) is the prime motivator and it will not be perceived that impressions received during teaching experiences in early years count very heavily. At the same time, staff must perceive the allocation as "fair" – for example, allocating five students who are all expected to graduate with third-class degrees to one individual is unlikely to be received enthusiastically, except by the most devoted teachers.

Loading and Coordination

In most instances, the allocation process is managed by an individual – it is difficult to see an organizationally acceptable way of distributing the core of this task. Like many administrative jobs, this is onerous and will not be popular. The choice of this individual can be critical, since whoever is chosen must have an insight into broader staff loading issues, and must have sufficient weight (or kudos) to be able to persuade or coerce colleagues into doing things that they may well not want to. Normally, this individual will have a senior member of staff as backup for the occasions when issues of seniority interfere with preferred allocations. These can be delicate managerial issues, dependent on local personalities and practices, for which it is difficult to plan.

What a "reasonable" load may be is likely to be a matter for local resource allocation [see 2.12 *Staff Deployment*], but experience suggests that if one individual is simultaneously supervising more than six independent projects, the resulting context-switching begins to disadvantage the students. Some mechanisms exist for streamlining the supervisory task, but when the system starts to creak because of shortage of supervisor time, it is usually time to consider a major rethink.

Special cases may arise in the event of, for example, M.Sc. projects conducted over the summer. These provoke a special tension in that they usually require supervisors to be specialist academic staff (precluding the use of peripheral staff) at the precise time they are accustomed to uninterrupted research and conference time.

Do not forget that the whole allocation process usually has to be repeated, at least in part, in respect of second markers, or shadow supervisors [see 2.9(iv) *Moderator* and *Supervisor Plus Another* and 2.11 *Coordination Structures for Supervision*]. Often this is overlooked and done in an unseemly hurry; this is a process that requires matching of staff to staff, with all the concomitant problems of local personality issues.

Especially, remember that you must have a contingency strategy. In less than 1% of cases, something will go wrong and a student/supervisor partnership will have to be changed. You must have a strategy so that you can react in time [see Section 5 *Stuff Happens*]. The sub-issue of allocation of students into teams and groups is considered in Section 8 *Team /Group Projects*, and particularly 8.2 and 8.3.

Unhappy Marriages – Topic Allocation

Much the most commonly experienced problem is the mismatch of staff to student "demand" areas or, conversely, the mismatch of student desires to topics offered by staff. The latter here may be at the coarse level ("I don't want to do AI") or finer grained, if the local practice is to publish lists of precise project possibilities ("I don't want to do a project on simulated annealing"). This is another aspect of the difficult cost-minimization task faced by the project coordinator or manager, and is intertwined with local expectations. Do students *expect* to be able to work in their chosen area? Do staff *expect* only to have to supervise in their research or cognate areas?

Other Connected Issues That Need Careful Thought Are the Handling of: . . .

- ... projects created or introduced by the students themselves. These are common, especially in the wake of a sandwich placement or specialist vacation employment, and represent an important opportunity for the student and department to reinforce useful links with outside organizations. Very often, however, student or company expectations are wildly unrealistic, and careful and tactful intervention is needed to rescale and refocus ideas.
- ... projects conducted on behalf of "outsiders". These may be other departments within the university or entirely independent companies – they have the same problem of definition as student-defined projects, but the secondary problem also of finding a student to take them on. It may be that the client is in some sense "cherished", in which case there may be pressure to allocate a student especially likely to succeed, implying cherry-picking of the talented end of the cohort. This will almost certainly be at variance with issues of fairness.

In both circumstances, the issue of first loyalty must be spelled out – that is, the project is being conducted in pursuit of a degree and may result in a useful product, not the other way around.

. . . Differing Student Ability

Orthogonally, problems often surround strong students taking on projects which do not challenge them, or weak students attempting something just too difficult [see 2.1 *Weighted Topics*].

When it is possible to gauge in advance how tough a project is likely to be, then some care can be taken to prevent this – it is not, of course, always the case that this will be possible. Another aspect of this issue is the *type* of project – many, and often the majority, are of the *design and build* kind preferred by accreditors, but examples of pure research projects are not uncommon, and many examples exist of very worthwhile activity conducted under the project heading, whose connection with computer science may be arguable. Some special care needs to be taken in matching students to things that are out of the ordinary.

Quality Assurance

Quality assurance in supervision (extracting, or hoping for, uniform treatment from the staff cohort) is a known problem [see Section 5 *Supervision*]. If it is practice to use non-academic staff as supervisors, the problem becomes more serious since often such people are unaware of the mechanisms that mainstream teaching staff take for granted – this is particularly the case if they are pursuing "pet" projects of their own, with the danger of the project becoming solely product-focused. This is, in fact, a special case of the general problem of non-uniform experience and expectations among supervisors.

4.1 Me and My Shadow . . .

Where projects are double marked, the second "supervisor" often doesn't see the project until it is completed and handed in.

○   ○   ○   ○

This bundle aims to fill any "gaps" that may be expected or anticipated by the allocation of a second member of staff to existing student-supervisor pairs. A secondary aim is to spread the talents of the supervising staff as widely as possible.

The way it works is to ensure that the allocation of shadows is done sufficiently early in the process to have meaning well before the final assessment, and to require some correspondingly early input. This gives an opportunity for tangible inputs both to supervisor and student.

The project coordinator (in almost all instances, a single individual) may be expected to have a reasonable idea of the talents of individuals, including skills of supervision (based on feedback from earlier years, or less formal understandings), experience (contrasting new with more established staff), experience with "how things are done here" ("enculturation"), as well as technical or specialist expertise. It is not unusual for the allocation process to result in projects being supervised by staff who are not specialists in the topic area, and likewise for some students to be supervised by "beginners". The allocation of shadows can then take this into account and insure that supervisor-student pairings of potential weakness are bolstered by the shadow having the appropriate skills.

Identification of likely "gaps" can be achieved by stipulating a brief, very early deliverable that itemizes the project's objectives and probable skills requirements – this can be the contract between the student(s) and their primary supervisor. Such a document permits the coordinator to see quickly where skill shortages might lie.

Early involvement of the shadow can be achieved by requiring an intermediate deliverable that gives fuller details of the project plan, perhaps with bibliography and progress report [see 7.2 *Mid-project Report*]. This report should be assessed, or at least scrutinized, by the shadow, requiring written feedback that both student and supervisor will see. This can be brief (in the form of "tick boxes", plus comments). This involves the shadow in partial "ownership" of the project at an early stage.

It is a very good way of getting experienced supervisors to talk directly to the less experienced, and provides a mechanism for ensuring that any "lame ducks" among supervisors are backed by a safe pair of hands. In the same way, inexperienced shadows can be allocated to supervisors known to be reliable and safe, to expose them to good practice.

It works best when the coordinator has a clear understanding of the strengths and weaknesses of the supervising staff, and the authority to make pairings as desired.

It doesn't work if the coordinator is short of some of this knowledge, or is not given sufficient information about the projects being conducted, or if affairs are conducted in a rush.

○ ○ ○ ○

So: use shadows for more than double marking, to plug the gaps that you know are going to occur.

4.2 "I'd Like To Do That"

Students often devise projects of their own, but with scant idea of what a project represents.

o o o o

This bundle aims to retain student enthusiasm while ensuring a student-proposed project has a prospect of academic success.

The way it works is that students often propose their own project ideas, and in some places these represent the majority of projects. The ideas may come from previous modules, from previous employment or placements, or other connections (*"My Dad's company needs . . ."*). These ideas are often ill formed and would not make successful projects – the reasons may be to do with scale, scope, content, divided loyalty, or a number of other possible causes. When ideas are over- or under-ambitious, it is important to put them back on the rails without losing student motivation for their own imagination.

You have to devise a clear proposal format in which student-originated ideas may be presented, and a protocol for their consideration by the department. This should mirror the local project practice as far as possible in respect of deliverables and, in particular, schedule. The undertaking on the part of the department is to make every effort to mold the proposal into something acceptable for proceeding – for example, by recommending changes to priorities or methods.

The benefits of the exercise can be great since the student is required to think well outside issues such as modules and grades in framing a persuasive proposal. Good things to require in a proposal include:

- an indication of the student's desired learning outcomes:

  "At the end of the project I will be able to . . ."

- a specification of curricular material that the project will exploit:

  If there is none, the project may easily be seen to be inappropriate

- a *student* estimate of how "hard" the project is:

  For example, will it win a First if well acquitted?

- an indication of staff who might supervise:

  This can lead to discussion of what input – technical or academic – the project actually needs, and where this might most suitably be found. For example, for "external" projects, technical help can be sought outside, but there must be a fair way of accounting for such input.

- resources, and their costing:

  Especially useful if hardware or software not commonly or publicly available is sought.

Such points can form the basis of useful negotiation along the lines of "You need to include some . . ..", or "If you want a respectable grade, you will need to . . .".

It works better when combined with a format which requires intermediate deliverables [see 7.2 *Mid-project Report*], which allow the project to be checkpointed regularly. *It works best with* a (potential) supervisor who is prepared to negotiate with the proposer.

It doesn't work if staff are unwilling. This is a real problem for many such proposals, particularly if they originate in a commercial domain removed from local interests. It will also founder if the primary loyalty of the student is not to the academic outcome – that is, if the project is seen primarily as a product generation exercise for some external organization.

See also: 2.1 *Externally-provided (or Negotiated) Topics*

o o o o

So: provide an explicit project framework to scaffold student enthusiasm and imagination, and use it as a basis for negotiation and contracting.

4.3 Project Sabbaticals

Like everything else in the academic cycle, projects can become a treadmill. Projects usually consume more than a term or semester (often well over half the academic year), and in most departments "there is no escape". It is important for staff to be able to get some relief from this treadmill.

○   ○   ○   ○

This bundle proposes periodic relief from some or all supervisory duties. The benefits for the staff are in an opportunity to recharge batteries, and for students in consequent renewed enthusiasm.

The way it works is for the department's workload allocation to recognize project supervision very explicitly and permit buyout from all or part of it. The precise "price" that might be paid is a matter for local definition, but obvious options are responsibility for all or part of some other teaching, or a suitable administrative task. It is not necessary for *all* supervision to be excused – a half-load can have a surprisingly rejuvenating effect on supervisors who have been responsible for, say, six projects a year for a decade.

It is not necessary for this to be part of a larger sabbatical arrangement; it is more in the way of a local rearrangement of duties.

It only works (obviously) if the department's managerial hierarchy are persuaded of the merits of the idea, and are prepared to see appropriate rearrangements of duties.

○   ○   ○   ○

So: provide mechanisms to give people a temporary break – they will come back to the task better motivated and with more energy.

4.4 Dynamic Matchmaking

"Free-for-all" allocation mechanisms which involve students (and/or staff) selecting projects themselves are always time consuming and often unsatisfactory for a substantial proportion of those involved.

○ ○ ○ ○

This bundle provides a mechanism for establishing student-supervisor pairings in an environment of large numbers of staff and students – probably unknown to each other – in which there is a possible skills and interest mismatch.

The way it works is to partition the *topic areas* that projects occupy as uniformly as possible (for example, AI, graphics, theory, etc.) – this partition is of necessity colored by local supply and demand, but may be amended each year on the basis of demand experienced the year before, and adjustments to the supervisors' profile. In most cases, the assignment of supervisors to areas is quite easy to determine, although it is probable that some supervisors will be more adaptable than others.

Students are invited to nominate three (say) topic areas in which they are prepared to work – these would normally be prioritized. Where pre-specified projects exist or have been negotiated, they will normally belong to one of these areas and a preference for one of them may be indicated by the student.

At this stage the complexity of the allocation problem is much reduced and it is a feasible task to construct by hand a supervisor-student pairing by matching on preferred topic areas. It is important that this is done by a single individual who has an overview of all the issues and personnel involved, and in whom both students and supervisors have trust. It is possible that software could ease this task, but it is likely that knowledge of local personalities (either student or staff) would always be needed to fine tune the allocation. The allocation may then be used as the basis of negotiation toward a full project specification – a nice feature is that the final project may potentially be nothing to do with the originally nominated topic areas, provided supervisor and student agree.

Given that there are staff to cover enough topics (not a problem in a moderate-sized community) this mechanism can remove the "beauty competition" aspect of allocation by making it difficult for students to pursue individual staff as supervisors.

It works better if the match of staff and student preferences coincides well with the topic areas defined. There is an obvious element of serendipity in this, but some preparation can be done by ensuring that all reference to the project in earlier years is in the vocabulary of the topic split preferred.

It doesn't work if significant numbers of students are unwilling or unable to complete forms (in which case their allocation has to be random), or if significant numbers of supervisors are very restrictive about the types of projects with which they are prepared to become involved. It is also necessary that all parties abide by the allocator's decisions.

○ ○ ○ ○

So: ensure allocation is under the control of a single individual, and give them a mechanism to make the task manageable.

4.5 Musical Chairs

If there are many students interested in one project, all but one will be losers.

○ ○ ○ ○

This bundle provides a mechanism for open and fair allocation of highly popular projects that has the side effect of preparing students for the job application process.

The way it works is based on the fact that it is to everyone's benefit (staff, students, commissioning companies) to insure that the student best suited to any given project is the one allocated. ("Best suited" might include extra-curricula skills.) In a competitive situation it is worth taking time to make that match.

The primary aim of this bundle is to optimize the match of skills to project, but its use also reduces discontent among disappointed students.

What you do is to use a competitive allocation mechanism for the projects that are heavily oversubscribed. Interested students are invited to regard the project as a job, and to submit a formal application.

Actual allocation may be done on the basis of the written applications or, if time and resources permit, by interview. The latter approach is preferable, both to extend the experience and to provide a more open mechanism. It is particularly useful if (where appropriate) employer representatives can be included in such an interview panel, both for the quality of the experience and because the employer then takes a responsibility, and consequent interest, in the identity of the student.

It doesn't work if the selection procedure is not detected by the students as properly "fair" – for example if it is rushed, or conducted behind closed doors. Feedback to unsuccessful applicants can alleviate this.

It doesn't work unless you can devote sufficient time.

○ ○ ○ ○

So: solve a problem of oversubscription by exercising skills which replicate allocation in the "real world".

4.6 Horses for Courses

Often a department will offer several types of project, but put them all through a single one-size-fits-all allocation mechanism.

○ ○ ○ ○

This bundle proposes that you use different (and differently appropriate) allocation mechanisms for different types of project.

The way it works is that you distinguish between "research" and "design and build" projects [see 1.5 and 1.6] with regard to the allocation process. If a research-type project is offered, then the allocation process should be along research (or research group) lines. Ways in which this can be implemented are: writing a formal proposal that is reviewed, an interview with the head of the appropriate research group, or a personal recommendation from a research supervisor. These methods are clearly inappropriate for design and build projects and should not be used for them.

It doesn't work if you only offer one type of project, or if your allocation mechanism is defined (by QA or other stipulations). It doesn't work if the types of project you offer are already confused (on paper, in presentation, or in the minds of students, or staff).

It works better if the "type" of the project is clearly distinguished in advance, so that students know what the difference is, and that the difference starts with allocation.

○ ○ ○ ○

So: use appropriate instruments for allocation.

4.7 Job Application

It is unnecessarily artificial to allocate students to projects on a "skills-blind" basis.

○ ○ ○ ○

This bundle provides a mechanism for allocating students to the best job for them, using a job application process.

The way it works is that students have to fill out job applications before entering the course (in its original form this was a course which ran over three quarters of a year). If their application is accepted, they may register for the course and start out as a fledgling worker; they can potentially work their way up to project manager. As they work, they focus on a specific portion of the project.

Even over three quarters of a year, they may not see the software to completion, so others continue the project after them. In order for others to continue, they need the thinking and reasoning of past team members recorded in the form of requirements, design, software, and test documents. These documents mature as the project progresses, but cannot be rewritten every term or progress on the project will not be maintained.

It doesn't work if your project is constrained (by professional body requirements or the like) so that every student must experience every part of the project lifecycle.

References This bundle is based on original practice developed in *Real-World Lab*, started by Melody Moore when she was at Georgia Tech. A variant was reported in the FASE newsletter (*Forum for Advancing Software Engineering Education* (FASE) Volume 9 Number 8 (115th Issue) August 15, 1999) by Susan Mengel of Texas Tech and further details can be found at http://www.se.cs.ttu.edu/

○ ○ ○ ○

So: respect and reflect the differences in student ability in the same way that industry does.

5 Supervision

Supervision

As student numbers have increased, many of the traditional forms of individual contact between staff and students have declined. Regular and continuing "tutorials" seem to have been largely abandoned in all but the best-funded universities; pressure on staff time has seriously curtailed availability for casual enquiries on an "open door" basis, and led to the uptake of "office hours". Today, one-to-one contact most often occurs in the context of project supervision, greatly adding to the significance of this role in the students' development.

Project supervision is an activity that encompasses several aspects, including:

- **technical assistance**
  Because project students typically rely (in the first instance) on their supervisor for detailed technical assistance it is most common that supervisors take on projects in their areas of expertise. There are several allocation mechanisms [see, for example, 2.1, 2.2, and 2.3] that address this. The driver for providing this sort of assistance is most often demand from the supervisee(s) and the supervisory input is reactive.

- **engineering processes**
  Especially in large-scale (or group) projects there is an increasing reliance on effective use of engineering processes by the students. Sometimes processes are prescribed (typically where all students are doing the same project) but where this is not the case, they are often required to choose appropriate processes for the demands of their task. The driver for giving this form of assistance is often failure (or imminent failure) of the students' process, spotted by the supervisor: the supervisory input is proactive.

- **personal and professional development**
  Many of the problems encountered by students during large-scale and long-term pieces of work are connected with external circumstances rather than the work itself. These may be concerned with the difficulties of working within a group, with legal, ethical or property rights, or with the students' real life. The drivers for giving personal or professional development assistance are as often concerns raised by other stakeholders as they are problems observed in (or by) the student immediately involved.

These aspects are rarely distinct or discrete, but are all part of the activity of supervising a project and must be taken into account.

Where more than One Member of Staff Supervises Projects, Look for Inconsistency among Them

Many project instances assume that there is a consensus amongst supervisors as to the aims and objectives of the instance, and a consistency of approach between supervisors in addressing those objectives. This can indeed be the case among a stable group of supervisors where such a consensus has been developed (maybe implicitly) over time, but the privacy of the supervisor-student relationship makes such a consistency difficult to demonstrate. In any event, new supervisors being bought into such a culture will not have the benefit of this history, and must (at least) be indoctrinated into the zeitgeist.

An apparent collective understanding may, without having a noticeable effect on assessment outcomes, conceal wide disparities in effective goals (of supervisors as well as students). Consequently, either:

- **formulate agreed goals for the project instance**
  This is in keeping with the current climate of specification of expected student learning outcomes and experience, but can be difficult to assure across a large pool of supervisors.

- **factor the disparate approaches of supervisors into the assessment criteria used**
  This can be easier to implement if the supervisory load is shared (as it often is) by a wide variety of staff, but it might require an additional step in the assessment process to account for the supervisor's contribution to the student's achievements, as well as recognition of the potential variability of that input.

- **use a smaller pool of supervisors, and expend more effort on training them in forming a consensus**
  This approach has been used successfully even with single supervisors taking on quite large cohorts, but requires dedication from the staff involved, and cooperation from those apportioning teaching loads. Unless care is taken, it can also lead to a decrease in the types of projects offered, to the detriment of the students' ability to express their enthusiasm.

Cost

Supervision is an expensive activity, both at a departmental and individual level. There are two principal ways to address this. One is to maximize the use of currently available resource (staff time), exemplified by bundle 5.2 *Loosely Coordinated Groups*; another is to supplement, augment or otherwise increase the scarce resource. An example of this is given in 5.4 *The Supervisor's Eyes and Ears*.

Projects Are (Usually) Conducted over a Long Period of Time for Large Credit; There Is a Need To Intercept Failure Early

At one extreme, it is possible to construe project supervision as simply a "fly on the wall" activity, with students being allowed to follow their own paths, even to the extent of being unable to deliver anything at the end of the day. This is rarely taken to be an effective learning process. Thus it is concomitant on the supervisor to attempt to detect such pathological behaviour, and to help the student to change it before it is too late. At the other extreme, supervisors can control students' behavior to the extent that students have no creative (high-level) input to the work they are doing and are effectively unable to fail.

It is particularly difficult to keep students on track if there is no track. The first task of a supervisor is thus to ensure that students make (or buy, or copy) a map. The second task is to help them follow it – to an appropriate extent. The simple existence of a map (whether a project plan or a series of interim deliverables) does not imply that students should always be penalized for deviation (there may be a better way), but does provide a common reference against which student and supervisor can reflect on and discuss progress. Such intermediate supervisory input can be useful in affecting working practices, whether it is to alter the bad or assist in the good.

Conflict Between Supervisor/Assessor Role

Where a supervisor is also responsible for assessing a project, there are inevitable tensions between the two roles. Students may perceive that advice given by the supervisor is colored by their separate duty to assess them. So they may form the perception that the supervisor is withholding (or giving) particular advice not to support and develop the students' own thinking, but as part of their role in assessment.

There may, in fact, be a conflict between what students should do in order to complete a project in its own terms, and what they should do in order to maximize the mark awarded. In an ideal world, with assessment strategies completely aligned with the work undertaken, this would not be the case, but projects are often deliberately artificial in their nature. For instance, it is often the case that quite small projects are used to give students practice in the deployment of software engineering processes only applicable to far larger instances. In this case, the rational supervisor would advise students that it was better to use much simpler processes in the work, but assessment objectives dictate otherwise.

In institutions where examinations are marked "blind", projects are probably the most significant pieces of work undertaken by students in which their identity is visible. Indeed, blind marking of exams is often adopted precisely to combat the unwanted effects of the relationship between students and staff that is claimed as a major benefit of the project experience.

Stuff Happens

Things always happen. They are always unexpected. This section has been compiled from anecdote, "war-stories" and bar-room discussions with many colleagues. None of the problems presented here may ever happen to you, but something will. The important thing is to retain the expectation that there will be an exceptional circumstance somewhere and to have (even half-formed) contingency strategies.

- the supervisor is not expert in the subject area or in regard to student process

The mix of projects which students are interested in undertaking often does not match the mix of staff available to supervise them. Research-oriented staff may have a partial understanding of the requirements of process-based projects [See also 4.6 *Horses for Courses*].

- **conflation of student problems**
  Some students will have problems in areas other than their project work. Equally, students (particularly "traditional" 18-year-old students) are not very good at separating areas of work and their emotional reactions to them. Given the personal nature of the supervisory process, these will often impact on project work – where they don't really belong [see also Section 9 *Motivation*].

- **student time management – conflicting priorities**
  Project work, especially undertaken in groups, can consume far more time than its assessment worth. Be prepared to make them work *less* on the project – even if it is your pet idea.

- **late breaking failure**
  Students are good at covering up lack of progress, both their own and that of other non-functioning members of their group. Potential failures discovered near the end of a large project are far more difficult to retrieve.

- **ducking for the tape**
  Where projects finish near the end of an assessment period there is no scope for extension. This is an artificial situation, leaving students having to make a decision about what to omit from their delivered work. This will be conditioned by assessment criteria rather than by software engineering realities.

- **project turns out too simple/complex**
  Especially where students specify their own projects it can be difficult to judge an appropriate and comparable level of complexity. [See also 4.2 – I'd Like To Do That]

- **group geography**
  Students who live together interact differently. So do students who live far apart.

- **role allocation – star and forced drone**
  In a group situation where students allocate their own roles, as well as the familiar reliance on the skills of one or two members there is a potential problem with a competent student being assigned (or taking on) a role which does not allow them to demonstrate their abilities.

5.1 Characterizing Supervisor Input

Variations in the student/supervisor relationship have an effect on the extent to which the project is "the student's own work"; these are (commonly) not visible, and therefore not factored into assessment.

○ ○ ○ ○

This bundle provides a mechanism by which the level and scope of supervisor assistance can be recorded and factored into assessment, and coincidentally provides a framework in which supervisors can reflect on their own approaches and effectiveness.

The way it works is that, as part of the assessment process, each supervisor is required to report (on a pre-printed form) the extent to which they have assisted students during the course of the project. In order to facilitate comparability, the supervisors are asked to characterize their role as (predominantly) one of four types:

- **observer/commentator**
  The student(s) run the project for themselves, sometimes in the presence of the supervisor. The supervisor gleans from their actions the roles that they have taken, and the success with which they are implementing these roles. The supervisor may suggest lines of attack or potential solutions to problems, but will not in general require that the students adopt them.

- **master/mentor**
  The traditional "apprentice master" role with the supervisor passing on skills and advising the student(s) on the approaches to be taken to specific tasks.

- **line manager**
  The student(s) manage and implement the project, but regularly report to the supervisor who tracks progress and dictates strategy but not tactics.

- **project manager**
  This is the traditional "science" model of project supervision, where (typically) a small aspect of the supervisor's research project or interest is marked off as the students' project, to be integrated on completion. The supervisor has a particular interest in the success of the students' project, and will guide them to that end, allocating sub-tasks and directing progress.

The supervisor's report is attached to the project before it is forwarded to the moderator, second or other assessor.

It works better if staff share an understanding of the contents and importance of the supervisory report, both as authors (supervisors) and readers (assessors).

It doesn't work unless projects are supervised by different members of staff.

It doesn't work if the supervisor alone assesses the project (although there may be a personal development gain for staff in the process of reflection).

○ ○ ○ ○

So: moderate, or at least make explicit, the amount and type of assistance being given to project students by their supervisor.

5.2 Loosely Coordinated Groups

Supervisor time is expensive and may be squandered by duplicating advice. It is important to maximize supervisory resources without impairing the quality of the interaction.

○ ○ ○ ○

In this bundle group projects are supervised not by meetings of individual groups with their supervisor, but by more formal meetings of multiple groups with a single staff member present.

The way it works is that overall staff time spent on supervising projects should reduce, time spent responding to technical (or other) queries outside the formal supervision period should not increase and students' requirements for advice/guidance outside scheduled sessions should reduce.

At each meeting, one representative of each group present makes a short report on the group's progress during the preceding period and its plans for near future. All present respond to this presentation and to any problems raised.

Meetings last one hour, with each group's presentation lasting 10–15 minutes (including Q&A/problem solving). Students take the role of chair and secretary for these meetings (on a rotating basis), with minutes and paper versions of the progress reports being circulated to all after the meeting.

Using this bundle makes staff/student interaction more focused, and hence more useful to both parties. It gives students the experience of chairing meetings and of taking minutes, gives them practice in the presentation of results outside formally assessed forums and introduces the idea of group monitoring. Additionally, it encourages students' responsibility to the cohort as a whole.

This means that staff time is saved by combining the function of similar meetings, students learn to support each other's work and working practices and the amount of input a student gets from a supervisor is made more visible.

It works better if each group undertakes a different project, or each group undertaking the same project is placed in a different loose group (avoiding cross-fertilization between instances of the same project). *It works better if* projects are similar enough that the students have some understanding of the work being undertaken, and the technical problems encountered, in other projects. *It also works better* for group projects, as meetings consisting of individuals each presenting their own projects would either run too long, or be too small to encourage interaction.

It doesn't work if students' preparation for the meeting consumes more effort than the benefits gained or if students do no work (despite warnings) and are absent from the meetings. *It doesn't work if* students come from different programs, or are undertaking projects with a different weighting; leading to a proportionately different amount of effort being spent on preparation for the meeting.

○ ○ ○ ○

So: appreciate that supervision does not have to be a one-to-one activity.

5.3 The Help They've Had along the Way

At the end of a project, only the deliverables are visible. It is difficult to gauge the amount or source of supplementary "help" or "technical assistance" that students have had.

○ ○ ○ ○

This bundle allows staff to record, and supervisors to quantify, the amount and extent of help given to students, and to factor this into the assessment process.

The way it works is that students undertaking a project are given a set number of "vouchers", which they can trade in for assistance from any qualified member of staff. The voucher is filled in by the staff member to indicate the purpose and extent of the help given (and to whom) and returned to the project supervisor for consideration in the assessment process. Thus every submitted project has an associated file of completed help vouchers (which will range from none to maximum).

Each piece of advice or assistance is worth one or more vouchers. The number of vouchers per student may be fixed at the outset, and no more issued.

An example voucher:

Help Voucher
Group/Student Name
Help Requested
Help Given
Signed   Date

By using this bundle, students can approach staff who have the required expertise, rather than being restricted to their project supervisor. Students know how much help they can expect with their work and at the same time an upper bound is placed on the commitment of staff to supporting that work (which, in extremis, can be factored into staff loading calculations). Records of what help students have required can be used to identify curriculum "weak spots".

It works better if there is a shared understanding of voucher currency (the voucher/advice exchange rate) amongst staff. It is particularly suitable in situations where all students undertake the same project (in order for comparison of the amount of help needed to be meaningful).

It doesn't work unless the market for help is accurately judged. If too few vouchers are handed out students will not get the assistance they need and/or a black market may emerge; if too many vouchers are handed out you risk a flood of "use it or lose it" queries.

o o o o

So: look for a mechanism which can record the formal (and semi-formal) help the students have received.

5.4 The Supervisor's Eyes and Ears

Managing group processes can absorb a lot of supervisor time.

○ ○ ○ ○

This bundle reduces the amount of supervisor time spent in managing group processes by using postgraduate students in an intermediate supervisory role.

The way it works is that each project group is allocated a postgraduate "advisor". These advisors give no technical input, but focus on group processes and the early identification of problems. Advisors are specifically told that their responsibility is to spot problems rather than fix them. The advisors are paid, so they turn up to meetings and send in reports much more reliably than academic staff.

Students meet with their advisor on a weekly basis; the agenda and minutes are included in the student's project log, which is an assessed deliverable (assessment of this is undertaken jointly between advisor and supervisor). An additional assessment benefit is that the advisor can provide independent evidence to moderate or justify extreme mark distributions within the group.

Each advisor sends the supervising member of staff a weekly report of their group's progress (which can provide early identification and evidence of non-performance so defaulters can be chased) making the advisor the supervisor's "eyes and ears" on the group.

When problems are identified, the supervisor talks it over with the advisor and agrees on the next step. This may take the form of ideas that the advisor can feed to the group, or it may involve the supervisor talking to some or all the group members. In extremis, the supervisor may sit in on a progress meeting or formally summon the group to a meeting with them.

It works better if the project is of sufficient length and complexity to require investment in process. It is most useful where the students have not worked together before and the groups are mixed or lacking in terms of group-working experience: ideal for second years.

It doesn't work if advisors act as project manager and therefore remove the need for the group to own their process. It doesn't work if they start to give technical advice – which is perceived as unfair by some students. It doesn't work if there are insufficient postgraduates available – in any case new advisors need to be recruited and briefed each year. There can be "advisor" problems with postgraduates who are not experienced enough to spot a group which blows up late in the project.

○ ○ ○ ○

So: see who else might be able to supervise the non-technical aspects of group projects.

5.5 Looking for the Early Wobble

Projects are (usually) conducted over a long period of time and for significant credit. Without mechanisms for tracking progress, there is much scope for things to go wrong – with dire consequences.

○   ○   ○   ○

This bundle assists students in producing final project reports by requiring them to submit well specified sections of the report at set times during the year, for example after the analysis, design and testing phases.

The way it works is that students submit reports on specific (perhaps negotiated) phases of their work at the end of that phase, rather than at the end of the project. Thus, they can be given feedback on their report writing and have a chance to revise their work before it is finally assessed. Students can't leave all the report writing until the end of the project and then be faced with the horrors of a blank sheet of paper. Conversely, if there is a major revision of the aims or requirements late in the project, the fact that earlier work has already been "validated" discourages students from perceiving it as wasted.

A variation of "stage by stage" is to link the staging to interim grades as well. A way to implement this, in situations where everyone does the same project, is to require weekly progress and then to provide "model solutions" at the end of each week so that everyone starts the following week at the same point and no-one's marks are disadvantaged cumulatively. [An example of this is described in: A. G. Sartori-Angus (University of Natal, Durban, S Africa) *Object-Oriented Design through Ray-tracing*, Proceedings of the 5th Annual Conference on the Teaching of Computing (26–29 August 1997) pp 220–222]

It works better with final-year, individual projects where the development of the project can be expected to show definite phases and require a substantial written report upon which much of the assessment will be based.

It doesn't work unless the requirement for staged delivery is common to all students and supervisors. The detailed content of the staged reports can be negotiated between the student and supervisor to be appropriate to the project's development method. Project supervisors must have sufficient time to give the necessary feedback; if they don't students may be resentful of the supervisor not keeping their side of an implicit bargain.

○   ○   ○   ○

So: institute mechanisms which trap early failure.

6 Assessment

Assessment

Assessment sits at the intersection of learning objectives, the deliverables which demonstrate those objectives and the criteria used to judge the quality of the deliverables:

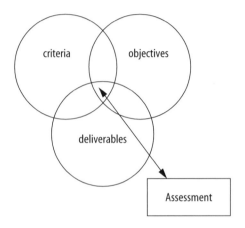

This relationship is not unique to assessing project work; it is common to all assessment. However, there are issues specific to project work that change these aspects.

Project work is, in general, on a larger scale than other assessed work; indeed, this is part of the rationale for having students undertake projects at all. Many of the problems of software development only become apparent as scale increases. Small-scale coursework typically consists of implementation from a given design, or design from a given specification, where there is neither scope for innovation nor necessity for multiple deliverables. This increase in scale also leads to a change in the nature of the required deliverables – large-scale projects inevitably require a more rigorous approach to the process of generation of the products, which process itself must produce assessable artifacts. This is congruent with the principles of software engineering.

In many cases (particularly with final-year projects), students are undertaking significantly different projects from one another, leading to a disparity in appropriate deliverables which must still be assessed under the same "rules". This can also make it especially difficult to generate criteria that are precise enough to be meaningful as aids to assessment, yet general enough to cover the range of projects undertaken in a particular instance.

In team and group projects "working together" is often an objective, and is often the first time that such methods have been required. This forces a change in the assessment criteria (especially in the minds of the students) where previously deprecated practices of producing joint work ("copying", "plagiarism") become an essential, assessed component.

Ensure that the Objectives, Deliverables and Criteria Are in Constructive Alignment

If one of the objectives of a project instance is that students learn process as well as produce products, then it is important that the deliverables of the project actually demonstrate stages and aspects of that process [see 6.5 *What Is a "Report" Anyway?*].

Marks Are the Only Thing We've Got that Students Want

~~Most~~ Some students are not motivated by the Joy of Learning. They are at university for the benefits that the qualification will give them in the job market, and therefore work primarily to maximize their marks. Staff can use this to their advantage in the assessment process by setting criteria and deliverables that manipulate students into learning the important bits, by giving them the most marks [see 6.4 *"Authentic" Assessment Criteria*].

Assessing Projects Is an Expensive Activity

Partly because of the scale of projects, partly because of the weighting they carry in the curriculum (from 3–30% of an undergraduate degree), partly because there is often a great variety of deliverables in a great variety of media (software artifacts, technical documentation, reports, code, oral presentations, etc.) and partly because several members of staff are commonly involved, assessment of projects is a time-consuming (and therefore expensive) activity.

~~Most~~ Some staff perceive the extra work that project assessment requires as excessive and unfair. One way to address this is to undertake an audit to see how long staff actually *do* spend reading reports, watching demonstrations, etc. This might prove that project assessment is both costly (it takes a lot of time) *and* cost-effective (it produces results which could not be gained in a different/cheaper way).

Conflict Between Supervisor and Assessor Role

Because project assessors are frequently the same as project supervisors, assessment may be colored by their knowledge of the students' effort. If they've "come a long way" should they get as many/more marks than another project that went further, but was easier? It is important to forge a consensus amongst supervisors and examiners as to the relative value of these two aspects.

It is important for the supervisor to have knowledge of where the "tricky bits" of the project fall so that apparently trivial pieces of implementation can be properly acknowledged, but it is equally important to have criteria that distinguish between effort and achievement.

Relationship of Individual Marks to Group Marks

There is a tension between assessing the products of a group and rewarding the efforts of individuals within that group, between "group products get a group mark" (every group member gets the same mark, regardless of contribution) and "only individual effort is rewarded" (attempting to completely determine individual contributions).

Although tempting on grounds of economy of assessment effort, "group" marking can be perceived by students as unfair, but is defended by its adherents on the grounds that if individual marks can be accrued from group work, then students will to work to maximize their own mark.

Mechanisms which reward individual effort in a group context are confounded by the difficulties which assessors have in determining what actually went on in the group, and by problems of determining appropriate weightings for different activities (e.g. "implementation" versus "documentation").

Between these two extremes, a proportion of the marks can be awarded for individual contribution to the work, with the rest going to the group as a whole. Many mechanisms have been devised to address this; commonly a proportion of the marks is handed over to the students to allocate amongst themselves so that they can reward the highest contributors (and punish the laggards).

6.1 Use Peer Assessment

Especially in projects that are returned to students near the end of their program of study, feedback tends to be ignored, and notice is only taken of the mark awarded.

○ ○ ○ ○

This bundle engages students in the process of assessing their own work against given criteria and generating feedback on the work of others against the same criteria. It encourages them to see their work with "others' eyes", appreciating their own strengths and weaknesses, and to evaluate the work of others in a domain (and against criteria) with which they are already familiar.

The way it works is that the project is developed to a set of detailed criteria (effectively a marking scheme). This focuses the students from the outset on how the work is going to be assessed. When they submit their work, students attach a self-assessment. They then undertake a peer evaluation of the work of another group who have done the same project.

Students peer-assessing a project do not receive the self-assessment that goes with it, although they will, of course, be informed by the experience of their own self-assessment.

The final mark awarded for a project is decided by the staff member involved, using the self-assessment to moderate the peer assessment, and referring to the original project (i.e. re-marking) in cases of gross disagreement. The results of the moderation are included with the peer assessment; thus the students receive the comments of their peers and of the "trusted" staff member.

It works better if students have some experience of peer assessment, and if the projects are the same or very similar in nature.

It doesn't work unless assessment criteria (including marking scales) are well understood and shared before the assessment process is begun.

○ ○ ○ ○

So: get students to use assessment as part of their learning.

6.2 Assessment Walkthrough

Especially where students are working in groups, or attempting the same or similar projects, it can be difficult to decide who really did what.

o   o   o   o

This bundle allows staff to validate that the work described/delivered is that of the student, to ensure that the claims made for the deliverables are correct, and to clarify any statements made in the final report.

The way it works is that students meet with staff to undertake a terminal "walkthrough" of their project deliverables, using any of the standard forms described in the software engineering literature, depending on the goals of the project as well as on how many students are involved. Possibilities include the review of designs against specifications, implementations against designs, or code against local standards (Pressman, 1992). It may take the form of a presentation (although there is still the possibility of students "hiding" here) or a dialog. The results of this process inform the assessment of the students' work, but are not necessarily assessed themselves.

It works better if students have had practice with, or are at least aware of, the form and function of software reviews, and hence in projects with a software engineering focus.

It doesn't work unless staff and students can commit the time to make it a collaborative, non-intimidating process.

Reference Pressman, R. S. (1992) *Software Engineering, a practitioner's approach*, McGraw-Hill, New York

o   o   o   o

So: use processes derived from software engineering to enhance assessment.

6.3 Increase the Granularity

The reliability of assessment suffers when the value of the marginal (unit) mark is small.

○   ○   ○   ○

This bundle focuses student (and staff) attention on the extent of the difference in achievement that is reflected by a single mark – and changes the way assessors award marks so as to ensure that the scale rises in appropriate steps.

The way it works is that if each category in the marking scheme (e.g. design, implementation, evaluation) has an associated maximum mark, and within each category marks in the range 0–100 are awarded then it is very difficult to achieve numerical agreement between one assessor's 57% and another's 52%. However, the granularity can be increased to reflect the marks "earned" by each component, i.e. if *design* carries 40% of the total project mark, mark it out of 40 instead of 100. Agreement between assessors on what 15/40 means is more likely, and the award of extra marks on appeal from the student becomes more meaningful.

It works better if there is agreement among the staff that granularity is a problem and if agreement about what the weightings should be has been secured.

It doesn't work unless you have a number of categories in the mark scheme.

Variation Students think that 1% on an assessment that counts for of 25% of 1/12th of their degree is worth arguing over. It isn't. Don't argue, but give it away freely.

○   ○   ○   ○

So: make the marginal mark worth something.

6.4 "Authentic" Assessment Criteria

If you set a problem that involves programming, students will construe it as being solely about programming.

○ ○ ○ ○

This bundle uses students' understanding of project life-cycles to characterize appropriate deliverables, and to weight the effort (and risk) involved in producing each one. The resulting list is then used to generate the assessment criteria (and associated weightings) for the deliverables of an assessed software project.

The way it works is that, before students start on a project (but after they know what the project will be), a "negotiation" session is undertaken in which the appropriate activities for such a project are discussed, listed, and relative weightings are agreed. This discussion can be "steered" and the outcome "stitched up" by the facilitator deprecating (and discarding) some suggestions and coalescing others, as well as making sure that all the necessary elements are present. This session can be undertaken with the entire cohort (if it's not *too* large) or in smaller groups with the facilitator combining and moderating the results.

The outcome of this should be a list of the activities, a weight for each activity (typically 5–15% of the total effort), and a list of where in the deliverables of the project evidence for the quality of that aspect might be found. This list can then be used to guide students' efforts and priorities in undertaking the project, as (they are told at the end of the session) the effort weightings are used as assessment weightings.

It works better if it is embedded in a software engineering module or program, so that discussions of weightings are guided by an understanding of the appropriate processes.

It doesn't work unless the project to be undertaken is process-centered, and the students already have an understanding of what this means. All students must be undertaking the same project, unless you are prepared to negotiate with each student.

○ ○ ○ ○

So: use pre-specified, agreed and published criteria to direct students' activities in assessed work.

6.5 What Is a "Report" Anyway?

The "report", which is the sole assessed deliverable of many projects, is often a mixture of technical and process documentation, and a reflection on achievement.

○ ○ ○ ○

This bundle reconciles the deliverables of a project with its learning goals, minimizing the extra work that students have to undertake purely to make their efforts assessable. It recognizes that a project is a learning exercise, not a production effort. It also minimizes duplication of material in the deliverables that assessors need to consider.

The way it works is that instead of characterizing the outcomes of a project as a "report", they are divided into two, separately delivered, sections:

- what the project should have delivered anyway, e.g. plans, records of investigations undertaken (requirements gathering), design documentation (including rationales for the choices made), and so on

- a reflective piece giving the students' perception of the success (or otherwise) of the work, and demonstrating what has been learnt from the process.

These deliverables are more appropriate, especially to projects with a substantial software engineering focus, and encourage students to discuss what they have done, rather than rehashing general descriptions of approaches (such as life-cycles) that they have adopted. They encourage students to submit documents describing what they intend to do (as part of plans and risk analyses) rather than a narrative description of what they eventually did.

The more useful aspect of the "report" – students' reflection on what they have achieved and how – is still captured (in the *reflective piece*), but does not have to be distilled from amongst the narrative description of their software development process.

It works better if the project is not entirely assessed against the final product.

It doesn't work unless there is a consensus among supervisors as to the appropriate deliverables from a project.

○ ○ ○ ○

So: ensure that the assessed deliverables of a project match the process which students are expected to employ.

6.6 Assess the Fact that They Did It

When students undertake a project for an external "client" there are problems with gauging and assessing the scope and difficulty of their work.

○ ○ ○ ○

This bundle identifies a series of tasks which, if completed, will count for the academic credit of the project, irrespective of what the student produces for the "client".

The way it works is that when the project is negotiated with the external (usually industrial) client, a series of tasks are identified whose completion will count for the academic credit of the project, irrespective of the marginal quality of the artifacts they deliver.

The tasks might be specified in the form of a "learning contract" where the student has to ensure that they fulfill the educational objectives of the project, or they might be set in the context of an existing framework (such as the BCS's Professional Development Scheme, see: http://www.bcs.org/pds). The fact that the student actually accomplishes the specified activities is certified by someone outside of the academic department (normally in the workplace).

It is assumed that the process and product of the work is satisfactory unless otherwise stated (by the external assessor). If satisfactory, it is sufficient that they have done the work; there is not enough added value in the detail to warrant a more fine-grained assessment process.

It doesn't work unless reliance is placed on the motivation and quality of the participants – students, academic supervisors and external (industrial) assessors.

○ ○ ○ ○

So: consider awarding academic credit for successful accomplishment of tasks, rather than assessing the products of those tasks.

6.7 Three Wise Monkeys

No matter how tightly specified the criteria for assessing a project, assessors will always find room to vary.

o   o   o   o

This bundle reduces the total variance between assessors by reducing the number of assessors.

The way it works is that you only have three assessors per project instance. They grade every project produced within a course (or module or cohort). In this way, they can then spend more time discussing the "implicit" criteria of the project, and are more likely to be able to form a consensus. Their grades will, probably, be closer and internally consistent.

It works better if there is a slow "turnover" of assessors; that is to say only one rotates out of the job every year. This ensures that the assessment culture of project work within the department ("the way things are done here") is maintained and disseminated. It also helps to solve the problem of longitudinal variation in assessment over time.

It doesn't work unless assessors receive "credit" for the work. It doesn't work unless the projects are such that all assessors are equally capable of assessing the technical content.

o   o   o   o

So: consider reducing the number of people who assess projects.

6.8 Assessing Something Is Not the Same as Measuring Something

No matter how tightly specified the criteria for assessing a project, assessors will always find room to vary. One assessor's 58% will be another assessor's 49%.

○ ○ ○ ○

This bundle addresses assessor inconsistency by decoupling numeric grades from more qualitative assessments of the work. This provides justification for (and, it is to be hoped, a basis for agreement on) the grade awarded.

The way it works is that everyone who marks the project completes a form which asks a number of questions, justifying the numeric mark(s) awarded. See following example.

These forms are then all returned to the assessor(s), and are used to inform their validation of the numeric mark(s) awarded.

It works better if all assessors are involved.

It doesn't work with particularly strong-willed individuals who will mark according to their own private criteria whatever guidance is given.

○ ○ ○ ○

So: consider separating numeric from subjective grading, so that one type of information informs and enhances the other.

Mark whichever box best describes the characteristics of the project report.				
The report shows that the student used the available literature . . .				
not at all	ineffectively	adequately	effectively	very effectively
The report shows that the student's overall grasp of the subject was . . .				
minimal	incomplete	satisfactory	good	excellent
The structure of the report is . . .				
abysmal	poor	average	good	excellent
The quality and style of the grammar used in the report is . . .				
abysmal	poor	average	good	excellent
The quality, relevance, and referencing of the tables and diagrams is . . .				
abysmal	poor	average	good	excellent
The use of references is . . .				
abysmal	poor	average	good	excellent
The way in which the discussion and conclusions of the project are presented is . . .				
abysmal	poor	average	good	excellent
The number of errors in the report is . . .				
excessive	numerous	acceptable	small	almost none
The definition of the project area is . . .				
non-existent	vague	adequate	succinct	sharply focused
To what extent are the ideas presented in a natural and orderly way . . .				
not at all	sometimes	satisfactorily	mostly	always
The review of the theoretical background to the project is . . .				
non-existent	vague	adequate	succinct	sharply focused
The report identifies the following proportion of the main issues . . .				
none	some	about half	most	all
The analysis is . . .				
vacuous	feeble	adequate	good	insightful
The report explains the rationale behind the design of any artefact . . .				
not at all	ineffectively	very adequately	effectively	very effectively
The report compares alternative designs and justifies choices . . .				
not at all	ineffectively	very adequately	effectively	very effectively
The report suggests that the project was . . .				
trivial	feeble	adequate	challenging	impossible
The evaluation of the work done was . . .				
vacuous	feeble	adequate	thorough	rigorous
The relationship between theory and practice was identified . . .				
not at all	weakly	adequately	strongly	everywhere

6.9 Never Make a Choice Without a Reason

Students often consider that their project work exists in isolation, and don't bother to situate it in the wider world.

○ ○ ○ ○

This bundle is concerned with ensuring that students undertake an appropriate amount of background reading.

The way it works is that students are required to deliver for assessment a justification of choices taken and decisions made against external material. They are required to show evidence of background reading in their project deliverables.

The most common occurrence of this is through the use of a literature survey in a research-type project [see 1.5]. However, it can have different qualities. For instance, a discussion of the merits of different notations, and a rationale for any choices made, may form a (required) part of the design documentation. This can also be a requirement if a structured analysis and design method is used, for example within the *Selection of Technical Options* stage in Structured Systems Analysis and Design Methodology (SSADM).

It works better if there is a shared understanding (between staff, and between staff and students) that no work exists in isolation. This can be addressed successfully in other teaching with regard to the ethical and "professional" aspects of academic work (such as the necessity for proper attribution and the problems of plagiarism) and related to their work on a project.

It doesn't work unless the requirement to produce the evidence is acknowledged in assessment.

○ ○ ○ ○

So: consider assessing students' understanding of the context of their project.

6.10 Phased Assessment (End-of-level Guardian)

Students often feel that objectives and associated assessment criteria are not clear.

○ ○ ○ ○

This bundle provides a mechanism whereby students can know what they have to do to achieve a particular grade and, at the same time, what their current level of achievement is.

The way it works is that associated with each deliverable (process or product) is an assessment checklist that defines what must be present in that deliverable, and an appropriate quality threshold. Deliverables have to conform to the appropriate assessment checklist before the grade is awarded, but conformance is sufficient.

Students begin work on the project by working on the lowest grade deliverables. The work is complete when the deliverable satisfies (by a process of student and/or supervisor inspection) all the items on the associated checklists. Students can begin working on the next higher grade deliverables while the inspection process is being carried out.

If a deliverable does not conform to all the items on its checklist it must be reworked and reinspected. This activity continues until the deliverable conforms to the checklist. The students gradually work through the deliverables corresponding to each grade in order.

If, later in the project, an earlier deliverable requires extension, it appears again at the higher grade. The deliverable is assessed against a checklist that takes account of the new requirements.

By including this type of inspection and rework mechanism, backtracking and improvement can be rewarded. Each deliverable has to satisfy all the requirements, expressed on the checklists, but to achieve the highest grade a student also has to complete all the deliverables.

It works better if staff are familiar and comfortable with a *deliverable inspection* process [see also 6.2 *Assessment Walkthrough*].

It doesn't work unless staff and students have the ability (and QA freedom) to negotiate, and renegotiate, learning outcomes. It doesn't work if students can skip stages and deliverables.

○ ○ ○ ○

So: allow students to accumulate credit by delivering to defined thresholds.

7 Reflection

Reflection

Reflection on experience underpins the process of successful learning and is essential to the success of education. The major problem here lies in the process being well removed from the technical content on which students fixate, and the fact that it is its own reward – allocating "marks" for reflective activity is likely only to divert attention from its true purpose.

While supervisors may be well aware of this, all too often students are not; reflection is an activity that does not carry explicit credit and it can be hard to convince students that the benefits of it will accrue, not least, ultimately, in raw grades. Since, to the inexperienced, the merits of reflection are not evident, there is sense in devising activities surrounding project conduct that will cause it to happen, perhaps covertly. It is common to see groups looking inwards, or for individual students to become over-absorbed, and coaxing them out of this is a supervisory duty that can have beneficial side effects in changing long-term practice. Another, lesser, problem is that students may well engage in reflective activity without realizing it, and hence not learn the merits of this approach to learning. This lends purpose to activities that involve the articulation of reflection.

It is probable that the project is the first truly large-scale piece of work a student has undertaken, and the adjustment to this mode of working can be difficult, or at least not obvious. Developing the skills to handle intermediate deliverables that may or may not be cumulative and to work in activities where interaction is positively beneficial is not easy or obvious. This is particularly true if all assessed work hitherto has been strictly individual, with penalties for plagiarism, and smaller scale, operating over no more than a few weeks. The transition can be eased significantly by a reflection on one's own knowledge, skills and working practices, followed by a suitable adjustment based on what is said.

The other aspect of scale is the longevity of the work. Quite unlike coursework, project work may well contribute to larger developments that have a longer and altogether more important existence. Where this is not the case, however, it is very useful to suggest to students that project deliverables can have a visible longer lifetime. If, at completion, the work is not mentally shelved it can be used as the basis of a reflective experience long after assessment and departure from the university.

Projects are conducted in a wide range of environments, some of which provide more support to encouraging reflection (and other desirable skills) than others. In particular, the active support of a university library can be a great spur to making the activity "serious" [see, for example, 7.7 *Cherish It*], but staff taking matters "seriously" at a departmental level can suffice. This requires broad agreement on what the project exercise is for (not just in written aims and objectives), and can be encouraged by a visible administrative and support structure that stands independent of, for example, coursework management.

There are many ideas that can be used in this area; a popular one is the logbook, which can, if properly implemented, have the full reflective effect of a personal diary, especially when there is a requirement to revisit it from time to time. Many formats are possible (paper, HTML, etc.), but a written journal provides discipline in expression and permits portability, especially as raw material is likely to be electronically available somewhere else. If this is used, it is a good idea, especially at the outset, to require a specific format since this will assist those inexperienced in this kind of activity; this is particularly true if students have difficulty focusing on process. Displaying a good example from earlier years is also useful, although there is often a problem with reuse of formats and words that are perceived by students to be "successful".

Logbooks can fail if students see them merely as an overhead on the project – a distraction from the "real" work of software production, and will not work effectively without adequate motivation and reward for the student. The reflection can be little more than superficial, particularly if the log does not hold much information. There is also a danger that it becomes literally a log, i.e. simply a history of what happened with no analysis or conclusions for the future. Without this analysis the log does not provide the full value for any reflective reports based on it. Significant events can occur in projects that no tutors are aware of; consequently the log might not include events which produce significant outcomes. It should not be expected that the log will contain everything of significance.

The general idea is applicable to group-based work as well; a team-based log may suffer particularly from incompleteness due to the reluctance of students to report problems associated with peers. The inverse problem may also appear, i.e. that one student's experience dominates the log [see 8.5 *Red Card/Yellow Card* and 8.6 *Moderation Using Student Input*].

Projects frequently require a range or number of deliverables; the "report" and/or a software product are common, but the specifics can vary and other options are available. The possibility of phasing deliverables provides an excellent opportunity for reflection and adjustment of practice where necessary [see 6.10 *Phased Assessment (End-of-level Guardian)*]. For example, students may be required to produce a progress report, a literature survey, a draft chapter of the final report, or a proposed future schedule. Any or all of these can be used as the basis of supervisory meetings and have great value in spurring reflection since they require an examination of achievement to date. Going one step further, such submissions may be made the subject of formal assessment (preferably by more than just the supervisor) – upon return, invaluable advice can be provided on how things are going. The return of the assessors' comments, while the project is still underway, can provoke self-examination and adjustment, and provide a handle for future reflection on progress.

The project experience is usually long, and provides many opportunities for reflection of various kinds:

- before: at project outset, it is likely that there will be some experience on which to build; constructing explicit reflection before the "real" work has commenced can be illustrative and good experience of the general practice
- during: projects may well run for some months, a major difference to coursework; there is therefore the opportunity for reflection on progress and adjustment of practice
- after: most of a project's life is after completion, but it is all too common for it to be put on a shelf and forgotten; there are many opportunities to use the project experience, both for the author and other students, and maximizing these aids reflection of the whole process.

7.1 Throw the Driver Under the Bus

Teams/groups should be resilient to changes in personnel, but in practice students often rely on the particular skills of a small number of key individuals.

○ ○ ○ ○

This bundle requires students to reflect explicitly on who can do what, by disturbing (or temporarily destroying) the natural or established allocation of duties.

The way it works is to set a project that requires different skills to be deployed, and, at a crucial moment, remove from the group an individual with a particular set of skills. (For example, set a programming task then remove the good programmers.) This determines whether someone other than the driver can keep the bus moving along the road. Once the person has been removed, ask the rest of the group to modify some of the person's work. Keep the key person occupied on some other activity. The task set while the person is removed needs to be small enough to be completed in the time available (e.g. hour, or half-day). This can also be extended to several groups.

It works better if the activity requires (and the group possesses) a diverse mixture of skills – for example, on a highly interdisciplinary course. For reasons of economy (and surprise) it is better, where this is applied to a number of groups, that they are in some form of synchrony – for example if all the groups are conducting the same work to the same schedule. It also works better if you have a good understanding of the dynamics of each group.

A variation is to swap students with the same key skill between groups.

It doesn't work unless you monitor how the groups tackle the problem: some may subcontract the task, others may complete it effortlessly using records that the key person left behind, and some groups may fabricate the results. Monitoring is important because you need to explain to students what has happened, and get them to reflect on it.

○ ○ ○ ○

So: ensure that groups recognize the value (and use of) process documentation, by making them rely on it.

7.2 Mid-project Report

If students have no formal feedback during the conduct of a project, there is no guide to keeping the show on the rails, and no spur to commencing or conducting the reflective process.

○ ○ ○ ○

This bundle requires reflective activity to begin well before project completion.

The way it works is to require students to deliver an interim report part way through the project. This should be significant but not overwhelming, and should be submitted to a strict deadline and assessed, preferably by more than just the supervisor. It will provide an early warning of impending problems, both among students and potential disagreements between assessors. Upon return to the student, invaluable advice can be provided on how things are going.

This practice is of great value in spurring reflection, since such a report requires an examination of achievement to date; furthermore, the return of the assessors' comments, while the project is still underway, can provoke self examination and adjustment, and provide a handle for future reflection on progress.

It works better if conducted a little before halfway through the project, with a swift turnaround. It also helps if the feedback contains comment on the perceived level of project difficulty (and ultimate maximum grade attainable).

It doesn't work unless you have sufficient resource, since the deliverable needs coordinating across the cohort, and staff time needs to be devoted to assessment. It is important that this is done briskly or the benefits are diluted.

○ ○ ○ ○

So: to require reflection to commence, introduce an interim, reflection-based, deliverable; feed it back with constructive comment and guidance.

7.3 Coordinated Supervision

The most accessible, and sometimes best, advice can come from the peer group. Student working practices do not always encourage this, though project work should engender the practice of asking for and providing support.

○ ○ ○ ○

This bundle requires students to account for their progress and discuss problems with each other.

The way it works is by the supervisor requiring groups of individual project students to meet in a structured setting, usually meaning a minuted meeting of fixed duration – an hour normally suffices.

Working partnerships can grow spontaneously, and mature problem-solving mechanisms can be developed. The formal presentation of progress requires student reflection on their achievement and plans, and usually provokes conversation and debate on possibilities that are often outside the supervisor's experience.

If the group meetings are formal (minuted) and of manageable size – 5 students can meet a supervisor and exchange business within an hour – the peer pressure to attend with something positive to say is an aid that is quite absent in individual supervisions. There can also be a significant time saving over a sequence of individual supervisions, but it is important not to let the students see this as a motivation for the practice.

A variant is to rotate the tasks of chair and secretary around the students, thereby giving them experience of these organizational roles. Another variation is to alternate group meetings with individual supervisions; this provides reassurance to those who might feel the need of specialist input.

This might not work if the group of students is studying projects in disparate areas, since they may not have interest or knowledge in the work of some others. In fact, this idea has been seen to work well in such scenarios but it is necessary for the supervisor to ensure that the organizational benefits are drawn out, and that no "lame ducks" develop. It may also, therefore, not work if the supervisor is wedded to the idea of one to one supervision.

○ ○ ○ ○

So: devise ways of encouraging "vicarious learning" by requiring students to explain their project triumphs and obstacles to each other.

7.4 Project Log

The raw skills of reflection are often absent or under-rehearsed in students.

○   ○   ○   ○

This bundle initiates reflective activity at project outset, and maintains it throughout.

The way it works is to make a diary (or log) a deliverable of the project. Use the content of the log of the immediately preceding week(s) as the agenda paper for supervisory meetings, thus requiring the student to reflect in conversation on what is being done. Furthermore, when the final report is written, the diary over a period of time should illustrate the scale and nature of achievement, and provides hard data for reflection on what has (and has not) been conducted.

The same idea can work just as well in group projects. A decision needs to be taken on whether there is one log for the group, or a number of individual logs, or a hybrid of the two approaches.

The scale of credit allocated to the log need not be great, since most credit will be won for achievements made whose progress it records. The credit does need to be sufficient to ensure the exercise is taken seriously.

It works better if there are clear intermediate milestones of the project that provoke explicit reflective recording.

It doesn't work if students see the log as an overhead on the project.

○   ○   ○   ○

So: catalyze reflection by requiring it to be recorded.

7.5 Sooner Rather than Later

Although reflection can often lead to an improvement in students' performance during the project, such opportunities will be lost if students view reflection as a process which only takes place after project work is completed.

○ ○ ○ ○

This bundle provides a structured mechanism within which students must exercise reflection through the conduct of the project.

The way it works is to have students use Watts Humphrey's *Personal Software Process* (Humphreys, 1997) to record the effort they have expended on individual tasks within a project, to use these records to assist them reflect on their work, to implement changes in the way they approach their work, and to track the effects of the changes.

This bundle fits with a project in which students are required to design, build and test a number of software modules, or similar deliverables. If used repeatedly, more benefits can accrue: assessors feel that students are working steadily producing real quantitative results and, over time, students' development strategies change.

It works better if the student is not penalized for attempting process improvement which does not have a beneficial outcome.

It doesn't work unless the project requires students to undertake a task or group of tasks on a number of occasions. It doesn't work if students leave the work until the last moment, and it requires a standardized set of documents. It doesn't work if students are able to exploit opportunities to fabricate results.

Reference Humphreys, W. S. (1997) *Introduction to the personal software process*, Addison-Wesley, Reading, Mass.

○ ○ ○ ○

So: employ mechanisms which require students to shorten the cycle of reflection.

7.6 "Follow That Plan"

Work schedules stretching over weeks or months are new to most students, who have little experience of estimating or measuring how long particular tasks may take.

○ ○ ○ ○

This bundle requires students to produce a time plan, to monitor their progress against it, and to amend it as necessary, noting the changes as they go.

The way it works is to make the production of a time plan the first project activity. This is then used on a regular basis in meetings to monitor progress. It is probable that modifications to the plan will become necessary as a result of project developments, or poor estimates; this provokes immediate reflection on how and why things need to be changed. At the end of the project, students are required to evaluate their performance on the project in respect of the project planning and time management skills.

This idea can be used in any project situation, individual or team based, where the work can be split into separate tasks.

A side effect is improved time management skills, and better understanding of the estimating of time taken to complete a task.

It works better if students have experience of following, or are strongly encouraged to follow, a clear, phased approach to project development.

○ ○ ○ ○

So: find ways to ensure the time consumed by project tasks is estimated, measured, and commented upon.

7.7 Cherish It

At project completion, many of the benefits of project experience can be lost if students think the exercise is "all over".

○ ○ ○ ○

This bundle encourages students to see project products as having a lifetime beyond assessment and their own university careers; this encourages greater pride in their work and more reflection on its production.

The way it works is to require project reports to be submitted in duplicate. After assessment, one is returned to the student and the other is filed somewhere visible for future reference. Electronic access could also work, and would have the merit of immediate international access. When students see their own work on (permanent or semi-permanent) public display, they are encouraged to take pride in it and may well revisit it from time to time. Such visits nearly always result in increasingly mature reflection on what they did, often with the benefit of intervening experience.

Over time, success can be judged by students examining the work of others and remarking "I could do better than that", or similar, or if they draw attention to the hazards and benefits of public availability during production. A more immediate test of success is an accumulation of reports from earlier years.

It works better if students are required to read one or more reports from earlier years from the accessible pool, since foreknowledge that the project deliverables will be filed publicly can also affect the sense of pride students take in project conduct.

It doesn't work if for some reason a project is of low quality, in which case "image" problems in its public availability may be expressed. It is possible that easy access to reports and grades may provoke comparisons leading to appeals (justified and unjustified), or that those taking especial pride may wish to update/edit their reports before public filing. If paper copies are filed for public access, significant filing space is necessary, and the material often (usually) ages after five or so years.

See also: 9.2 Well *they* managed

○ ○ ○ ○

So: ensure something outlives the project that students can point to and cherish.

7.8 "I Thought that . . ."

Reflection on the project process should include staff. Often this does not occur even when students participate.

○ ○ ○ ○

This bundle encourages students to reflect formally on the project process, and provides material to assist staff and project managers in reviewing and improving it.

The way it works is to encourage (or require) students, on completion, to complete a survey in questionnaire form of their perception of the project process and outcomes. The precise questions asked will depend upon local feelings about short-comings or problems in affairs, but standard guidelines in the preparation of questionnaires (Oppenheim, 1992) obviously apply. The act of completing the exercise is of immediate benefit to the students, and the outcomes usually point to adjustments that departments might make to improve. The outcomes can also be of value as pre-publicity to students.

It works better if the largest possible percentage of the cohort can be surveyed; one approach is to make the return of a private copy of the project report contingent on this action having been taken. It also assists if students operate in a culture of responsible feedback in which coercion is not necessary to encourage them to state frank and responsible views.

It doesn't work if too much credence is given to student opinion, which is often an unreliable source of quality information, and it may not work if the survey is conducted prior to assessment, when frank opinions may not be forthcoming. There may be a problem in extracting opinions after assessment when students are under-motivated to engage in this kind of exercise.

Reference Oppenheim, A. N. (1992) *Questionnaire Design, Interviewing and Attitude Measurement,* Pinter, London

○ ○ ○ ○

So: obtain the widest inputs you can to surveys of project process and outcomes. Use them to improve and inform, and to initiate reflective thought.

7.9 Last Year's Punters

The project provides a wealth of experience, often intangible, that might not be recognized. Simultaneously, this experience is of potential value to junior students and may go untapped.

○ ○ ○ ○

This bundle recognizes that a lot of the process of project conduct is learned very well during its course, but this may go without proper recognition by the student. It is also the sort of experience that is very hard to "teach", but may well be communicated effectively by a peer.

The way it works is by realizing that both those problems are soluble by facilitating interaction between students at different levels. One way of doing this is to make a presentation or poster a project deliverable, and getting the junior students to take part in assessment, although actual interaction between the groups helps more. Getting senior students to talk to groups (large or small) of junior students about "how it was for me" is another variant. This may be done as part of a formal lecture, or to ad hoc groups in, for example, tutorials. If the group is small enough, very fruitful conversation can ensue. Of necessity, the senior students must have thought about their experience, and thus reflection is stimulated.

It is necessary to ensure that the presenting students have actually conducted the reflection necessary to inspire such interaction.

A side effect is rehearsal of presentation techniques.

You'll know this is working if junior students make remarks such as "That chap warned me that this might happen", or if senior students remark on how much they learned outside the technical necessities.

It doesn't work if there are problems in scheduling such interactions, especially if senior students are at the end of their university careers soon after project submission. It is also possible that they will communicate things that contradict what supervisors might wish.

A variant is to use newly recruited Ph.D. students who will in all probability have recent project experience. Possible problems with this are that their experience may not map directly onto local conditions, and that they are self-selecting in being at the highly academic end of their cohort, and may not communicate what is required by the broader mass.

Another variant was given by one of the anonymous reviewers of this book: "My particular variant of *Last Year's Punters* is to introduce an open day, when finishing students can demonstrate their products, both to staff and students from the previous year. This will introduce an aspect of continuity and inter-year contact."

○ ○ ○ ○

So: find ways of getting last year's students to talk to this year's, to the benefit of both.

7.10 "If I Had My Time Again"

Students rarely re-examine their project progress and ask how they might have done it differently with improved (or different) outcomes.

○ ○ ○ ○

This bundle makes explicit reflective activity a deliverable by asking students to note opinion on the whole project process.

The way it works is to require a section of the project report to address the question "How might the work have been conducted differently?". Some element of guidance is necessary when encouraging answers to this, to prevent responses being at a superficial or purely technical level.

It is possible to ask for other questions to be addressed as well – "What have you learned?" is a good example.

It works better if there has been genuine reflection on the whole project process, perhaps, but not necessarily, conducted within a supervisory session. It is even better if this is conducted in company with other students of the same cohort, since this encourages them to see differences and similarities in their individual experiences.

It doesn't work unless the reflective practice is genuine. This can easily be undermined if, for example, the responses are seen as part of assessment, in which case formulaic phrases from earlier years that are seen as "successful" may well be delivered instead of true opinion.

○ ○ ○ ○

So: devise ways to make students answer the question "What if I had done it differently?".

8 Team/Group Projects

Team/Group Projects

It is a truth universally acknowledged by employers and professional bodies alike that an element of group work in a practical subject like computer science is A Good Thing. Yet group work sometimes sits uneasily in an environment where individual achievement is prized and collaborative activity (of the variety labeled "academic misconduct") is deplored.

"Group work" is the name given to a variety of projects in which groups of students collaborate to achieve a single goal. It manifests itself in laboratory work (often involving pairs of students working on small laboratory-based exercises), in so-called team projects (involving a large cohort of students divided into groups of at least three engaged in collaborative activity, often the construction of some artifact), and in places where groups of students collaborate to work on an individual project of a scale that they could not have attempted individually (often, a final-year or postgraduate activity).

Group work is valued within degree programs, not only for its intrinsic learning goals, but also because it is perceived to inculcate in the participants an awareness of the needs, difficulties, opportunities and complexities of an activity essential to the professional engineer in the computing discipline. Conversely, although group work often has a large profile within a degree program, the marks that it attracts may be a small proportion of a student's final classification, so students and staff have to balance effort against the potential reward.

You Can't Avoid Process

As soon as group or team working is required in a project, then working with others – the technical and personal collaboration necessary to build a joint product – cannot be avoided. This means that students will expect support in this way of working.

Supervisors (and institutions) vary in their approach to this requirement, from very prescriptive ways to manage process provided by continuous quality process documentation, to the laissez-faire "this is what group working is, you must expect problems, just get on and do it" [see also 5.1 *Characterizing Supervisor Input*]. Students may also be empowered with mechanisms to address internal group problems which do not require supervisor intervention [for example, see 8.5 *Red Card/Yellow Card*].

Whatever approach (in whatever degree) is taken, the simple fact of the *way* in which the students are working (in groups) adds a dimension which is quite absent from typical forms of learning in the rest of the curriculum – that is in coursework or in individual projects.

Devising Activities Suitable for Groups . . .

. . . From Within Academia

This involves devising activities that are suitable for groups of students to complete in the time available, while still achieving the educational objectives. The work typically exposes students to as much of the product life-cycle as possible, yet remains small enough to allow them to both encounter challenges and have time to reflect on their achievements (or otherwise) at the end of the activity [see Section 7 *Reflection*, especially 7.7 *Cherish It*]. The activity must subdivide to enable a division of the task between the members of a group. Where a cohort is large, there will typically be many groups attempting the same task, which must therefore be capable of solution in a variety of ways to avoid excessive duplication between groups.

. . . From External Sources

A desire for realism may encourage the supervisor to consider introducing some element of "real world" input. This can be a mixed blessing; the obvious advantage of exposing students to a problem that they might have tackled had they been in employment is to be welcomed, but input from companies (say) is necessarily circumscribed by real commercial constraints. This might mean that the scale or scope of the project proposed, or the outcomes expected (i.e. a robust commercial quality product) are unrealistic [see 4.2 *"I'd Like to Do That"*]. Other problems can occur in the student-industry interaction. For example, a response to a student question from an external "client" or "manager" is often not as prompt nor as detailed as a local supervisor might give. All of these problems can be useful educational experiences, of course, assuming that there is an opportunity for appropriate reflection and debriefing. In practice, real world input is often most effective when moderated by someone in close contact with the students tackling the project [see 3.3 *Creating a Real Company*].

Achieving Balanced Groups

The key problem here is to attempt to allocate students to groups so that each group has an equal chance of doing well. Those who have read Belbin's work on the structure of teams (Belbin, 1981) will appreciate that the aim is to form teams that have a good balance of skills; this is not necessarily the same as a good balance of academic ability. Students easily perceive that allocations are unfair, typically because they perceive one team as having more academically able students than another. Staff, however, perceive that this can be unfair for different reasons – a team with the most academically able students in it may be one with too many strong characters to form an effective and harmonious team. It has been shown (Thorn, 1998) that when allowed to self select, students may not work to maximize the skill set of the group for the task in hand, but instead may choose to work with their friends.

Getting Started

Once the allocations are done, all groups need an initialization strategy to get them going. The issue here is whether to let the students simply get on with the task set (which may be too much to expect of less mature students), and hope either that a natural leader will emerge to take control, or appoint someone with the specific task of leading the group. Another, less intrusive, method is to require that the team have named roles, but let them decide (by whatever mechanism they choose) who is to take on which role. If tasks are specifically allocated, they may rotate between members of the team or be negotiated with the supervisor; an election or job application process may also take place. Whatever your choice, it is helpful to students if you tell them which initialization strategy you are adopting [see 2.7 *Roles in groups*].

Consistency in Supervision

The issues surrounding the supervision of group projects can be clustered around the role of staff, the activities of students, and a small number of special circumstances. Where a large cohort is engaged in a group project it is likely that several staff will need to be involved in supervising the cohort. Where different staff have different skills, experiences, and approaches, it can be difficult to get all the staff to give advice in a consistent way. Recognizing and using those different skills, for example by allocating staff to a functional role rather than to a group of students, can mitigate this [see also 2.12 *Staff Deployment*, 4.1 *Me and My Shadow* and 5.1 *Characterizing Supervisor Input*].

Whatever role is allocated to staff, they need to check that every student within a group is making a contribution, and that the group as a whole has the opportunity to reflect on the process as it proceeds. Occasionally a student will become isolated from the rest of the group. Sometimes it is because they think they can complete the task on their own (which may be true, but that's not the point of the exercise), sometimes it is because their personality or culture makes it difficult for them to interact effectively with their peers, or sometimes it happens that other team members become unavailable (for example, through illness) [see also Section 5 *Stuff Happens*]. Supervisors need to be aware of these problems and offer appropriate encouragement; they should also make sure that groups are not so small that they become individuals [although see 9.1 *Going Solo*].

Individual Credit for Group Effort

Of all the issues surrounding group work, that of assessment is perhaps the most problematic because it is the issue on which students, staff, institutions, professional bodies, and external examiners alike have the strongest views.

It must be a prerequisite that it is acceptable that marks awarded for group activity can be counted towards the degree classification of individual students. The extent to which they count varies: 5% would be unexceptional, more than 20% may require considerable discussion. It is common for students to engage in a group activity, but nevertheless be assessed, at least in part, by an individual assessment reflecting on the experience [see also 6.1 *Use Peer Assessment*].

Where identical marks are given to individuals for the work of a group, it is often for the construction of an artifact, but this raises the issue of whether all students made an equal contribution to the activity. This can be addressed by moderating the marks awarded for the group activity by student input, allowing a group of students to agree that individuals made greater or lesser contributions to the activity. Getting the students to agree, or where they cannot agree, having a clear method of resolution, is key [see also 2.9(ii) *Group Assessment*]. Where a group project has involved industrial input, an industrial contribution to the assessment may be appropriate. Here, a shared understanding between the academic and industrial views is essential. Industrial input in the form of a prize may mitigate potential differences between academic and industrial views [see also 2.8 *Motivation*].

Did They Get the Point?

At the end of the project, the participants should have an awareness of the needs, difficulties, opportunities, and complexities of working as a group. If you are the supervisor, you need to know whether this has happened. You also need to know whether the activity was too easy (so that students have not experienced enough of the problems), too challenging (so that students have been over-occupied with too limited a range of activities) or just right.

If the project was just right, students will feel that they have been challenged to face problems, but have been able to overcome them, and that they gained understanding and useful experience. You will know all this by having been involved in the project, by soliciting feedback from students and colleagues, and by engaging in your own reflective activity. More negatively, some of your students may have hated the group work experience, so reflection, and getting them to realize that they may have learned something from the experience, is important. At its most positive, your students will obtain jobs by being able to articulate their experiences of group work in an interview, and this seems to be important to students (and potential employers) at the present time [see also 7.10 *"If I Had My Time Again"*].

References

Belbin, R. M. (1981) *Management teams: why they succeed or fail*, Heinemann.
Thorn, K. (1998) In *Projects in the Computing Curriculum* Holcombe, M., Stratton, A., Fincher, S. and Griffiths, G.(Eds), Springer-Verlag, London, pp. 217–224.

8.1 Managing Staff Input

Group projects are often of such a scale that several members of staff need to be involved in supporting students doing the project. Members of staff need to give consistent advice (in terms of content and amount) to all teams.

o   o   o   o

This bundle mitigates potential differences in the input that different staff can provide to different groups of students.

The way it works is that, rather than allocate members of staff to individual groups, they are allocated by functional role (for example, one to deal with requirements specification issues, another with implementation and another with testing; or in a multidisciplinary project, one to act as finance director, another as technical director, and so on). Student interaction with staff is by email only, and by their role, not as individuals, making it easier for individual members of staff to give consistent advice across a single functional area.

It works better if you have available staff with appropriate functional skills, but it can also help use staff who lack the breadth of skills to advise a group throughout the complete project life-cycle.

It doesn't work if students would really benefit from the physical presence of a member of staff in the laboratory (for example, because very detailed instructions need to be given), though staff can be briefed to tell students to ask detailed questions via the email system.

See also: 5.4 *The Supervisor's Eyes and Ears* and 5.3 *The Help They've Had Along the Way.*

o   o   o   o

So: give careful consideration to *which* staff are to be deployed in managing group projects, and *how* that deployment might be most effective.

8.2 Fair Allocation

It is important to allocate students to groups fairly.

o   o   o   o

This bundle allocates students to groups so that no group is perceived to be stronger or "better" than any other.

The way it works is that the supervisor compiles a list of the students in the cohort ranked by ability (for example, by the previous year's examination marks). If the cohort needs to be divided into G groups, numbered 0 to G −1, the student ranked R is put into group (R mod G). If this initial division produces a group that the supervisor knows is unsatisfactory (for example, it comprises a group of close friends, or has unfortunate gender divisions) some tweaking by hand may be beneficial to achieve the final allocation.

Alternatively, you can simply rank the students in alphabetical order and divide as above.

It works better if you have a large cohort of students; it is also a very cheap mechanism to implement and perceived to be no less fair than any other random allocation.

It doesn't work unless you assume (perhaps erroneously) that examination marks are a guide to how well individuals will perform in a team context.

o   o   o   o

So: use an allocation mechanism that disadvantages neither an individual student nor a student group.

8.3 Maximal Allocation

In group projects it is necessary to divide a cohort of students into groups. Students and staff would like each group to be equally able to complete the group task. It is important to maximize each group's chances of doing well.

○ ○ ○ ○

This bundle helps to identify individual characteristics that might be combined to make successful teams.

The way it works is that students complete a Belbin questionnaire (Belbin, 1981), that will form a profile of their potential contribution to the team across eight broad areas: implementer (makes decisions or plans happen in a sensible and practical way), coordinator (makes sure everyone is clear about what is to be done), shaper (driven by urge to get things done), plant (source of new and unusual ideas, suggestions and plans), resource investigator (makes friends easily and has masses of contacts), monitor-evaluator (steady person who thinks things through), team worker (makes sure everyone works together well) and finisher (meets deadlines at all costs).

Use the scores for individual students to allocate students to groups so that each group contains one coordinator, one strong plant or shaper, one finisher, one team worker and one monitor-evaluator.

It works better if no group contains two strong plants without a very strong coordinator, and also if the groups are roughly comparable in overall technical ability.

It doesn't work unless you read one of the texts that include a copy of the Belbin questionnaire, and an explanation of the scoring system. It also requires a fairly large cohort of students and is more time consuming to administer than some other allocation mechanisms. It is useful, however, for students to use the questionnaire to reflect on their own traits. Sometimes the distribution of Belbin categories is very uneven.

Variation: Alan Jones from the University of Teesside has used this technique in a Master's level course (Jones, 1999).

References Belbin, R. M. (1981) *Management teams: why they succeed or fail*, Heinemann. Jones, A. (1999); Experiences of Profile-Based Group Composition, *Computer Science Education*, Volume 9, No. 3, 242–255

○ ○ ○ ○

So: invest a little time in reading about Belbin's questionnaire and use it to build good teams.

8.4 Battle-scarred Veteran

When students undertake their first group project, they often have no idea of where to start or how to proceed.

○ ○ ○ ○

This bundle provides the group with experience by introducing, as a leader, a student from a later year who has undertaken (sometimes several) group projects in similar contexts.

The way it works is that the earlier-year students are allocated to groups by the normal process. Each group is then allocated a later-year student to act as leader. (If there are more students in the later year than there are groups in the earlier year, another exercise will have to be devised for those who have no group to manage. Also, a selection process must be established – for example writing an application: "Why I want to do this, and why I would be good at it"). The later-year students provide what input they think the project needs.

It works better if the project is reasonably short (5-6 weeks). It works better over time, as the managing students will have experienced "being managed" earlier in their program (and are often eager to participate). It works better if the management is also part of a credit-bearing course (for which the assessment might be a log of the project, and/or a reflective piece). If such a system is adopted, a collateral benefit of having the later-year management logbooks is that it makes staff assessment the project itself much easier.

It doesn't work unless the two cohorts are available at the same time of the year.

See also: 7.9 *Last Year's Punters.*

○ ○ ○ ○

So: provide support for initial group work from a perspective with which the students can readily identify.

8.5 Red Card/Yellow Card

Students and staff alike are reluctant to reward group members who do not contribute, although some groups seem perfectly happy to "carry" a hitch-hiker. In either case, it is impossible for staff to know precisely how much work each team member did; only the students involved know this.

○ ○ ○ ○

This bundle gives students some control over the behavior of members of their project group and allows their non-performance to be factored into the assessment.

The way it works is that students are allowed to issue others in their project group with yellow, and in extremis, red cards. A yellow card is "shown" to a student who is deficient in effort or attitude or in other ways not making a full contribution to the group and is then lodged with the project supervisor. Being "shown a yellow card" results in a known penalty being applied to the student (for example a fixed number of marks lost), though a yellow card may be canceled by increased effort, or at a boundary between phases of the project, or after a set time. A student who attracts the maximum number of yellow cards can be "shown a red card", which excludes the student from the rest of the project and sets the mark awarded to zero. There is no recovery from a red card.

These cards are public documents and their issue is a formal process. They must be ratified by a majority of the students in the group, and the final step of the process (actually issuing the card) can only be undertaken by the supervisor. A collateral benefit of this process is that the number of yellow cards received by a student across a program can be used as a monitoring tool.

It works better if staff set the parameters of control (the penalty, the number of yellow cards that can be carried).

It doesn't work if the system leads to the frivolous use of penalties. It doesn't work unless day-to-day management of the resource/role allocation is in the hands of the group themselves.

○ ○ ○ ○

So: find a mechanism which devolves some control over the performance of group members to the groups themselves.

8.6 Moderation Using Student Input

Students' awareness of their own group processes can be poor (or absent). It is difficult for staff to require (or encourage) such awareness without giving students both the tools, and the motivation to use them.

○ ○ ○ ○

This bundle allows students to give feedback on the contribution made by each team member (including themselves) under headings related to both the technical and managerial aspects of their work.

The way it works is that peer- and self-evaluation forms are issued to team members after the submission of each deliverable. Each student completes (anonymously) a form for each member of their team and for themselves. For each student, the response to each of the scaled questions is scored (−3, 0, +3) and an average taken. Within each team, individual average scores are compared with the team average. The supervisor moderates the individual mark for the assessment (by a maximum of ±5% from the team mark) for students with a large deviation, taking additional account of free-form comments on the form (see following example).

It works better if students have training in how to assess, and are practised at reflecting on process issues.

It doesn't work unless students are producing at least one substantial, well documented group-produced deliverable.

See also: 3.5 *Emphasis on Personal Transferable Skills*

○ ○ ○ ○

So: use peer- and self-evaluation forms to moderate group marks according to individual contribution.

Peer and Self Evaluation Form

You should complete this **Peer and Self Evaluation** form for **each member of your team and yourself** and hand them in to the Departmental Office in the normal way.

Name of Student:
Please indicate for the team member their management characteristics:

time management

highly organised — unreliable

responsiveness to others

respects views — domineering

coping with stress

always calm — panics easily

decision making

decisive — unable to commit

cooperation

always cooperates — goes own way

self-confidence

able to take criticism — can't take criticism

leadership

takes initiative — follows others

problem analysis

incisive — woolly

project management

best practice — activity lacks coordination

project evaluation

systematic and objective — casual and subjective

Comments:

Please indicate for the team member their technical contribution

Task Analysis

well above average   average   well below average

Conceptual Design

well above average   average   well below average

VDM

well above average   average   well below average

Manager's Meetings

well above average   average   well below average

Team Meetings

well above average   average   well below average

Low Level Design

well above average   average   well below average

Coding

well above average   average   well below average

Testing

well above average   average   well below average

Documentation

well above average   average   well below average

Demonstration

well above average   average   well below average

Comments:

8.7 Quick Off the Mark

When students have been allocated to groups they often spend the early part of the project not knowing quite what to do. They will achieve more if the roles they are expected to take are made explicit, and they are encouraged to take a role to which they feel suited.

○ ○ ○ ○

This bundle helps groups get started by encouraging each member to apply for a specific role in a group.

The way it works is that a number of roles are described by means of job descriptions. The roles can be chosen from managerial or technical specialisms: manager/coordinator/leader, requirements analyzer, designer, implementer, tester, interfacer, integrator, researcher, secretary, librarian, resource controller. Job descriptions are publicized and students invited to identify a small number of roles to which they feel themselves suited. The students are allocated to groups by particular jobs within the group.

It works better if there is a good balance between what students feel themselves suitable for and the roles that need to be filled.

It doesn't work if the students have to cover a broad range of activities within the group rather than concentrating on one particular role.

○ ○ ○ ○

So: find ways of making group roles explicit.

9 Motivation: the Achilles Heel of Learning

Motivation

There are only a limited number of things staff can do – interventions they can make or advice they can give – which will affect motivation. Where there is no, or low, motivation in a student there is little or no learning. Paradoxically, where student motivation is high, students can overcome most difficulties, many deficiencies (in the teaching process) and some disasters.

The best projects undoubtedly result from real interest and enthusiasm on the part of the student. Traditionally, it might be expected that intrinsic motivation is not a problem for students in higher education, and, indeed, for many that is still the case. For them, project work is frequently very enabling – where previously their performance might have exceeded the expected standard considerably, with projects they can achieve as highly as they wish (Roberts, 2000). However, it is recognized increasingly that, as the number of students in higher education grows and the range of abilities broadens, project supervisors must be more proactive in helping students to find the motivation to perform to the best of their ability.

Although individuals are different, students' motivation is often related to feeling that what they are doing is valued by others and feeling a sense of partnership with the person, or people, for whom the work is being done. So, although extrinsic motivators (such as awarding a prize for the best project and other types of rewards [see: 2.8 *Motivation*] may have an impact, they are likely to focus students' efforts on earning the rewards rather than on learning and achievement. Rather, the best work is likely to result from students being able to motivate themselves intrinsically, i.e. each individual should find personal satisfaction in achieving whatever it is they set out to do.

Motivation may be addressed at several points in the cycle of learning. Keller identifies four particular points: students' motivation can be affected by their *Interest* in the work, their perception of its *Relevance*, their *Expectation* that they will succeed and their *Satisfaction* in their achievement (Keller, 1983).

It is important to distinguish unmotivation, which may be associated with remarks such as *"What's the point of doing a project?"* (Interest and Relevance) from demotivation, which may result from difficulties experienced while undertaking the current project, or may be the residual effect of prior experience of project work (Expectation and Satisfaction).

Unmotivation may be associated with the degree program as a whole rather than just the project component and this can be difficult to overcome. However, projects can represent an opportunity for individuals to exercise more control over their work, particularly in terms of the scheduling and location of work and sometimes even in terms of the choice of subject matter and methods to be used as well. Projects can, therefore, be a real opportunity to help individuals get motivated.

Demotivation is a likely, perhaps inevitable, consequence of failure to match the requirements of the project to the abilities and skills of the student; if the project is either too hard or too easy motivation will be lost quickly. Similarly, it is important that students understand at an early stage in the project, the nature and range of the demands that they will face. Many students will become demotivated if the demands of the project turn out to be at odds with their expectations.

Giving Students More Control Means that Staff Have Less Control

In attempting to create an environment that helps to stimulate intrinsic motivation a key issue is that *giving students more control over their work means that staff have less control.* For example, involving students in the choice of project topic [see 2.1 *Allocation of Topics to Students* and 4.2 *"I'd Like To Do That"*] may help their motivation but it may also lead to staff working outside their areas of expertise. This might have implications for both the quality of supervision and the willingness of staff to take on supervisory responsibilities.

Similarly, it may be construed as motivating to allow students to determine the schedule for handing in interim deliverables [see also 2.9(iii) *Basis of Assessment: Deliverables*]. This would allow students to take ownership by deciding when to work on the different aspects of the project requirements – but it necessarily means that staff work around the schedules devised by individual students. This will make it difficult for staff to plan their own work schedule and may bring project supervision into conflict with other aspects of staff workloads.

Clearly, it is necessary to balance staff and student control but achieving the optimal balance is problematic.

Demotivation Involves Contingency Action

Unmotivated students are likely to have made themselves known in other parts of the course but demotivation can be related to some aspect of the task in hand. Students become demotivated for different reasons, and often the reasons relate to the individual's perception, rather than the reality, of how the project is going. Measures to cope with demotivation must address the cause and this means that supervisors must be adept in identifying the real reasons for demotivation (these may not be the most obvious or even those given by the student) and then tailoring strategy and tactics to the needs of the individual.

Indeed, used indiscriminately, measures to improve motivation may do more harm than good. For every student motivated by competition, for example, there may be one (or more) students who are turned off completely (Lepper, 1988). Publishing student work [see 7.7 *Cherish It*] may spur some students to insure that it is of high quality, but for others this is an unnecessary extra pressure. There will always be some students who just do not respond to the invitation to negotiate aspects of their project.

One Size Does Not Fit All

Helping students to motivate themselves is very difficult because there is no panacea; one size does not fit all, and matching ideas and approaches to individual students is a key skill for teaching staff generally and for project supervisors in particular. Further, in attempting to stimulate intrinsic motivation teaching staff can do no more than serve as a catalyst; individual students must take responsibility for their own motivation eventually. Each of the bundles in this section, therefore, comes with a "health warning": it will not work for everyone.

References

Keller, J. M. (1983) In *Instructional-Design Theories and Models* Reigeluth, C. M. (Ed), Lawrence Erlbaum, Hillsdale, New Jersey.

Lepper, M. R. (1988) *Cognition and Instruction*, 5, 289–309.

Roberts, E. (2000) In *31st SIGCSE Technical Symposium on Computer Science Education* ACM, Austin, Texas, pp. 295–299.

9.1 Going Solo

Some students lose motivation when they find it impossible to feel ownership of a group project. In extreme cases this can mean that an individual achieves nothing and might, as a result, be in danger of failing a course which they would otherwise complete successfully.

○ ○ ○ ○

This bundle offers a contingency solution for dealing with extreme cases of group-work-related motivation problems.

How it works is that you supervise the groups in the usual way but pay particular attention to students' reactions to being required to work in groups. Identify individuals who would be motivated to do the work but for their extreme reaction to group work. (They might manifest themselves by extreme disengagement and non-attendance, or perhaps by trying to "take over" and do all the work themselves, or in some other way). If undertaking this particular task in a group is not a specific requirement of the assessment criteria for the module, allow the individual in question to drop out of the group and pursue an individual project.

The individual then pursues a solo project based on the original group project but "cut down" to be manageable by one person in the time available. The group continues as before but with a negotiated reduction in the project requirements to take account of the group being smaller.

Although it is an extreme measure, this may allow a greatly demotivated student to achieve at least something. This may also have a beneficial effect for the group from which they drop out.

This works better if the majority of the cohort are motivated to work in groups since, once it is apparent that going solo is an option, students who to this point were working effectively in groups may want to work alone.

It doesn't work if prohibited by institutional requirements (particularly assessment criteria) and it will not work unless there is sufficient time for an individual project that satisfies institutional criteria to be instigated and pursued. Also, it must be possible for the group to continue unaffected.

○ ○ ○ ○

So: be sensitive to how the choice of teaching methods and assessment instruments can affect students' results.

9.2 Well, *They* Managed

In projects which are substantial pieces of work, students find it difficult to judge accurately the scale and scope of what is required. They may lose motivation because they cannot visualize the outcome or, if they can, find the process and the required deliverables intimidating.

○ ○ ○ ○

This bundle offers a way to show students that other students have managed to achieve something worthwhile and that they can too, affecting confidence and motivating performance.

How it works is that project reports submitted by previous cohorts are placed in the library. If you judge that a student you are supervising has motivation problems arising from an inability to visualize the outcome or by being overawed take them to the library and show them where the previous cohort's reports are kept.

Get them to take a report to read, and tell them that it will be discussed it at the next supervision meeting. At the next meeting get them to talk about the project they've read, focusing the conversation on the deliverables and the processes required to produce them. Wherever possible get the student to work out how things were done rather than telling them. Ask the student to "compare and contrast" the completed project with the challenges they will face in their own project.

Students get a much clearer idea of what is expected of them and find it much easier to see themselves completing the project successfully.

It works better if the ability and diligence of the current and previous student are reasonably closely matched as this helps to give the student a realistic view of what they can expect to achieve. It works better if grades of earlier projects are also available so that their lack of confidence can be attributed to real or imagined deficiencies.

It doesn't work if reports generated by previous cohorts are not available and it will not work unless the current student perceives the report to be relevant to their work. Also, it will not work if staff merely deliver a lecture on how the previous student went about the project; the student should work out as much as possible for themselves.

See also: 7.7 *Cherish It*, and 7.9 *Last Year's Punters*

○ ○ ○ ○

So: use deliverables from previous years to help students get an idea of what they have to do.

9.3 You've Done It Before

A lack of motivation can be due to an individual's perception that the project is beyond their ability. This can be true even if the student has successful prior experience of project work.

○ ○ ○ ○

This bundle aims to use the student's previous experience as a means of showing them that they can survive and thrive in project work, building on their satisfaction in previous performance to affect their expectation of future success.

How it works is that if you judge that an individual's motivation problems stem from a feeling that they just cannot do it, use a supervision meeting to talk about the student's prior experience of project work.

In one-to-one conversation get them to identify other projects they have undertaken either in a group or individually. Ask them to think about what went well and what was less successful, ask about the problems encountered and how they were overcome. Get the student to make connections between prior experience and the current project.

The idea is to leave the student feeling that their previous experience is relevant to what they're doing in the current project and that they *can* do the current work.

It works better if the previous project was reasonably successful and it helps for the relevant member of staff to have detailed information about the student's previous project work.

It doesn't work if the student has no such prior experience. Also, if the previous experience of project work was completely disastrous it may not be motivating to revisit it.

Variation: substitute aspects of other types of work, e.g. coursework, practical work, etc. in which the student may have successful experience and which can be seen as analogous to specific aspects of project work.

○ ○ ○ ○

So: try to change the student's perception of their ability by getting them to reflect on previous successful experience.

9.4 This Is for Real

Some students are unmotivated because they regard academic work as artificial, and academic staff as lacking in "real world" skills.

○ ○ ○ ○

This bundle bridges the gap between university and industry/commerce by using "real life" trainers to teach the key skills necessary for good project work.

How it works is that you get staff from the training departments of companies with a large IT base to provide learning opportunities in non-technical skills such as presentation skills, report writing, team skills, project management or time management.

Because the sessions are run by experts in the field of training for these key skills, students accept their importance, and their real world relevance, more readily than they would from academic staff. Useful company contacts are also made.

It works better if key skills are assessed as part of the project and if the sessions are scheduled such that the students need to use their newly acquired skills soon afterwards.

It doesn't work if companies misunderstand the purpose of the session, so close liaison is necessary.

○ ○ ○ ○

So: help students see the relevance of the processes and production of university project work by involving people from the "real" world in projects.

9.5 Get to Know Them

Motivation can be associated with feelings of belonging and security but students are often allocated a project supervisor who, being both an authority figure and a complete stranger, is to be distrusted.

○ ○ ○ ○

This bundle recognizes that when students, especially adults, sign up for a course they do not do so to fulfill the desires of their teachers; students have their own objectives in taking a course. This is why we must get to know them. This bundle also recognizes that student motivation can be altered as much by general encouragement and support as by specific intellectual guidance and academic intervention.

How it works is that if you judge that the student's motivation would be helped by a closer relationship, find out about the student before the first meeting. Consult the student's academic records and talk to the student's tutors or colleagues who have taught them. At the first meeting make a point of introducing yourself – don't stick to professional issues, let them know you're human and have other interests. If it is possible, meet project students socially.

This works better if staff-student relations generally are friendly and if teaching staff take an interest in individual students.

It doesn't work if students perceive insincerity or if they have a chip on their shoulder about academics and the "real world". Students must understand that good relationships are no substitute for quality work.

○ ○ ○ ○

So: help students to feel they belong.

9.6 Here's One I Prepared Earlier

For some students a lack of motivation can derive from a lack of confidence in their ability to use certain tools or techniques.

○ ○ ○ ○

This bundle gives students the opportunity to boost their confidence by practising the skills required for their project in a way that does not affect their marks.

How it works is that you take a previously completed project and ask the student to make a relatively small alteration to some part of it in such a way that they have the opportunity to practice using the relevant tool or technique. This enables the students to become more confident in using the software tools and methods of software development that they will later be required to use in their own work.

This works better if it requires a short amount of time and effort in comparison with the main project work and if it can be done concurrently with other aspects of the main project.

It doesn't work unless the previous project has been carefully designed and executed to match the learning goals. This can be a problem in the first instance, but once developed it can be reused and/or enhanced in subsequent years.

○ ○ ○ ○

So: build their confidence using practice exercises.

Coda

How To Write This Book

You have good ideas which others may find useful, but how will you make them available?

○ ○ ○ ○

This bundle provides a mechanism for the capture and presentation of good practice in computing project work.

The way it works is having seen the way that pieces of practice are abstracted from their context to make them easy for other practitioners to adopt, use the form of a bundle to identify and reflect on your own good practices. This is useful in itself.

If you think in terms of the phrases which introduce each section of a bundle they should act as levers to help extract the core features of your practice from its context – as well as making them visible and more accessible to others.

If you then write them down, you have a bundle that can be shared.

It works better if the title is relevant and memorable. *It works better if* the problem statement rings bells with your audience and the solution statement really is a solution to that problem. *It also works better if* the body of your bundle gives enough detail to give the reader confidence that they can use your practice, but not so much that it binds the solution to your context only.

It doesn't work if you don't then publish your bundle.

○ ○ ○ ○

So: use this format to capture your practice and put it on the web page:

http://www.cs.ukc.ac.uk/national/EPCOS

Index